THE AVENGER
TAKES HIS PLACE

ALSO BY HOWARD MEANS

◆

Colin Powell:
Soldier/Statesman, Statesman/Soldier

◆

C.S.A.:
Confederate States of America

◆

Money & Power:
The History of Business

◆

The Banana Sculptor, the Purple Lady,
and the All-Night Swimmer (coauthor)

HOWARD MEANS

THE AVENGER
TAKES HIS PLACE

Andrew Johnson

and the 45 Days

That Changed the Nation

HARCOURT, INC.

Orlando · Austin · New York · San Diego · Toronto · London

ISBN-13: 978-0-15-101212-1   ISBN-10: 0-15-101212-1

Text set in Adobe Jenson
Designed by April Ward

Printed in the United States of America

For my brother, Tom

Contents

THE AVENGER
TAKES HIS PLACE

Preface

NEARLY A CENTURY and a half after John Wilkes Booth's derringer promoted him to the presidency, Andrew Johnson comes down to us as the failed president who followed the martyred one. Yet Johnson was "the greatest man of his age," a *New York Times* correspondent wrote in March 1861. From the beginning of the Civil War to the end, he was nearly as polarizing a figure as Abraham Lincoln himself. On the Black Easter after Lincoln's assassination, Northern pulpits rang with the message that the nation had been delivered to a man better able to see the unfinished business of the war through. It was Johnson—not Lincoln, not Congress—who got the first crack at determining what form of peace would prevail and what kind of nation America would be in the decades and even centuries to come.

All that is largely forgotten now. The terrible event that brought Andrew Johnson to the presidency is enshrined in the American consciousness; the terrible times that followed seem obscure, half remembered. Once a towering figure to whom the nation turned its eyes with equal parts expectation (in the North) and fear (in the South), Johnson has been reduced to little more than a cartoon figure, a national embarrassment. What was it about his considerable strengths and maddening flaws, and their intersection with this crucial moment in American history, that condemned him? That is the question this book attemps to answer.

Part of the explanation, though only part, is that Johnson gave his detractors so much to work with. He was drunk when he was sworn in as vice president—drunk and loquacious. What was to have been an address of perhaps seven minutes stretched into an often-incoherent harangue more than twice that long. Abraham Lincoln, whom Johnson would replace six weeks later at one of the darkest moments in American history, forgave him for the lapse. Mary Todd Lincoln never did. Other presidents have been threatened with impeachment. One, Bill Clinton, endured a Senate trial; but only Johnson escaped being removed from office by a single vote, a heartbeat away from terminal shame. Reconstruction, that disastrous epoch that was to forge a new postwar South but instead perpetuated the old one, had many architects of failure—individuals, impersonal forces, the overwhelming nature of the task—but chief among them had to have been Andrew Johnson. The great historians of the period, Eric McKitrick and Eric Foner most prominently, treat Johnson poorly, and with cause. At a time that called for malleability, Johnson was rigid. For a lifetime politician, he lacked even fundamental political skills. Compromise was beyond him. Accommodation, impossible. "Undoubtedly the greatest misfortune that ever befell Andrew Johnson was the assassination of President Lincoln," the *New York Times* noted in Johnson's obituary. "It promoted him to the eminent position of President of the nation, it is true, but the student of history is forced to conclude that his posthumous fame would have been brighter without this high honor and the consequences it entailed."

Always, too, there was Abraham Lincoln to contend with. There's more poetry in the Gettysburg Address or in Lincoln's Second Inaugural Address than can be found in all the collective writings and speeches of Andrew Johnson combined; more wit, it sometimes seems, in a single Lincoln quip than Johnson managed in an entire lifetime. We'll never know whether Lincoln would have had any more success than Johnson did facing down the Radical Republicans in Congress after the war, but the battle would have been more tactical, less the slugfest it turned into. Johnson lacked the nuance of the man who came before him; he had nothing like the sixteenth president's deeply textured character. Those haunting photographs of Lincoln in his last years capture the heart and soul of human suffering. Light and shadow play off each other in so many ways, across so many declivities, that you see a slightly new personality from each fresh angle. Meanwhile, what's beneath looks bottomless, filled with secret spaces, beyond knowing or nearly so. Almost friendless in life, Lincoln was beloved in death. One of the most inspirational figures in American history, he was an unmatched political manipulator. Famous in his day as a jokester, Lincoln had a face that looked as if it were permanently etched in grief.

With Andy Johnson, what you saw was what you got. "Mr Johnson was about 5 feet 10 inches in height, and weighed near 175 pounds," Oliver Perry Temple, who had once lost a congressional race to Johnson, wrote in a lengthy profile for his book *Notable Men of Tennessee.*

> His limbs were strong and muscular, his movements active, indicating superior physical strength. His power of endurance was exceptionally great. His shoulders were large, his head massive, round and broad, his neck short and stout. His forehead was not exceptionally high, but very wide and perpendicular. Above his eyes, at the point where the phrenologists locate the reasoning faculties (causality) were two remarkable bumps or protuberances swelling out from his brow. His complexion was dark, his eyes black and piercing; his countenance, when in repose, gloomy; when lighted up by a smile, it became attractive. In ordinary conversation his voice was low and soft. His action, while not stately, was easy and rather graceful. In appearance he was far from being rustic. On the whole, nature stamped him as a remarkable man.

Remarkable, indeed, especially those vast "causality" protuberances swelling out from his brow. Look hard at photographs of Johnson, and you can almost see the ambition rising up in him as well as something close to anger smoldering just beneath it, but that's where the depth seems to stop. In Lincoln's house were many mansions. His successor's psyche, by comparison, was only a few rooms wide. Johnson was something quite common to modern Washington: a workaholic, happiest when crisis prevailed, without humor or recreation or even a known vice save for one improbable drunk at the very moment above all others when sobriety should have prevailed. Little wonder he will never be able to walk out from under the long shadow his predecessor has cast over him. Historians race by Johnson, but they give up Lincoln reluctantly, even when he has left the stage. In a December 11, 1973, letter to the novelist Walker Percy, Shelby Foote laments the moment when, almost at the end of his monumental three-volume "narrative history" of the Civil War, he finally has to say good-bye to Father Abraham. "I killed Lincoln last week. . . . Killed him and had Stanton say, 'Now he belongs to the ages.' A strange feeling, though. I have another 70-odd pages to go, and have a fear they'll be like *Hamlet* with Hamlet left out." A month and a half later, in another letter to Percy, Foote is still racing through the void, panting for the finish line: "Captured Jeff Davis yesterday, locked him up in Ft [*sic*] Monroe today. Now on to Andy Johnson, who looks to me as if he's headed for impeachment. Strike the tent!" (The last sentence is a play on Robert E. Lee's final words: "Let the tent be struck.") In his history of the closing month of the Civil War, *April 1865*, Jay Winik devotes fewer than a dozen of his 388 pages to Andrew Johnson, despite Johnson's having been president for half the month Winik writes about. Filmmaker Ken Burns seems to have barely noticed Johnson. In "The Better Angels of Our Nature," the final episode of Burns's nine-part PBS epic *The Civil War*, the president who succeeded Lincoln is mentioned only in passing and never seen. It's as if Johnson were a ghost drifting through his own times, but that's looking backward, as history both must and too often does.

His contemporaries saw Johnson differently. They had a far clearer sense of the challenge history and fate had placed before the new president. And they knew that, above all, Andrew Johnson was impossible to ignore. He had been the only Southern senator to declare for the Union in those tumultuous months before the Civil War. His fiery speeches on the Senate floor, his thunderous denunciations of secession, helped steel Northern resolve when the American Experiment was pulling apart. The war itself only added to his luster. No politician risked more or endured more during the fighting than Johnson; none was in the thick of it as thoroughly as he. Appointed by Lincoln to serve as military governor of eastern Tennessee, Johnson spent three years in Nashville, surrounded by the enemy much of that time. The qualities that plagued his presidency—his obstinacy, an iron will—were his strengths in the midst of combat. Nor was any politician more vocal or insistent that the South be made to pay for its sins. The Confederacy's leaders were "traitors," their crimes "odious." Only one punishment fit.

"In President Johnson . . . the country has a man of courage, of sound judgment and of a patriotism which has stood the test of the most terrible trials," the *New York Times* assured its readers on April 17, 1865, two days after the assassination. "His sympathies are with the people, and all his actions will be for their good. . . . No man ever came suddenly to power with a plainer path before him than that which lies before the new President. And no one need fear for a moment that the rebellion is to gain anything by the death of President Lincoln or by the ascendancy to power of Andrew Johnson as his successor." Clearly, the *Times* was closing ranks, nudging the new president along, but this was an era when newspapers didn't pull editorial punches. If the *Times* had had reservations about Johnson, its readers would have known.

Four months later, alarmed by two extended illnesses and fearful that Johnson's stern work ethic was endangering his health, the *Times* upped its rhetoric: "No patriot was ever more solemnly called upon to die for country than he is to live for country," the newspaper noted of Johnson on August 15. "Since this republic had an existence, never was there a life of such consequence to it as his. This comes not from his special personal qualifications for the office, great though they are, but from the peculiar circumstances in which he holds that office. There is no Vice-Presidency behind him to furnish a successor to his place for the rest of his Presidential term should he be taken away.... The death of President Johnson would be the greatest of public calamities, because it would force the country into all the fierce excitements and agitations of a Presidential canvass, in this transitional period of reconstruction."

Harper's Weekly, the self-appointed Journal of Civilization, with a circulation in the mid-1860s that sometimes topped 200,000 copies an issue, had many reservations about Johnson's policies, but about his role in history, the editors had no doubt. "We have had in our political life four eminently critical Presidential administrations," the magazine noted in its September 1866 issue: "Washington's, in which the Constitution, established in 1787, was first tested in operation; Jackson's, in which this Constitution was for the first time seriously threatened by Calhoun's adherents in South Carolina; Lincoln's, in which Calhoun's doctrines, finding support in eleven Southern States, culminated in open rebellion against the Constitution; and Johnson's, in which the rebellion, having been suppressed... it became necessary for the General Government to step in and, under the Constitution, to guarantee to disorganized States 'a republican form of government,' and to secure the peace of the country and the perfect allegiance of all its citizens, which had been obtained by military conquest." The effectiveness of Johnson's administration "remains yet to be decided," the magazine opined in the same article, but in Johnson, America had at its helm "probably as remarkable a man as our country has produced."

Johnson was the only president to be entirely self-taught, the only one who never had a single day of formal education. Even in an age of uncertain orthography, the first letter included in the multivolume *Papers of Andrew Johnson* is an absolute adventure in spelling: "cum" for "come," "sumthing" for "something," "git" for "get." And that was in June 1832, when Johnson was twenty-three years old and already launched on his political career. Lincoln's humble origins remain legendary: the log cabin, the railsplitter. Johnson—fatherless at three, indentured before age ten—out-humbled him by a mile. Indeed, his life story combines so many of the great themes of American biography—up from the bootstraps, self-reliance, the faith that, Jay Gatsby-like, Americans can spring from our Platonic conception of ourselves. Like so many American heroes, Johnson succeeded because he wouldn't let himself fail. He also spent a lifetime fostering the seeds of his own destruction.

Johnson was the third vice president to succeed to the top office through the death or resignation of the incumbent. He was the first of four to achieve the office through assassination. But no vice president before or since has been elevated to the presidency at a more challenging moment. Six days before Lincoln was assassinated, Robert E. Lee had surrendered his Army of Northern Virginia to Ulysses Grant at the courthouse at Appomattox. The Rebel capital at Richmond lay smoldering, burned nearly to the ground. But the war refused to end. Jefferson Davis and the Confederate government were in flight—from Richmond to Danville, Virginia, then scattering south and westward. Nearly 200,000 Rebel soldiers remained under arms, in three armies yet to surrender under terms still to be worked out.

The final battle of the war would not be fought for another twenty-four days, a skirmish along the Rio Grande at the far edge of the short-lived Southern empire. The last Confederate army, Kirby Smith's Trans-Mississippi Division, wouldn't surrender until early June. The freshly wounded on both sides would linger and die for months thereafter. But the statistics were staggering. Since the first shot of the Civil War had been fired on Fort Sumter, at the mouth of Charleston Harbor in South Carolina, at four thirty on the morning of April 12, 1861, more than 600,000 Americans had been killed in battle or died of war-related injuries or illnesses: one in every fifty persons in the land, ten times the American deaths in Vietnam, 200,000 more Americans than were killed in World War II, and this in a country with one-tenth the population it has today.

In the North, jubilation had just begun to seize the land—Victory at hand!—when news flashed over the telegraph lines that the president had been shot and had little chance of surviving the night. In the South, whatever joy the shooting brought (and the news was tortoise-slow to arrive in many quarters) was tempered by the fear of retaliation, of a harsh peace, and the hard reality of lives pared down to the bone. In the last months of the war, inflation in the South had topped 9,000 percent; with the collapse of the Confederacy, its currency was worthless. Meanwhile, the vanguard of a mostly illiterate throng of four million people had begun wandering the streets and country roads of the would-be nation it had only recently been forced to serve as slaves.

From Virginia to Mississippi, rain poured through roofs that couldn't be repaired and broken windows for which there was neither new glass nor the money to purchase it with. Boards that popped off buildings went untended. There were no nails, anywhere. The fighting had exhausted not just funds and supplies, but the earth itself and the people. Edmund Ruffin, a Virginia planter and agronomist—he's credited with being the father of soil chemistry—had pulled the lanyard that sent the first salvo of the war arcing across the predawn sky toward Fort Sumter. Four years and two months later, by then in his early seventies, Ruffin shot himself dead rather than submit to Union rule.

Anger, despair, revenge, fear, hysteria—they all sold wholesale as word of Lincoln's assassination spread out from the capital. But in the war's dénouement, bad news was never in short supply. From March through May, prison camps North and South disgorged sometimes terrifying secrets. Andersonville in Georgia was a cabinet of horrors such as the nation had never witnessed before. Nearly a tenth of the American population had served in one army or the other. Now, hundreds of thousands of them were trudging home to uncertain futures. The nation itself was virtually without form. Were the defeated states still states in good standing? Or would they become territories? Military districts? Who would govern? Who would vote?

Into this volatile mix now stepped Andy Johnson, as contradictory a marriage of man and moment as American history has ever served up. With the North victorious at last, a Southerner born and bred would occupy the White House. In a war fought at least in part over the argument of slavery—if not to free the slaves themselves—Booth's actions had turned the presidency over to a man who at the outset of hostilities had owned five slaves outright. No man—not Lincoln, not Grant, not "Little" Phil Sheridan, not even the prince of darkness himself, William Tecumseh Sherman—stuck more in the craw of the failed Confederacy than Johnson, yet none was more of the South than he.

Johnson's politics were always hard to pin down. He was a Jeffersonian agrarian, for slavery and for the Union, a radical and a strict constructionist, an Andy Jackson Democrat, yet never entirely anything, it seemed. The streak of independent thinking ran too deeply through him, or maybe it was just his ambition that was so great it resisted labeling. Speaking before a Cincinnati crowd in February 1865, only weeks before he was sworn in as vice president, Johnson declared himself a "radical Democrat...none of your pseudo, hermaphroditish Vallandigham Democrats, but a Jacksonian Democrat." (The reference is to Clement Larid Vallandigham, an Ohio congressman and war opponent whom Lincoln had banished to the Confederacy in May 1863.) What Johnson was not, decidedly, was a Republican, but that is the banner under which Lincoln had been elected in 1860. Now in death, he would be succeeded by a man who had campaigned against him a little over four years earlier, the only time in American history the presidency has changed political parties other than through the ballot box.

John Wilkes Booth never meant for Johnson to succeed Lincoln. The vice president had been marked for assassination as well, along with Grant and Secretary of State William Seward, a night of murder that would have left the North leaderless on and off the battlefield. That part of the plot failed, barely so in Seward's case. As Johnson slept soundly in his suite at the Kirkwood House on Pennsylvania Avenue, the highest office in the land was about to be handed over to the Confederacy's worst nightmare. Now it would be up to Andrew Johnson to determine the peace—its shape and dimensions. The stage was his. For forty-five days, Johnson would keep the nation waiting to see whether vision or division, mercy or vengeance prevailed.

CHAPTER I

Kirkwood House

*T*HE BILL AT FORD'S THEATRE on April 14 featured light comedy and high celebrity. The newspapers had served notice that the president and Mrs. Lincoln and General and Mrs. Grant would be attending that evening's performance of Laura Keene in *My American Cousin.* The Grants didn't make it. They'd left for Burlington, New Jersey, that afternoon to visit their children. Their place in the presidential box was taken by a young military couple, Army Major Henry Rathbone and his fiancée, Clara Harris. Flags were draped on either side of the balcony. The partition that normally divided it into two boxes was gone and more comfortable furniture had been hauled in for the Lincoln party, including a rocking chair for the long-legged, theater-loving president. Richmond had been captured, the end was at hand. A festive spirit prevailed.

All that ended at ten fifteen with the muffled crack of Booth's derringer, although at first no one knew for certain what had happened. Booth, after all, was a well-known actor around the capital. Only four weeks earlier, he'd performed at Ford's Theatre. The dramatic leap to the stage, his raised dagger (the one he had just used to slash Henry Rathbone after shooting the president), the shouted oath "Sic Semper Tyrannis" (Thus Always to Tyrants, the state motto of Virginia) were so theatrical they might have been part of the show, a skit added to amuse or startle Lincoln. Even the paid actors that night were initially uncertain about what John Wilkes Booth was doing among them.

That seems to explain why no one bothered to stop him. Ford's Theatre on the evening of April 14 bristled with men carrying sidearms, men who had used them recently in battle and were certainly ready to use them again. It is a mark of the sheer audacity of Booth's act—its un-thinkability—that he wasn't cut down before he could clear the stage and get to the horse he had waiting in the alley behind the theater. Booth came, he fired, and left, with an ease breathtaking in comparison to our own time, when presidents are hermetically sealed away during public appearances.

It wasn't long before the shock wore off and reality set in. Henry Rathbone shouted, "Stop that man!" Mrs. Lincoln cried out miserably, "They have shot the president!" There was no mistaking the message this time. Booth had used a wooden bar to block anyone from entering behind him into the presidential box. Bleeding freely from a deep gash that ran nearly from shoulder to elbow, Major Rathbone finally knocked the bar loose, and with that, the balcony swelled with doctors, officers, government officials, well-wishers, the morbidly curious, gawkers. Even Laura Keene, the star of the show, came up for a look. The place was as unprotected after Booth struck as it had been before he had arrived, and everyone wanted to lend a hand. In the days afterward, hundreds of those attending the performance—and some who had never come near the theater that evening—would claim to have helped lift Lincoln from the rocker he had been sitting in, or to have carried him down the stairs and out into the street, or to have aided in settling him in the Peterson house across the way, at 453 Tenth Street, where nine hours later he would finally die.

Those who couldn't get a hand on the president rushed to police headquarters farther down Tenth Street, to add their recollections of the moment to what quickly became a tidal wave of often conflicting testimony. A deeply human man, Lincoln was on his way to immortal-ity from the moment Booth pulled the trigger. It was only natural to want to put your oar in at the moment of transformation.

———

Almost alone among the crowd at Fords Theatre that evening, Leonard James Farwell seems to have worried less about the dying president than the man who would be replacing him. Farwell and Andrew Johnson had suites down the hall from each other at Kirkwood House on the northeast corner of Pennsylvania Avenue and Twelfth Street, four blocks from the White House and a short walk from Ford's Theatre. They were both ex-governors, Farwell of Wisconsin and Johnson of Tennessee. Although the vice president had been living at the hotel for only a month, the two men had come to know each other, and as Lincoln was being carried down the stairs and across the street, Farwell rushed back to the hotel to be by Johnson's side. The *Dictionary of Wisconsin History* concludes its brief entry on Farwell with the observation that he "saved Vice President Andrew Johnson's life on the night Lincoln was assassinated by warning him of an attack." That's not the case. The vice president's would-be assailant lost his nerve—or drank it away—before Farwell ever arrived. The exaggeration is understandable, though. It was a night of excess all the way around.

Leonard Farwell, Johnson's would-be savior, was born in Watertown, in upstate New York, in 1819. Around 1840 he showed up in Milwaukee, where he launched a successful career as a hardware merchant and real-estate entrepreneur. In 1847, two years before Wisconsin became a state, he began amassing large tracts of land east of the future capital at Madison. Farwell would be the state's second governor, serving from 1852 through 1854. A progressive, he helped establish the state's first institute for the deaf and mute. Wisconsin abolished capital punishment under his watch. Mostly Farwell was a one-man chamber of commerce for Madison itself. He built a mill to lure farmers into the city, drained marshes, graded and widened the streets, planted 6,000 maple and cottonwood trees, and sat on the boards of both the Dane County Bank and the Madison Gas Light & Coke Company. For good measure, he also set about giving the bodies of water that surround Madison more easily pronounced names. The largest of the Yahara chain, which the Winnebago had called Wonk-sheck-ho-mik-la, or "where the Indians live," became Lake Mendota, Chippewa for "large" or "great." For himself, Farwell built the grandest house Madison had ever seen in its brief history, a three-story octagonal mansion on what was known as the Third Lake Ridge.

Inevitably, since railroads were America's newest engine of great wealth, Farwell got deeply involved in one: a forty-two mile stretch of track known as the Watertown and Madison Railroad Company. The railroad is what wiped him out. On August 24, 1857, the New York City branch of the Ohio Life Insurance and Trust Company collapsed under the weight of massive embezzlement, and the Panic of 1857 was on. Foreign investors pulled their capital out of American banks, grain prices collapsed, inventory piled up in the factories. Already overbuilt, the smaller railroads went under one by one, and as they did, so vanished the value of all the speculative real estate the railroads were to open up.

Somewhere along the way late in that bottomless year of 1857, Leonard Farwell, who only three years earlier had been Wisconsin's celebrated governor and its capital's most ardent booster, lost his bid for election to the Madison Board of Alderman by nine votes. Bankrupt and in disgrace, he sold his mansion to three men from Milwaukee. The Civil War that began four years later gave Farwell a second chance, and Washington was the place to seize it.

The nation's capital was still in its raw youth at the outbreak of the war. Thomas Jefferson had been the first president to be inaugurated in Washington, on March 4, 1801, less than a year after the seat of power had been officially moved from New York City. Sixty years later, the capital had a grand plan—Pierre Charles L'Enfant's masterwork—but little to show for it. Funds were in chronically short supply. So was interest in a nation that still cared more for its state capitals, places like Farwell's Madison, than its national one. As the late historian Shelby Foote pointed out, it wasn't until after the Civil War that the United States was generally regarded as grammatically singular. Before the war, sentences would commonly begin: "The United States of America are..."

The U.S. Census of 1860 recorded 61,122 people living in the

District of Columbia—1,245 fewer residents than Albany, New York; about half the residents of Chicago; 100,000 fewer than Cincinnati; a little better than one-twentieth the population of New York City and Brooklyn (then a separate municipality) combined. Washington city maps of the time show a populated area that stretched from the Potomac River to Boundary Street, now Florida Avenue. North of Rhode Island Avenue, though, travelers were already in the sticks.

The U.S. Capitol had two new wings by the time the 1860s began, but not yet its current dome. A plan to erect a privately financed grand equestrian monument to George Washington had petered out in 1855 for lack of contributions. Thus far, there was only a stub to honor the first president. A block west of it, the National Mall extended like a thumb out into the river. The Mall itself was split lengthwise by a grimy canal. Everything south of what is now Constitution Avenue and west of Seventeenth Street was swamp. The Potomac sat mostly stagnant over the current sites of the Lincoln Memorial, the FDR Memorial, and the memorials to the Vietnam and Korean wars, at an average depth of about one foot—a breeding ground for mosquitoes and the malaria they carried. One building survives today on the Mall from that era— the red brick, castlelike Smithsonian, designed by James Renwick and built with funds bequeathed to the new nation by Scotsman James Smithson.

The Civil War changed all that: not the topography, not the grandeur—least of all that—but the population, the scope, the power of the city. With the enemy staring at it from across the Potomac, with the Custis mansion once occupied by Robert E. Lee looking down on the White House, Washington became in effect the forward headquarters of the vast, two-million-man Union army: a military base, the center of war strategy and political intrigue, a communications hub, and a hospital grounds accessible by both rail and steamship. Suddenly the capital was a business hub, too, because the government—as governments do in wartime—was printing money and in the market for everything from mules to muslin, hardtack to cannonballs. Then, as now, the place crawled with lawyers advertising themselves, to cite just a few examples, as "Collectors of Claims Against the Government & Negotiators of Contracts" and to "Procure Pensions, Bounty, Back Pay, & Arrears of Pay on Reasonable Terms."

In four short years, as the war raged around it, Washington's population doubled. Hotels and rooming houses scrambled to expand capacity. A newspaper advertisement from the spring of 1865 notes in capital letters that the Kirkwood House "has been thoroughly renovated and repaired and contains all the requisites of a first-class hotel, is centrally located, and convenient to the business portion of the city and public buildings, city railways, &c." An accompanying sketch shows a four-story wooden facade with a recessed fifth floor on top, six windows wide on Pennsylvania Avenue and twelve windows deep heading back north on Twelfth Street. The Kirkwood had its own restaurant, a saloon, a billiards room. It was a hotel for politicians and businessmen. Deal makers, preference seekers, and profiteers flowed to its doors. Among them was Leonard Farwell.

By 1863, Farwell had landed a job as an assistant examiner in the U.S. Patent Office, the sort of patronage post a once-prominent Whig down on his luck might find in a rapidly expanding federal government, especially one controlled by the Whig's successor party, the Republicans. He would stay at the Patent Office for the next seven years, rising ultimately to become a principal examiner, one cog among many, in one office among many, in a bureaucracy that cared little for individual achievement. The night of April 14 and morning of April 15, 1865, were Farwell's time to shine, and he made the most of it.

Seven weeks later, on June 3, 1865, Farwell told the military tribunal trying the alleged plotters, the assassins, and the would-be assassins, that on the evening of April 14 he had gone immediately from Ford's Theatre to Kirkwood House, arriving there sometime between "ten and half-past ten o'clock...I ran as soon as possible for Johnson's door." The door, he said, appeared to be locked, although he couldn't swear to the fact. Nor could he swear that no one was lying in wait although he didn't recall seeing anyone. "I rapped and received no answer," Farwell told the commission. "I then rapped again and said in a loud voice, 'Governor Johnson, if you are in the room, I must see you." After rousing Johnson from a deep sleep, Farwell remained in his room about half an hour, keeping the door bolted from the inside and carefully screening anyone who sought entry. At his insistence, the front desk provided a guard just outside the door.

Farwell would later recall that his first words to Johnson once he had gained entry to the room were, "Someone has shot and murdered the President." With that, he said, the two men fell into each other's arms and clung together for support while Johnson wept. A surviving image of Farwell—a head-and-shoulders portrait executed a dozen years earlier when he was governor of Wisconsin—gives him a high forehead, a prominent nose, and an elongated oval of a face, all framed by a crown of dark hair and a full beard. It's hard to envision him or anyone else holding the mercurial, square-bodied, scowling Johnson in his arms at a moment of such high emotion. The vice president was not a man constructed for comforting.

Few events in American history have been more pored over than the Lincoln assassination, yet despite the almost obsessive examination, questions still remain. Did Mary Surratt deserve to die for her part in the conspiracy—the first American woman ever executed under federal mandate? Or was it merely happenstance or not quite full culpability, that so much of the planning for the murders seemed to have taken place at the boarding house she owned and ran at 541 H Street in Washington, in what is now Chinatown? Was it cruel and unusual punishment to condemn Dr. Samuel Mudd to that most distant of American prisons, Fort Jefferson in the Dry Tortugas, for the simple act of setting John Wilkes Booth's broken leg? Or was Dr. Mudd—the origin of the phrase "his name is mud"—a fellow traveler?

The challenge of sorting out the actual conspirators from those who might have been merely guilty by association is compounded by the fact that the plot was so long unfolding. Booth had been hanging around the capital since well before the inaugural, looking first for an opening to kidnap the president and others, then when Lee's surrender and the fall of Richmond made kidnapping impractical, plotting to kill the lot of them. He knew scores of people around town by first name, and in the immediate aftermath of the assassination, merely to have been associated with Lincoln's assassin was grounds for suspicion. Booth was also part of a web of Confederate sympathizers and operatives who traveled back and forth across the easily navigable river that separated North and South. Indeed, the webs of deceit hung so heavily over the enterprise and were so entangled that at some distant point on the horizon all the lingering questions about the conspiracy seem to converge. Samuel Mudd, for example, had been the first person to introduce John Wilkes Booth to Mary Surratt's son, John, who was initially suspected of the attack on William Seward and his family.

The before-and-after questions—who helped plan and to what extent? who abetted the escapes and to what degree?—will never be answered to everyone's satisfaction. History isn't that simple, nor is human nature. Yet the actual details of the murders and attempted murders are largely beyond question. When the moment to strike finally presented itself, Booth took Lincoln, the biggest prize, and succeeded spectacularly.

The task of murdering Seward, already bedridden from a carriage accident, fell to Lewis Powell, one of the more frightening minor figures in American history, who was assisted by David Herold. The one thirty A.M. update on the attack that the *New York Herald* offered its readers the next morning is a miracle of accuracy, considering that the events described had occurred only a little more than three hours earlier, in a city consumed by wild speculation and innuendo:

> About ten o'clock a man rang the bell, and the call having been answered by a colored servant, he said he had come from Dr. Verdi, Secretary Seward's family physician, with a prescription,

at the same time holding in his hand a small piece of folded paper, and saying, in answer to a refusal, that he must see the Secretary, as he was entrusted with particular directions concerning the medicine.

He still insisted on going up, although repeatedly informed that no one could enter the chamber. The man pushed the servant aside, and walked hastily towards the Secretary's room, and was then met by Mr. Frederick Seward [one of William Seward's sons], of whom he demanded to see the Secretary making the same representation which he did to the servant.

What further passed in the way of colloquy is not known; but the man struck him on the head with a billy, severely injuring the skull and felling him almost senseless.

The assassin then rushed into the chamber and attacked Major Seward [another son], Paymaster United States Army, and Mr. Hansell, a messenger of the State Department, and two male nurses, disabling them all.

He then rushed upon the Secretary, who was lying in bed in the same room, and inflicted three stabs in the neck, but severing, it is thought and hoped, no arteries, though he bled profusely.

The assassin then rushed down the stairs, ran out the door, mounted his horse, and rode off before [an] alarm could be sounded, and in [the] same manner as the assassin of the President.

A modern account of the same events offered by Michael W. Kauffman in *American Brutus*, his exhaustively researched study of the Lincoln assassination conspiracies, differs only marginally on the facts, but is less squeamish. Instead of a billy, Powell produced a pistol, pressed it against Frederick Seward's temple, and pulled the trigger. When the gun failed to fire, he brought it crashing down on Frederick's skull, pushed his way into the secretary of state's bedroom, slashed his male nurse (in fact, an

Army private named George Robinson) with a large knife, and then attacked Seward himself, twisting his head so he could get to the jugular vein. Robinson and another son, Augustus, finally pinned Powell to the floor, but when Augustus left to get his pistol, Powell threw off Robinson, made for the stairs, knocked down Hansell the messenger and stabbed him, too, in the back, and burst out the front door, screaming "I'm mad! I'm mad!"

Mad, he might well have been, or at least temporarily crazed. Lewis Powell was handsome, powerfully built, and in other circumstances a man who readily impressed people. Amazingly enough, though, he failed in his task. Seward was already in his midsixties at the time of the attack. His lower face would be forever disfigured by the wounds. Yet Seward did survive—long enough to fulfill his second term as secretary of state, long enough to buy Alaska from the Russian czars for the ridiculous, bargain-basement price of $7.2 million, long enough indeed to stand by Johnson's side through all the ugliness to follow. Still, William Seward paid a terrible price for what happened that night of April 14, 1865, worse in some ways than Mary Todd Lincoln herself. Already incapacitated, Seward's wife never recovered from the shock of having her home invaded and her loved ones attacked. She died a few months later. His only daughter, Fanny, who had been in the bedroom with her father when Powell broke in and whose screams had brought Augustus running, didn't recover from the experience, either. She was dead within the year.

The attack on Andrew Johnson, the projected third victim (or fourth, if Grant is included) on what was to have been a night of murder, produced fewer dramatics for the simple reason that nothing ever really happened.

The task fell, or was supposed to fall, to George Atzerodt, a carriage-maker who split his time between the capital and his home in Port Tobacco, Maryland, southeast of the capital at the top of a long inlet of the lower Potomac River. In his early thirties by the time the war drew to a close, Atzerodt had been an active supporter of the Confederate cause, helping to smuggle spies across the river into Union territory. Like many in the border regions, he also came from a family of divided loyalties. His brother-in-law, a detective on the staff of the provost marshal of Baltimore, would help to run him down after the assassination. However, nothing in George Atzerodt's life or in his character seems to have prepared him for the assignment Booth had handed him.

Atzerodt did check into the Kirkwood House on the morning he was to murder the vice president, paid cash in advance, and was assigned to room 126, one floor above Johnson's suite. What's more, he had access to the necessary tools to do the job. At his trial, John Lee, chief of detectives to the provost marshal of Washington, testified about what he discovered at Kirkwood House on the very early morning of April 15. Atzerodt had signed in at the hotel under his own name, written so badly that Lee at first couldn't read it. Room 126 was locked, and since no key was available, Lee busted down the door. Inside he found a black coat hanging on the wall, new gloves, a piece of licorice and a toothbrush, two collars, a pair of socks and a brass spur, and three boxes of Colt cartridges. A revolver, loaded and capped, was hidden beneath the pillow; a bowie knife, stuffed between the sheets and the mattress. Lee also uncovered a bank book that showed $455 deposited with the Ontario Bank of Canada by a Mr. J. Wilkes Booth.

Just as clearly, Atzerodt had set about doing the basics of his business, almost certainly at Booth's urging. A Colonel W. R. Nevins, age sixty-two, testified at the same trial that on the late afternoon of April 12 he had come across George Atzerodt at the Kirkwood House, in the hallway that led from Johnson's suite to the dining room. "He asked me if I knew where Vice-President Johnson or his room was. I do not remember which he asked first, and I showed him on the left-hand side where the room was, and told him that the Vice-President was then at dinner. There was no other person excepting the Vice-President in the dining room at the time.... I thought he was a stranger and referred him to the vice-president's servant, who was a yellow man, standing behind him…He looked in the dining room. I do not know whether he went in or not."

When asked to describe the man he had encountered that afternoon, Colonel Nevins noted that the subject had been wearing dark clothes and a low-crowned black felt hat. As for his appearance, Nevins testified that he could pick Atzerodt out from among 50,000 men. "I think you would have to look at a great many before you would see one exactly the same."

Atzerodt also had the opportunity to carry out his mission, indeed more than enough of it. John Lee, who examined room 126 within hours of the time appointed for murdering Johnson, noted that the steps down to the first floor led directly to Johnson's room. "When I came down, there was a soldier at the door. A man of any courage coming right down the stairs could throw a handful of snuff in the soldier's eyes and get right into Mr. Johnson's room."

Courage, though, seems to be exactly what Atzerodt did lack in any measure. To kill the toughest of the three targets who remained after Grant's departure, the only one who was battle tested, Booth sent less a desperado than a bundle of desperations. A close-up photo of Atzerodt shows a ferret-faced man with puffy, oddly asymmetrical eyes. He's half-shaven with a moustache and the makings of a sneer, and the same low-crowned felt hat that Nevins described, this time jammed tight down on his head as if he were afraid it might fly off in a breeze. It's a face that looks like it has just stepped out of one bar and is about to step into another one, which is essentially what George Atzerodt did on the evening in question. Booth had recruited Atzerodt months earlier to help kidnap Lincoln; now he was being told to assassinate the vice president, and assured that even if he didn't make the attempt, he would hang should the conspirators be caught. It was a dilemma, and Atzerodt responded, at least in part, by trying to drink it away.

The charges and specifications ultimately brought against Atzerodt would include: "lying in wait with intent maliciously, unlawfully, and traitorously to kill and murder the said Andrew Johnson." In fact, the closest Atzerodt came to actually lying in wait for Johnson was the tavern at the Kirkwood House. By ten P.M., as Lewis Powell was preparing to force his way into Seward's house, and Booth was advancing on the presidential box at Ford's Theatre—and at the moment he himself should have been closing in for the kill in suite sixty-eight—Atzerodt was instead presenting himself at J. Naylor's livery stable at Fourteenth and E streets, three blocks away. Atzerodt had earlier directed the foreman, John Fletcher, to keep a mare saddled and ready for him: a getaway horse, presumably. Instead of claiming his ride, Atzerodt asked Fletcher to join him for a drink at the nearby Union Hotel, at the corner of Thirteen-and-a-half and E streets.

"I told him I would have a glass of beer. He took some whisky," Fletcher would later testify. "Returning to the stable he said, 'If this thing happens tonight, you will hear of a present.' He seemed to me as if he was about half-tight, and I did not pay much attention to him." At Naylor's stable, Atzerodt mounted the mare that was waiting for him there and rode the few blocks to Kirkwood House. Fletcher watched him walk inside and walk out again after only a few minutes. The drinks meant to give him nerve had instead dissolved it.

An hour or so later, sometime between eleven thirty and midnight, another acquaintance, Washington Briscoe, came across Atzerodt on a "car," a horse-drawn omnibus, headed for the Navy Yard on the far eastern side of the city. "I judged from his manner he was a little excited," Briscoe told the court. As for whether Atzerodt had been drinking, "I hardly know," he said. "I did not notice him very particularly." Atzerodt begged Briscoe to let him sleep in the store near the Navy Yard that doubled as his home, but Briscoe refused. The two talked briefly about the assassination—everyone in Washington was talking about it by then— before Atzerodt caught a car back toward the center of town.

By no later than one that evening, again mounted, Atzerodt appeared at another of his old haunts, the Pennsylvania Hotel on C Street, where he asked James Walker, a black waiter and stable hand, to hold his horse while he went into the bar. After he'd had more to drink, Atzerodt rode off. By the middle of the night, roughly between two and three, he was back, on foot this time, asking for a room, even though he had already paid in advance for one at the Kirkwood House.

Atzerodt would later testify that the weapons left behind in room 126 belonged to another of the co-conspirators, David Herold, who had ridden off with Powell. Since Atzerodt was carrying his own revolver and bowie knife on the night of fourteenth and the morning of the fifteenth, the claim is likely accurate. Nonetheless, Atzerodt was shedding evidence fast and furiously. The knife, by his own admission, he threw in the gutter opposite the Patent Office on F Street, between Eighth and Ninth streets. A woman who lived along the street saw it lying there about six A.M. from her third floor window and sent her maid down to recover it. At eight Saturday morning, John Caldwell was at work at the Matthews & Co. store at 49 High Street in Georgetown, when Atzerodt came in and borrowed ten dollars, leaving his revolver behind as security. By then he was on his way out of town, headed up the Frederick Road to Germantown, Maryland, where he was known as Andrew Atwood. (Powell, too, traveled with a pocketful of false names: That seems to be about the only thing the two men had in common.) In Germantown, Atzerodt was finally run to ground, on April 20.

He had struck no blow or directly helped anyone escape, yet such an ineluctable chain of evidence—from numerous public meetings, to horse rentals, and way too much more—tied Atzerodt to Lincoln's assassin that he must have realized from the moment of his arrest that his life was over. He did try to cooperate with the government, talking freely in prison. With the help of his brother-in-law, the same government agent who had helped arrest him, Atzerodt even put together a statement, a confession of sorts, in which he implicated Dr. Mudd while denying any advance knowledge of Lincoln's murder and the attempted murder of Seward, and any involvement in the plot to murder the vice president. The confession, though, rambled all over the place. In it, and in all his other statements, Atzerodt was open about his involvement in the plot to kidnap the president, but his revelations were contradictory, the lies plentiful. In the end, he had nothing to trade, nothing the government could use. Even his information on Mudd was secondhand.

It didn't help that Atzerodt cut so poor a figure in the courtroom and everywhere else. A *Washington Evening Star* report on his capture and transfer to Washington concludes: "He has a thoroughly bad face and repulsive manners." Nor did it help Atzerodt that he was being tried by a nine-man military commission that required only a simple majority, and only six votes to impose the death penalty. Or that the commission had been created upon a proclamation issued by the man he was accused of being sent to murder. Ultimately the military commission would hear from 366 witnesses. Testimony would fill almost 5,000 pages; the trial dragged on for more than seven weeks. For George Atzerodt, though, as for the other principals, this was a stacked deck from day one.

The most effective defense Atzerodt's legal representative could muster was that he wasn't man enough to undertake the mission. Two acquaintances, Alexander Brawner and Louis Harkins, testified that Atzerodt was apt to run from a fight and widely considered to be lacking in nerve. Washington Briscoe, who denied Atzerodt lodging the night of attacks, said it best: Atzerodt "was always called a man of not much courage." Asked outright if Atzerodt was "considered remarkable for cowardice," Briscoe answered, "Yes, sir; he was."

For the defendant, this must have made for painful listening. In the end, none of it was enough to prevent Atzerodt from being found guilty on June 30 and sentenced "to be hanged by the neck until he be dead, at such time and place as the President of the United States shall direct." The time chosen was July 7, 1865; the place, the yard of the Old Arsenal, the first United States penitentiary. There, at one in the afternoon, Atzerodt died in the company of Lewis Powell, David Herold, and Mary Surratt—surely the most famous mass execution in American history, faithfully recorded in an unsettling series of photos by Alexander Gardner.

One more piece of the Johnson nonassassination story remains to be mentioned. On the afternoon of the day he was to murder the president of the United States, John Wilkes Booth walked over to the Kirkwood House, asked the desk clerk for a card to write on, and left a note for Andrew Johnson: "Don't wish to disturb you. Are you at home? J. Wilkes Booth."

Forensically, the note was—and remains—meaningless. Booth was shot at point-blank range inside a burning barn and died before he could be asked about the note's intent. Perhaps Booth was trying to cover his tracks, although such tracks were just what he wanted. Not long before he left the note for Johnson, he had asked an acquaintance to deliver a letter the next morning to the *National Intelligencer* in which Booth took credit for the crimes about to be committed, adding Powell, Herold, and Atzerodt's names with his own, although as a show of rank Booth named his three co-conspirators by last name only. More likely, he was just sowing confusion, shoving a burr under the loathed vice president's saddle.

If the latter was his aim, it worked, Mary Todd Lincoln took the few words as evidence that the vice president was in some way in league with the man who had murdered her husband, and she often spoke and wrote of her suspicions—to War Secretary Edwin Stanton, who would in time become Johnson's implacable enemy; to her personal friends and associates; to anyone, it seemed, who would stop and listen. "That, that miserable inebriate Johnson, had cognizance of my husband's death," she wrote to her friend Sally Orne in March 1866. "Why, was that card of Booth's, found in his box, some acquaintance certainly existed. I have been deeply impressed, with the harrowing thought, that he, had an understanding with the conspirators & they knew their man. As sure, as you & I live, Johnson, had some hand, in all this." In fact, the president's murder seems finally to have broken Mrs. Lincoln with woe. Their eleven-year-old son, Willie, had died of typhoid in 1862. Another son, Eddie, had perished a dozen years earlier, not yet four years old. Now her husband had joined them. In the summer of 1866, when Johnson was touring through Illinois, the still-grieving widow would accuse him of "desecrating" Lincoln's grave.

Johnson wasn't alone in bearing the brunt of Mrs. Lincoln's suspicions. Inconsolable in her grief and despair, she leveled many of the same charges against Charles Forbes, a White House messenger who had been sitting outside the president's box and had allowed Booth entry—although "allowed" stretches the facts, since Lincoln had neither bodyguards that evening nor any formal security apparatus. The United States Secret Service wouldn't come into existence for another two and a half months, and then to run down currency counterfeiters, not to protect a president, though one had just been assassinated.

Mrs. Lincoln was not the only one in the president's box on April 14 who became a secondhand victim of Booth. Henry Rathbone and Clara Harris married two years after the attack. The two had three children and eventually, under Grover Cleveland, Henry became United States consul general to Germany. Demons had haunted him ever since the assassination, though. His behavior grew increasingly erratic. On December 23, 1883, in Hanover, Germany, Henry murdered Clara and was only prevented from murdering their children as well by a nurse. In the aftermath, he stabbed himself six times, survived, and was committed to an asylum for the criminally insane, where he died twenty-eight years later, in 1911, in his mid-seventies.

In the cool light of history, we can tease out the separate strands of the Lincoln assassination conspiracy and examine them one by one: Powell went here, Booth was there, so-and-so held horses for them. Addled by drink, Atzerodt failed his end of the bargain miserably. A logic runs between the various elements; threads begin to connect. We can see the plot in part and in whole. (And the preceding pages represent only a submicroscopic particle of the immense body of scholarship and writing devoted to the conspiracy.)

It's possible, even, to argue that the assassination should have been expected, or at least the possibility better defended against. The Confederacy had resisted the North at every turn, had sacrificed a frightening proportion of its sons and fathers—a quarter of all Southern white males of military age—and virtually all its resources. Robert E. Lee might have been ready to lay down arms, but Jefferson Davis wasn't, and his government might have been expected to be more dangerous the more cornered it became. Seward himself had talked about the possibility with Attorney General James Speed eleven days earlier. The fall of Richmond had left Southerners feeling as if the world had come to an end; if the war was to end in assassinations, now was the time. In Europe, attacks on heads of state had become almost commonplace by midcentury. Why not in Washington, too, especially since the capital had been a sump of intrigue throughout the entire war?

In the heat of the moment, though, when faces were pressed up against the window, everything was a jumble. Along with John Surratt, George Atzerodt was widely suspected of having inflicted the savage attack on William Seward and his family. Although Ulysses Grant had left town by the time the conspirators struck, word persisted that he had been included in the attacks. One rumor held that Grant had been murdered in his railroad car as the train sat at the station in Havre de Grace, Maryland, halfway between Baltimore and Wilmington, Delaware. Indeed, when Atzerodt arrived on the fifteenth in Germantown, eighteen miles from the White House on a well-traveled road, one of the first questions he was asked was whether it was true that Grant, too, was dead. (Grant was already back in Washington when the question was asked. He'd gotten word of the attacks in Philadelphia and immediately reversed course.) Across the Potomac in Virginia, word flew through one Wisconsin artillery unit that Lincoln had been shot in the hand and Andrew Johnson killed. On most matters, everyone from the highest level to the lowest was equally in the dark.

The diary kept by Gideon Welles, a former Connecticut newspaper editor and part owner (*The Hartford Times*) and secretary of the navy under Lincoln and Johnson, captures perfectly the dark chaos of the time. Welles's home, like Seward's, was on Lafayette Square, and the

Square itself is directly across Pennsylvania Avenue from the White House. More central one cannot be.

I had retired to bed about half past ten on the evening of the 14th of April—was just getting to sleep when my wife said someone was at our door. Sitting up in bed, I heard a voice twice call to John, my son whose sleeping room was on the second floor directly over the front entrance. I arose at once and raised a window, when my messenger James Smith called to me that Mr. Lincoln the president had been shot; and said Secretary Seward and his son, Assistant Secretary Frederick Seward, were assassinated. James was much alarmed and excited. I told him his story was very incoherent and improbable—that he was associating men who were not together and liable to attack at the same time. "Where," I inquired, "was the President when shot?" James said he was at Ford's Theatre on 10th Street. "Well," said I, "Secretary Seward is an invalid in bed in his house yonder on 15th Street." James said he had been there—stopped in at the house to make inquiry before alarming me.

I immediately dressed myself, and against the earnest remonstrance and appeals of my wife went directly to Mr. Seward's, whose residence was on the east side of the Square, mine being on the north. James accompanied me. As we were crossing 15th St. I saw four or five men in earnest consultation, standing under the lamp on the corner of St. John's Church. Before I had got half way across the street, the lamp was suddenly extinguished and the knot of persons rapidly dispersed. For a moment and but a moment, I was disconcerted to find myself in darkness but recollecting that it was late and about time for the moon to rise, I proceeded on, not having lost 5 steps, merely making a pause without stopping....

Entering the house, I found the lower hall and office full of persons, and among them most of the foreign legations, all anxiously inquiring what truth there was in the horrible rumor afloat. I explained that my object was to ascertain the facts.

Upstairs, Welles learned that Frederick Seward had indeed been attacked and saw with his own eyes the grievously injured secretary of state being attended by Dr. Verdi: "The bed was saturated with blood. The Secretary was lying on his back, the upper part of his head covered by a cloth, which extended over the eyes. His mouth was open, the lower jaw dropping down."

Welles was leaving Seward's house just as Edwin Stanton arrived. As secretary of war, Stanton controlled the Military Telegraph Service, which brought the most pressing news to Washington. Lincoln spent half the Civil War, it seemed, in Stanton's office, keeping up with events. Stanton had his finger on every pulse. He was ready to act. Indeed, before midnight orders would go out to the seventy-two forts encircling Washington to seal the city's boundaries, including the roads and bridges out of town. Yet it soon became apparent that Stanton had little more idea what was going on than Welles. Like the Navy secretary, he had heard the rumor that the president had been shot, had even talked with a man who claimed to have been present when it happened. Yet although Stanton told Welles that he was heading to Ford's Theatre next, he had hurried to Seward's house first, an indication that he considered it the greater crime scene or perhaps just a sign of Stanton's shock.

In all the confusion of the night of April 14, 1865, and morning of the fifteenth amid all the uncertainties and panic and freshly hatching conspiracy theories, one fact was absolutely clear to everyone who had seen him: Though breathing, Abraham Lincoln was a dead man. By noon, if not earlier, Andrew Johnson would be president of the United States. "The president is still alive but in precarious condition," the *New York Herald* informed readers in its earliest edition. A one A.M. dispatch confirmed that Lincoln was "perfectly senseless, and there is not the slightest hope of his surviving." By one thirty A.M., the details of the initial discovery of the wound had become horribly graphic. "On a hasty examination it was found that the President had been shot through the head, above and back of the temporal bone, and that some of the brain was oozing out."

The scene at the president's bedside, meanwhile, was "described by those who witnessed it as most affecting," the reporter wrote.

[The President] was surrounded by his Cabinet ministers, all of whom were bathed in tears, not even excepting Mr. Stan[t]on, who when informed by Surgeon General Barnes, that the President would not live until morning, exclaimed "Oh, no, General, no-no," and with an impulse natural as it was unaffected, immediately sat down on a chair near his bedside and wept like a child.

Senator Sumner was seated on the right of the President's couch, near the head, holding the right hand of the President in his own. He was sobbing like a woman, with his head bowed down almost on the pillow of the bed on which the President was lying.

At Kirkwood House, as many as 500 people had gathered to wait out events, poised between the dying president and the one-to-be. Behind his closed door, Johnson paced back and forth, bemoaning Lincoln and cursing those who had committed the crime. At Johnson's urging, Farwell, who really does seem to have been the picture of efficiency that night, had gone over to the Peterson house to inquire about Lincoln's condition and to consult with officials there about a guard detail for the vice president.

Sometime after one in the morning, word was sent back to Johnson: He was to attend President Lincoln. How he went, how large was his detail, is told in various ways, depending on how the teller regarded Andrew Johnson. In his generally admiring and jauntily written 1928 biography of Johnson, Robert W. Winston describes the scene thus:

"Against the remonstrance of friends the Vice-president insisted on going to President Lincoln's bedside. Accompanied by Major O'Beirne, Andrew Johnson left his apartments and made his way through vast crowds to the deathbed." In his more authoritative 1989 biography on Johnson, Hans L. Trefousse largely agrees with Winston's account: Although his friends urged him to be more careful, Johnson simply buttoned his coat, pulled his hat low, perhaps to shield his face, and left for the Peterson house with only O'Beirne and Farwell for company.

Both accounts are certainly consistent with Johnson's personal bravery—another element George Atzerodt would have had to contend with had he gotten up the nerve to burst through the vice president's door. Johnson seems to have been constitutionally incapable of running from a fight. In Nashville, as military governor, he had faced constant danger. Walking those three blocks to the dying president's bedside through teeming crowds accompanied only by James R. O'Beirne, the provost marshal of Washington, or perhaps by O'Beirne and Farwell, would have been an almost predictable act of courage.

And yet the crowds were more than teeming. They were agitated and vengeful, a volatile combination. Walt Whitman, who spent much of the war in the nation's capital helping to nurse the wounded, describes in his journals a near lynching that took place in the streets outside Ford's Theatre that night, a few blocks from Kirkwood House and within an hour or two of the time Johnson would have been heading that way on foot.

> The infuriated crowd, through some chance, got started against one man, either for words he utter'd, or perhaps without any cause at all, and were proceeding at once to actually hang him on a neighboring lamp post, when he was rescued by a few heroic policemen, who placed him in their midst and fought their way slowly and amid great peril toward the Station House.... The night, the yells, the pale faces, many frighten'd people trying in vain to extricate themselves—the attack'd man,

not yet freed from the jaws of death, looking like a corpse—the silent resolute half-dozen policemen, with no weapons but their little clubs, yet stern and steady through all those eddying swarms—made indeed a fitting side-scene to the grand tragedy of the murder.

Lincoln was fatally wounded; Seward, near death for all that most people knew. The evidence that Johnson was to have been included among their numbers was already mounting. The capital sat a mere hundred yards across the Potomac from the enemy. To have allowed Johnson to walk virtually unaccompanied to the Peterson house on such a night, in such circumstances, among such people, seems unthinkable in retrospect. Johnson was, after all, soon to be the next president. Even by his own exalted standards of obstinacy, to have insisted on going virtually alone would seem nearly insane. One newspaper drawing of the time shows Johnson at the middle of a tight cluster of guards. Whether accurate or not, the depiction seems at least a more reasonable course of action.

Then there are those who contend that Johnson never went to visit the dying president at all, that he never left his rooms because he was on a bender and had been on one for weeks. Johnson, in this version, was every inch the "miserable inebriate" Mary Lincoln would later decry in her letter to Sally Orne. The charge hung around for decades after the event, threatened to die out, then was revived in 1908 when William Morris Stewart, who came to the Senate in 1864 to represent the new state of Nevada and would stay for two terms, published his *Reminiscences*. Johnson, he wrote, "did not know of the President's death until seven or eight o'clock next day," and then only because Stewart himself woke the vice president from a drunken sleep and dragged him to the White House, where Edwin Stanton sent for a tailor, a barber, and a doctor to make him presentable enough to swear into office a few hours later. Like Stanton, Stewart would become an arch political enemy of the new president.

Johnson did call on the president, at about two in the morning. Every reputable source has him there, including Charles Sumner, who sat weeping by Lincoln's side. A Currier & Ives print published later in the year shows Johnson standing in the foreground by the president's bedside when Lincoln finally died. That, in fact, is not so. Johnson stayed a brief while and might have stayed longer, but word arrived that the First Lady was coming to be with her husband, and Stanton hurried Johnson from the room. The secretary of war knew Mary Lincoln couldn't abide the man in the best of times; in these, the worst, it was impossible to predict to what extremes her enmity might reach.

Truncated as the visit was, it must have been awkward for Johnson. He barely knew some of the people in the room with Lincoln, and he'd been drunk and on public display the last time he'd seen most of the others. One or two of them almost certainly shared the First Lady's concern that the vice president's hands were less than clean. However much he had sacrificed for the Union cause, he was a Southerner. Who else had more to gain than Johnson by the death now playing itself out?

Back at Kirkwood House, again behind closed doors, Johnson paced more, sent up more oaths: "They shall suffer for this; they shall suffer for this." He was still at it, sleepless, at 7:22 that morning when Abraham Lincoln breathed his last, Surgeon General Barnes placed silver half dollars on the dead president's eyes, and Stanton uttered his famous benediction: "Now he belongs to the ages."

Secretary of the Treasury Hugh McCulloch and Attorney General James Speed brought official word to Kirkwood House that the president was dead. With them was written notification that Andrew Johnson was to be the nation's seventeenth president. Both men had signed it, along with Secretary of War Stanton, Secretary of the Navy Welles, Interior Secretary John Usher, and William Dennison, the postmaster general. Secretary of State Seward, the missing member of what was then a seven-person cabinet, was too grievously wounded to sign his name.

Johnson suggested that the swearing in be held in his rooms at the hotel, and thus at eleven on the morning of April 15, 1865—in the presence of McCulloch, Speed, Francis Preston Blair Sr. (of Blair House fame today) and his son, Montgomery, and a handful of others—Chief Justice Salmon Chase administered the oath of office. As every president before and since him has, Johnson vowed to "preserve, protect, and defend the Constitution of the United States." The ritual had become by then almost a familiar event in Washington. Of the last seven vice presidents, three, including Johnson, had been called on to assume the highest office upon the death of the president. Yet if the nation had become inured to the mechanics of succession, this was without precedent.

Ford's Theatre is today a working theater, a museum, and a national historic site. Tour buses bring students from around the country to gape at Booth's derringer and the clothes Lincoln wore that night. Peterson House, across the street, is now both a museum and a maudlin shrine, home, among other objects, to the bloodstained pillow where the president last rested his head. Kirkwood House, by contrast, is long gone— an office building stands there now—and every artifact of Johnson's swearing in has disappeared along with it.

A drawing for the January 6, 1866, edition of *Frank Leslie's Illustrated Newspaper* shows eight men standing in a small room with heavy draperies covering the windows at the far end. Johnson and Salmon Chase are standing at the center, under a chandelier. Johnson has his left hand resting on an open Bible, his right one slightly raised. His legs are spread, as if he were trying to keep his balance on a lightly rolling ship. Chase, the chief justice, is ramrod straight.

On its Web site, the Joint Congressional Committee on Inaugural Ceremonies notes that while the origin of the Bible used in the ceremony is unknown, it was thought to have been opened to Proverbs 20 and 21. Perhaps the committee is trying to assure posterity that Johnson had learned the lesson of his egregious behavior six weeks earlier, for Proverbs 20 begins: "Wine is a mocker, strong drink is raging; and whosoever is deceived thereby, is not wise." The Bible used in the ceremony was indeed turned to the Old Testament. The scant evidence available, however, suggests that it was opened not to Proverbs, but to the book of the prophet Ezekiel—to chapter 11, with special emphasis on the twenty-first verse: "But *as for them* whose heart walketh after the heart of their detestable things and their abominations, I will recompense their way upon their own heads, saith the Lord God."

Certainly, that sounds more like Johnson. Beyond doubt, too, the verse reflects the expectations for a Johnson presidency. When word finally did penetrate to the nooks and crannies of the South that Lincoln was murdered and the Tennessean was president, more than a few Confederate patriots cursed Booth for the fate he had visited on the failed nation he professed to love. The war wasn't over, but Lincoln had won it—Lincoln and Grant and Sherman and Sheridan and others in the field. Now, the task of determining what the terms of peace would be, and thus what a rejoined America would be like years and decades hence and even in centuries to come, had fallen to Andrew Johnson.

In an April 15 letter, Edward Bates, attorney general in the first Lincoln administration, wrote Johnson that he was assuming office "in the most critical moment in all our history." Three days after he had sworn Johnson into office, Salmon Chase wrote a note of his own: "Everything now, under God, must depend on you."

CHAPTER 2

Apprentice Boy

ANDREW JOHNSON WAS BORN on December 29, 1808, in Raleigh, North Carolina, then a town of not many more than a thousand people, a third of whom were slaves. In December 1811, his father, Jacob, leapt fearlessly into a pond to save three boaters whose canoe had overturned. Though he succeeded, Jacob died within a month of exposure to the icy water.

That much of Johnson's biography everyone seems able to agree on. Yet it is still another indication of the scant regard history has held for the seventeenth president that even the most basic details of Johnson's earliest years seem sketchy in the extreme. For more than a century after his death, it was widely believed that Johnson had been born at a rambling Raleigh hotel known as Casso's Inn, where Jacob worked as a porter. A wedding party was said to be underway when Mary McDonough Johnson, known as Polly, gave birth to her third child and second son in a small cabin behind the hotel. In the extended version, the new bride left her own reception to visit Polly and suggested she name the boy for Andy Jackson, later to be Johnson's role model and hero.

In fact, as Hans L. Trefousse argues convincingly, the birth took place at the Johnson family's two-and-a-half-story log cabin on Carrabus Street, not in the hotel yard. Jacob wasn't merely a hotel porter. A January 12, 1812, obituary in the *Raleigh Star*—written by its owner, Colonel Thomas Henderson, who had been among the boaters rescued by Jacob Johnson—notes that he had "occupied a humble but useful station" as city constable, sexton, and porter to the state bank. "None lament him, except perhaps his own relatives, more than the publisher of this newspaper," Henderson wrote, "for he owes his life . . . to the kindness and humanity of Johnson." Nor did Andy Johnson simply rise up from the dust of obscurity and endless generational poverty as so often is written when his story does get told. The future president could trace his lineage back to Silvanus Johnson, who farmed nearly a thousand acres in Amelia County, Virginia. His great-grandfather, William, had 700 acres of his own. By Jacob Johnson's time, though, the land was gone, sold at sheriff's sale to satisfy debts, and with Jacob's early death, the descent was complete.

Left nearly penniless with two boys—her daughter had already died—Polly bought a loom and with it scraped out a bare living. Around Raleigh, she was known as Polly the Weaver. She married again, to a man named Turner Doughtry. The union, though, seems to have improved neither partner's economic prospects. Polly apprenticed her older son, Willie, to Colonel Henderson, whose life her husband had saved; when the colonel died not long thereafter, Willie was apprenticed to a local tailor, James J. Selby. The younger son, Andrew, mostly ran wild. One tale has him whipped on orders of a local gentleman for running naked across his path, or perhaps for stealing fruit from his daughter. If it's true, the incident must have been early fuel for the lifelong class anger that would drive Johnson. School was out of the question. There was no money for education and none provided free. In November 1818, Polly did with Andrew as she had done with Willie, binding him over to James Selby "till he arrive at lawful age to earn the trade of a Tailor." Johnson was a month shy of ten years old at the time. By contract, he essentially belonged to Selby until he reached age twenty-one.

To the credit of Selby and the other tailors he worked under, Johnson would learn the trade well. More than three decades later, shortly after being sworn in as governor of Tennessee and long after he had given up practicing his trade, Johnson received from a high-ranking state official a set of elaborate fire irons the man had forged himself. Immediately, the new governor set out to make the man a gift in kind. First, he bought some of the finest black broadcloth to be found in all Nashville. Then he took his benefactor's measurements and made him a complete suit, sewing every stitch himself. The anecdote might be apocryphal, the sort of glorifying item campaign biographies are always packed with, and indeed this one does appear in an 1865 book, hastily brought to market upon Johnson's ascension to the presidency by T. B. Peterson & Brothers of Philadelphia, whose bold motto was Cheapest Book House in the World. Yet the story sounds like Johnson: his refusal to owe any man, to put on airs, to be seen as other than what he was. In Nashville, at the start of his first term as governor, he had insisted on walking rather than riding in a carriage to his own inauguration, just as 122 years later, another Southern governor, Jimmy Carter, would insist on walking from the U.S. Capitol to the White House after being sworn in as president.

Tailoring gave Andy Johnson a way of looking at the world: He was always the common man's everyman, the worker's champion, the mechanic's and artisan's best friend. The trade gave him a way of talking about the world, too. The biographer Robert Winston tells of attending as a boy a commencement address Johnson gave in June 1867 on the campus of the University of North Carolina at Chapel Hill. "I have no other ambition in life," the then-embattled president declared, "than to mend and repair the breaches in the torn and tattered Constitution of my country." So compelling was the metaphor, Winston writes, that an elderly woman standing nearby commented, "Bless his dear heart, Andy's going to come back home and open up his tailor shop again."

Tailoring also gave the bluebloods and aristocrats whom Johnson railed against a way of viewing him, of fitting him into a niche. Of the many unforgivable things about the man, perhaps the most egregious—the one that explained his character more thoroughly than any other—was that he had been a "mudsill tailor," that is, he had once plied his trade in a shop with an earthen floor. Mudsills were considered the white trash of the nineteenth century, the lowest of the low. Although Johnson would eventually serve five terms in the U.S. House of Representatives; though he would be a governor, a senator, and finally vice president and president of the United States; though he would leave an estate at his death valued in the several millions of dollars by contemporary calculations; and though he would appear to have come by every penny of his wealth honestly, Johnson could never escape the term in some quarters. Once a mudsill, always a mudsill. He never forgot the insult, either, or was he ever allowed to. More than any other single factor, the disdain visited on him for his poor origins would color his under‑standing of why the Civil War had been fought and what the terms of peace should therefore be.

Johnson was still a tailor's apprentice when he got his first taste of education, a hint at something beyond the grind of his daily life. "A gentleman of Raleigh was in the habit of going into the tailor's shop and reading while the apprentice and journeymen were at work," the *Washington Evening Star* informed its readers on April 17, 1865, in a "Biographical Sketch of His Excellency President Andrew Johnson." "He was an excellent reader, and his favorite book was a volume of speeches, principally of British statesmen. Johnson became interested, and his first ambition was to equal [the gentleman] as a reader and become familiar with those speeches. He took up the alphabet without an instructor, but by applying to the journeymen with whom he worked, he obtained a little assistance. Having acquired a knowledge of the letter, he applied for the loan of the book which he had so often heard read. The owner made him a present of it."

Like the fire-iron story just above, this one sounds spin doctored, massaged into life by some PR staff: character and opportunity flowing together in a perfect expression of the meritocracy at work. It wasn't doctored—the story is accurate in its particulars—but the *Evening Star* doesn't spoil the effect for readers by recounting what happened next. Johnson and Selby the Tailor had some sort of an altercation. One version maintains that Johnson and some other boys had been pelting the house of an old woman named Wells with sticks, either because they were mad at her, or trying to impress her daughters, or just being boys. The pelting story circulated around Raleigh for decades: Mrs. Wells had threatened to sue; Selby was enraged at his indentured apprentices. Whatever the exact impetus, Johnson, his older brother, and two other boys took off running. Five and a half years after Johnson had been legally bound over to him, Selby posted a notice in the Raleigh *Gazette* of June 24, 1824, under the boldface headline TEN DOLLARS REWARD. "Ran away from the Subscriber, on the night of the 15th instant, two apprentice boys, legally bound, named William and Andrew Johnson....I will pay the above Reward to any person who will deliver said apprentices to me in Raleigh, or I will give the above reward for Andrew Johnson alone. All persons are cautioned against harboring or employing said apprentices on pain of being prosecuted." According to the posted notice, Johnson was then about five feet four or five inches tall, "of dark complexion, black hair, eyes, and habits." Of the many possible meanings of "black...habits," one suspects Selby was referring to Johnson's disposition, that smoldering quality he would never lose. In any event, the phrase remains hauntingly ambiguous.

The Johnson brothers got as far as the tiny town of Carthage, some sixty miles southwest of Raleigh. There, they stayed just long enough for Andy to open a tailor shop in a rented shack—mudsill, for sure—then lit out for Laurens, South Carolina, where they figured to be well out of the reach of Selby. In Laurens, Andy found work as a tailor journeyman, fell in love with a local beauty named Mary Word, made her a quilt, and followed that up by proposing marriage. While Mary was apparently agreeable, her parents were not. Johnson was without resources, slowly learning to read, still unable to sign his own name—hardly a proper catch. Two years after he had fled Raleigh, Johnson returned, hoping to make peace with Selby so that he could find work in a shop owned by the tailor's old foreman. To settle the dispute, Selby wanted the one thing Andy didn't have: money.

Spurned in love and out of work options, the future president set out on a peripatetic westward ramble, almost as if he were searching for some spot on the continent commensurate with his own inchoate ambitions. His travels took him first to Chapel Hill, thirty miles west of the capital, then over the Great Smokies to Knoxville, where he boarded a flatboat and drifted down the Tennessee River to Decatur, Alabama. At Decatur, Johnson recrossed the river, then headed north to Mooresville, where he found work as a tailor's assistant; and then on to Columbia, Tennessee, where another tailor took him on while his wife provided the struggling journeyman with room and board. Within six months Johnson was back in Raleigh, checking up on his family. His first trip west had been a whirlwind, with barely time to put his feet up anywhere.

Soon Johnson was heading to Tennessee again, hoping to reunite with his brother and with an uncle. On this trip he brought along his mother and stepfather and a fellow tailor, and this time he left for good. As his biographer Robert Winston so nicely writes, "One August day in 1826, dumping their earthly belongings into a two-wheeled cart, without cover against rain or shine, they set out for their new home. No covered wagon, no barking, prancing dog, no romance."

No romance, maybe. At age seventeen, though, Andy Johnson had joined the great westward migration. This was 1826: Tennessee had been admitted to the Union three decades earlier, but the first permanent settlement in the state was less than sixty years old. A blind pony is said to have pulled the Johnson-Doughtry cart along. Perhaps that part of the story is legend; perhaps more of the details of these early years are, too. If so, Johnson never bothered to correct the record. One account even has the two apprentice tailors fighting off a bear as they camped in the Great Smoky Mountains, near their journey's end.

The trek ended in September 1826 when the exhausted travelers camped by a sweet-water spring in the town of Greeneville, Tennessee. Johnson liked the town. He found a position with a tailor almost immediately and settled his family in a room rented from the Russell family. He even met a girl to make him forget Mary Word, but he still wasn't ready to settle down. Before long, Andy pushed on yet again, to another mountain town, Rutledge, where he found more work. (Johnson's tailoring skills must have been impressive; he never seemed to want for employment.) Finally, in the spring of 1827, he returned to Greeneville and put down roots. Whether it was fate or circumstance or dumb blind luck, Johnson seems finally to have found the place he was looking for.

Greeneville had been settled in 1783 in what was then the far reaches of North Carolina, an area so remote, so cut off from the rest of the state by the Great Smokies that in 1785 it literally formed its own little world. North Carolina's effort to cede its western territory to the general government so enraged the good citizens of Greeneville and the surrounding region that they elected their own governor, passed numerous laws, declared themselves inhabitants of the new state of Franklin with Greeneville as its capital, and petitioned Congress for admission to the Union. Congress refused, North Carolina had second thoughts, and soon enough Tennessee as we know it was formed and recognized. For four years, though, Franklin had its own governor and thus was born a habit of adamantly independent thinking. (Davy Crockett was born in 1786 on a mountaintop in what then considered itself Franklin State, not Tennessee, just a few miles from Greeneville.)

In Greeneville, Andy Johnson found a people as hard-nosed as he was and as ill-inclined to respect the authority of the state's cotton planters, who controlled the central and western parts of the state. Indeed, a decade and a half after he had settled there, by then a member of the Tennessee legislature, Johnson proposed reconstituting the old state of Franklin, this time with contiguous areas of North Carolina and Virginia added, under the slightly altered name of Frankland. Johnson also found in Greeneville the remedy to his own hobbling lack of learning: the woman whom he had earlier met and now actually did marry, Eliza McCardle. He was eighteen when they were introduced; she was just sixteen, with a background only marginally better than his. Her shoemaker father, John, died when she was still a girl; her mother, Sarah, like Andy's mother, was forced to learn a trade to provide for her family.

From her earliest teens, Eliza stayed home to help her mother sew quilts and manufacture a cloth-topped sandal that had been one of her father's mainstays. Still, for a few years Eliza somehow managed to attend a local school, an exposure to formal education that would go a long way to advance her husband's learning.

First Lady lore is filled with fairy tales, and Eliza's has one, too. Young Andy Johnson was supposedly leading his blind pony when she first laid eyes on him and, so the story goes, declared then and there to a friend, "There goes my beau!" In fact, they seem to have been well matched. Both shunned society, although Eliza seems to have done so to an almost pathological degree. She visited Washington, D.C., only once during the sixteen years her husband served in the House and Senate. In the nearly four years she lived in the upstairs residency rooms of the White House, she attended exactly two public functions downstairs: once to greet Queen Emma of Hawai'i and once to preside over a children's ball marking her husband's sixtieth birthday. Andy Johnson was quick to remind one and all that he was without pretension. Eliza lived what he loved to talk about.

Where they differed most dramatically was in their constitutions. He was indefatigable. She suffered from tuberculosis much of her adult life and spent her later years as an invalid, a convenient pretext for avoiding people she had little desire to see. Her health certainly didn't prevent her from reading stacks of newspapers and magazines each day during her tenure as First Lady, clipping all the relevant articles and sorting them into two piles. The good ones she gave to her husband each evening. The bad ones she saved for morning when his temper was more manageable.

Andy and Eliza were married in Greeneville May 17, 1827, by Mordecai Lincoln, a justice of the peace and first cousin once removed of Abraham; they then took up residence in a two-room house. The front room became his tailor shop, the back was their home. During the day, Eliza read to him as he sewed, or sometimes a hired boy took over the reading. Evenings, Johnson read on his own and with Eliza's help worked on basic mathematics and other disciplines. Having found the right wife and the perfect place to realize his ambitions, Andy Johnson began an upward ascent made all the more remarkable by where he had begun. In 1828, in town only two years and not yet twenty years old, he was elected a Greeneville alderman. He won the post again in 1830, and then in 1834 his fellow aldermen elected him mayor of the town. That same year, after lobbying for the post, he was named a trustee of the local Rhea Academy, a special honor for a man who had never had a day of formal schooling. The next year, 1835, still twenty-six years old, Johnson trounced his opponent in the race for a seat newly added to the state legislature. He served one term and then lost his reelection bid largely because he had opposed an ambitious slate of internal improvements on the grounds they would fail, saddling Tennessee with an onerous debt. They mostly did just as he had predicted, and in 1839 Johnson was sent back to the legislature by a whopping majority.

The record is uncertain about Johnson's earliest political affiliations. He might have won his first statewide race backed by the Whig Party. Formed in 1834 out of the National Republicans and other elements, the Whigs still had echoes of their earlier incarnation as antiroyalists during the American Revolution. By 1840, though, Johnson was the Whig's opposite: an Andy Jackson Democrat; a populist or a dema-gogue, depending on where one stands on Johnson (and Jackson); and like his hero, a foe of central banking and an ardent proponent of a strong executive branch. Clearly, the voters of Tennessee liked the fit. Until the presidency ruined his reputation, Johnson never lost another election: the state senate in 1840; the U.S. House of Representatives for five consecutive terms beginning in 1842; a pair of two-year terms as governor of Tennessee after his congressional district had been gerry-mandered out from under him; the U.S Senate in 1858, from a state that would cease considering itself a member of the Union before his term was up; and finally, the vice presidency in 1864. Even after leaving Wash-ington in disgrace and twice losing elections that would have returned him there, for the Senate and for a seat in Congress, Johnson regained his Senate seat again in 1874.

Financially, Johnson went from strength to strength as well. He sold the tailoring business in the early 1840s but held on to the shop his entire life—a simple building with a plain sign that read A. JOHNSON, TAILOR. With the profits from his tailoring work, he dabbled in railroad stocks and expanded into local real estate, buying a hotel and an office where he could conduct his political affairs. By 1856, he owned twenty-five acres out in the countryside, $2,800 worth of lots in town, and another $6,400 in taxable property. He launched a newspaper, too—the *Greeneville Spy*—in large part to advance his own political ambitions. Soon, he was being referred to as Colonel Johnson, a rank he earned through his involvement in the local militia. As the editors of the Johnson papers note, "a not inaccurate index of his comparative prosperity" can be found in the fact that he didn't seem to suffer when he lost $2,000 in cash in a Nashville fire.

The tiny backroom where he and Eliza had first lived yielded to a larger, still humble house on Water Street, and then in 1851, in another of those storybook moments that probably hover between truth and legend, Johnson bought between one-half and three-quarter acre of land right on the main street, including an unfinished brick building and the sweet-water spring where he, his brother, mother, and stepfather had first camped in Greeneville a quarter century earlier. (The deed does show a spring house, but springs are plentiful in that part of Tennessee, and there's no documentation to prove that this is the same spring the family had first camped beside.) The unfinished structure Johnson turned into a home: two rooms up, two down, a pantry and serving room attached to the back, a separate kitchen beyond them, and a veranda off to the side, overlooking his new domain. "It delighted him to see his humble neighbors gather on the premises, drinking from the spring and carrying pails filled with the cool water to their homes," Winston writes, and indeed that sounds like Johnson to a T.

Wealth bought him more than real estate: Dolly, his first slave, for whom he paid $500, presumably after she had picked him out at auction as a likely benign owner; Dolly's half-brother Sam, Johnson's favorite, who, according to one account, became the best-dressed church janitor in Greeneville after emancipation; Dolly's son Bill, who took over the tailor shop after the war and kept the same A. JOHNSON sign out front; Bill's wife, who cooked for the family; and others. In all, as many as nine slaves might have worked in the Johnson household over the years.

There were also five children born to Andy and Eliza: Martha, who would marry David Patterson, a circuit judge and later U.S. senator almost a decade older than her; Charles, a doctor and druggist; Robert, an attorney and politician; Mary, who married a local farmer and landowner named Dan Stover; and finally, Andrew Jr., born when his parents were already in their mid and late forties.

The male side of the family proved a tragic lot. Charles and Robert both took to whiskey—"the curse of the Old South," Winston calls it. Charles was thrown from a horse and killed in 1863 while serving as an assistant surgeon with the Middle Tennessee Union Infantry. Dismissed from the First Tennessee Union Calvary for his drunken antics, Robert signed on as his father's private secretary for the remainder of the war and later joined him in that capacity in Washington. Despite promises to his father, Robert never gave up drinking. In 1869, at age thirty-five, he committed suicide. Andrew, the youngest, called Frank, founded a newspaper after the war, the *Greeneville Intelligencer*, just as his father had, and watched it flounder and fail within two years. Consumptive as a child, Frank was dead by age twenty-seven.

The female Johnsons weren't spared misery either. Mary's husband, Dan, won fame as a bridge burner for the Union cause, but consumption claimed him, too, before the war was half over. Of the five children, Martha seems to have been both the strongest and the most worldly. Educated in Washington at the Georgetown Female Seminary, she took over hostess duties at the White House while her mother sought refuge upstairs, attended the Washington galas her parents shunned, and did her best to win over a skeptical society. It was Martha, not Eliza, who wrote her father from Nashville on noon of April 15, 1865, an hour after he had been sworn in as president:

My dear, dear Father,

The sad, sad news has just reached us, announcing the death of President Lincoln. Are you safe, and do you feel secure? Our City is wild with excitement. It presented a gala appearance this morning but our joy was suddenly "turned into grief." The stars and stripes have all been taken down, and now nothing but the booming of cannon is heard and returning soldiers to camp. I never felt so sad, in all my life, and poor Mother she is almost deranged fearing that you will be assassinated. Our distracted and torn up country. How I long to be with you this sad day, that we might weep together at a Nation's calamity.

Though Johnson yearned for respectability, it seemed always to have to be on his terms. He never took to organized religion, never even joined a church. Indeed one of his first stands as a state representative was in opposition to opening each session with a prayer. Later, in the House, he unsuccessfully proposed that congressional chaplains be paid out of voluntary contributions, not federal funds. His political enemies heaped abuse on Johnson for it—he was anti-Christian—but in fact, he was only trying to save taxpayers money.

Culture was largely lost on him. Museums, art, and the like smacked too much of what he once called the "purse-proud set . . . not half as good as the man who earns his bread by the sweat of his brow." During his long and generally tightfisted career in politics, Johnson voted against funding an expedition to study an eclipse of the sun, tried to get rid of the Congressional franking privilege, spoke out against acquiring George Washington's farewell address, and opposed excessive spending for presidential portraits in the White House. As a U.S. senator, he even opposed using James Smithson's famous bequest to establish a cultural institution on the Mall in Washington, arguing that the institution would become a burden on the taxpayers and that the money and the space would be better used for an industrial school.

As a legislator and governor, Johnson supported public schools, public libraries, state fairs—anything to give the working man a leg up, anything to level the playing field. He opposed convict laborers, too, because they took paying jobs away from law-abiding ones. He railed against the service academies, West Point and Annapolis, for accepting too many "sons of members of Congress, many of them almost imbecile," while excluding "lads who are blessed by nature with talents." He also proposed rotating federal employees every eight years so that everyone got a chance at the public trough, and so that those already there didn't grow too fat at their posts. In December 1860 he even advanced a constitutional amendment that would have limited the terms of all federal judges, including Supreme Court justices, to twelve years. Anything longer, he believed, created a judicial aristocracy.

At various times in his political career, Johnson also advocated direct, popular election of the president and vice president and of U.S. senators, who were then chosen by state legislatures. One man, one vote: To Johnson, this just made sense. The Founding Fathers planned otherwise, for good reason. Johnson, though, wanted a government that read the will of the people—the *real* people—like some constitutionally mandated tuning fork.

Johnson's was a lifelong fight against the swells, the bluebloods, the pocket liners and influence wielders and schemers. That "illegitimate, swaggering, bastard, scrub aristocracy," Johnson had called it during his first term in Congress. The object of his anger that day was another first-termer, Jefferson Davis of Mississippi—a clash that set the tone between the two men for decades to come. Always, too, it was personal with Johnson. He had no ability to laugh at himself, no facility for sloughing off insults or ignoring them—bad traits in a politician at a time when insults were common and often scurrilous, and ultimately paralyzing ones for the nation when Johnson squared off against the Radical Republicans after the war. To oppose the president's plan for, say, the reconstruction of North Carolina was to oppose the president himself. There was no separation, no buffer zone; every attack on policy was an attack on self. Of all the things Johnson lacked that Lincoln had, a gallows humor might have been the most useful.

Johnson, according to one widely circulated insult, was the bastard son of a distinguished Raleigh lawyer, perhaps John Haywood, to whom he bore some likeness and in whose house Polly had once worked. (How else to explain Johnson's obvious aptitude, his innate talent despite a miserable upbringing, or that Andrew bore so little resemblance to his fleshy, fair-skinned, and freckled brother, Willie?) Other insults contended that he was an infidel, a secret Catholic, an abolitionist, a Northern sympathizer. Lincoln might have made a joke of the allegations. Johnson couldn't. He actually took time in an open letter to point out soberly how unlikely it would be for him to be both an infidel *and* an ardent Catholic. The higher he climbed, the longer he served in public office, the more inventive the insults grew, and the more they seemed to enrage him. As thickheaded as he could be, his skin never seemed to toughen at all. "When I reflect upon my past life and that of my family," he wrote from Washington to a friend back in Greeneville in October 1845, "and know that it has been my constant aim and desire to steer them and myself through society in as unoffending a manner as possible—this though it seems I have most signally failed—when I sum up the many taunts, the jeers, the gotten-up and intended slights to me and mine, all without cause so far as know[n], I wish from the bottom of my heart that we were all blotted out of existence, and even the remembrance of things that were."

As for his adopted home and the slights he and his had suffered at the hands of its grandees, Johnson went on: "I never want to own another foot of dirt in the *dam* [*sic*] town while I live—If I should happen

to die among the dam spirits that infest Greeneville . . . I would be-
queath the last dollar to some negro to pay to take my dirty, stinky car-
cass after death, out on some mountain peak and there leave it to be
devoured by the vultures and wolves, or that it might pass off in smoke
and ride upon the wind in triumph over the god-forsaken and Hell-
deserving, money-loving, hypocritical, back-biting, Sunday-praying,
scoundrels of the town of Greeneville."

Clearly, Johnson got over it—he never left Greeneville except for
Washington and to serve as governor and later military governor in
Nashville. Inherent in those words, however, is a dark side and a temper
of extraordinary magnitude. Watching Johnson rage one day against the
Confederate traitors, Michigan senator Zachariah Chandler remarked
to then Vice President Hannibal Hamlin that "Johnson has the nightmare." More than once he carried a pistol with him to some political debate or another. That was hardly uncommon in those days. America was
a violent place, and politics have always been incendiary. Still, it seems
almost a miracle that Johnson never used his. Maybe it helped that he
was an absolute stranger to fear. One apparent eyewitness account from
Andy Johnson's two terms as governor in Nashville goes as follows:

[Johnson] was announced to speak on one of the exciting questions of the day, and loud threats were uttered that if he dared
to appear he should not leave the hall alive. At the appointed
hour, he ascended to the platform, and advancing to the desk
laid his pistol upon it. He then addressed the audience, in terms
as near like the following as our informant could recollect:
"Fellow-citizens, it is proper when freemen assemble for the
discussion of important public interests, that every thing
should be done decently and in order. I have been informed that
part of the business to be transacted on the present occasion is
the assassination of the individual who now has the honor of
addressing you. I beg respectfully to propose this be the first
business in order. Therefore, if any man has come here to-night

for the purpose indicated, I do not say to him, 'Let him speak,' but 'let him shoot.'"

Here he paused with his right hand on his pistol, and the other holding open his coat, while with his eyes he blankly surveyed the assembly. After a pause of half a minute, he resumed: "Gentlemen, it appears that I have been misinformed."

Perhaps that's why George Atzerodt drank away his chance to assassinate Johnson a decade later. He might have known that if he ever got face to face with the vice president, he wouldn't have stood a chance.

Johnson's great legislative cause was the Homestead Act: 160 acres of the surveyed public domain to any adult citizen or alien intending to become a citizen who was willing and able to pay a ten-dollar claim fee and then reside on or cultivate the land for a period of five years. It wasn't an ideal piece of legislation: For one thing, so much of the good land was already being worked or was in the hands of speculators. But it was an ideal cause for Andy Johnson—a chance for the common man to share in the great American land grab. "Every man is entitled to a home," Johnson declared in a July 1850 speech in the House. "... Like the air or like the heat, the public domain is the property of all, intended to be used and enjoyed by all."

He advocated one version or another of the Homestead Act repeatedly from his earliest days in politics. At first, he was opposed by Eastern industrialists and big-city slumlords. If the workers all lit out for free land, who would fill the tenements of New York and Boston, and what would happen to pay scales in the textile mills? The huddled masses of cheap labor concentrated along the Atlantic seaboard were money in the bank for them. As the 1850s wore on and political fault lines shifted, the Homestead debate shifted with them. Republicans and New Englanders suddenly were all for free land and westward expansion, so long as antislavery provisions traveled westward with them. When a Homestead Act was passed in 1860, James Buchanan vetoed it rather than provoke the Southern states. Two years later, with the South no longer represented, Congress finally did pass and a new president signed the Homestead Act. By then, though, its chief proponent was gone from the Senate because his home state was no longer part of the Union.

On the leading moral issue of the day—the great and still unresolved matter of American history—Andrew Johnson was both a catalogue of conventionalities and a living embodiment of all the illogic that surrounded the question of slavery. He was a slave owner, yet he loathed the great planters who were the largest slaveholders and the greatest beneficiaries of America's "peculiar institution." Nor was he any stranger to abolitionist sentiment. Greeneville, his adopted home, had been the site in November 1816 of the second convention of the Quaker-backed Tennessee Manumission Society, the oldest antislavery organization in America. *The Emancipator* and *The Genius of Universal Emancipation*, groundbreaking antislavery journals, had been published briefly in Greeneville not long before Andy Johnson arrived in town.

According to Robert Winston, Johnson was an enthusiast for a remarkable book first published in 1856 and now largely forgotten: *Compendium of the Impending Crisis of the South*, written by a North Carolinian named Hinton Rowan Helper. Helper's purpose, he proclaimed in the opening paragraph, was not to write a philosophical or moral treatise on slavery or on the ethics of slavery, "nor to waste time in pressing a universally admitted truism—that virtue is preferable to vice. Self-evident truths require no argumentative demonstration." His purpose rather was to use the new tools of the social sciences to create a statistical portrait of the effects of slavery on the Southern economy.

In 1790, he noted, New York had less than half the population of Virginia and half a million dollars fewer in exports; yet sixty years later, by the U.S. Census of 1850, New York had twice the population of the Old Dominion and more than forty times its exports. By then, the total value of real and personal property in Virginia, even including slaves as property, was a little more than a third the total value of New York property "exclusive of any monetary valuation of human beings." Massachusetts and North Carolina had had roughly similar populations in 1790.

Both had harbors favored by nature: Boston and Beaufort. North Carolina had almost seven times the land mass, yet Massachusetts, hotbed of abolitionism, led the Tar Heel State in every important economic and growth category.

So it went on, page after page. By virtually every critical measure other than slavery-dependent tobacco and cotton, the free states slaughtered the slave states. Newspapers and periodicals in the free states printed ten times the copies annually of their counterparts; free state inventors in 1856 received seven times the patents of slave state ones. As for manufactured goods and the finer objects of life, the South could simply forget anything even approaching a standoff: "It is a fact well known to every intelligent Southerner that we are compelled to go to the North for almost every article of utility and adornment, from matches, shoepegs and paintings up to cotton-mills, steamships and statuary."

Winston's assertion that Johnson made the *Compendium* his *vade mecum*—his "arsenal of facts"—seems overblown. Johnson never would have accepted that the South itself was inferior to the New England states. In fact, in March 1860, when a New Hampshire senator invoked Helper's theories in comparing the relative prosperity of his own free state, despite its poor soil, with Tennessee, blessed with natural resources yet blighted by slavery, Johnson took sharp exception. Johnson also would have resisted being associated with the Black Republicans who promoted Helper's work so ardently, but he was certainly familiar with the book. The *Compendium* was so popular among Lincoln's supporters that a committee of private citizens sought to raise $16,000 to help distribute 100,000 free copies of the *Compendium* in the states generally thought to hold the swing vote in the 1860 presidential election: Pennsylvania, New Jersey, Indiana, and Illinois. In the South, where for a time an abolitionist was just as likely to be known disparagingly as a Helperite, copies of the book were burned from Virginia to Mississippi. Congress got in the act as well—Helper and his *Compendium* were the subject of raucous debate.

Not only would Johnson have known the book, he would have agreed with Helper that the mechanics and yeomen and artisans of the South had suffered nearly as much as the slaves themselves under the yoke of the aristocrats. Johnson saw clearly, too, before the first shot of the Civil War was ever fired, that if slavery led to secession and secession to war, the Southerners who would suffer most and die in the greatest numbers by far would be the "six millions of non-slaveholding whites from the second degree of slavery," as Helper put it, the ones cajoled into fighting by "a selfish and domineering oligarchy." Johnson could have written the words himself.

In September 1864, after Johnson had been nominated for the vice presidency, Hinton Helper wrote from Buenos Aires, where he was serving as U.S. consul, to congratulate Johnson on the honor and to praise both his "well-tested and well-proved patriotism" and the foresight he had shown in the months leading up to the war. "Four or five years ago, that is to say, some time during the year 1859, or the year 1860 ... to me at least, it became apparent that, as a distinguished member of the United States Senate, you were acting upon a much better knowledge of the inevitable drift of affairs in our country, than seemed to be possessed by any other Southern Senator."

Yet to loathe where slavery had led the South was not to loathe slavery itself. For Johnson, it never broke down that simply. Slaves were property, not citizens. By its silence, the Constitution said as much. So had Chief Justice of the U.S. Supreme Court Roger Brooke Taney in his majority opinion in that 1856 judicial disgrace known as the Dred Scott case. For good measure, Taney had been appointed to the court by Johnson's hero, Andy Jackson. That was point one. Point two was that states had the right to determine the destiny of those living within their borders. It was an article of faith with Johnson. Where he drew the line was where Jackson had drawn it against John C. Calhoun: States' rights were not nullification rights. The Constitution was a sacred covenant; the Union, forever. Otherwise, authority, as Johnson perceived it—and almost certainly desired it—was all on the side of slavery.

Time and again, in the House and in the Senate, Johnson lent his vote to measures that would extend slavery, or at least not limit its reach. Beginning in the late 1840s, he cast forty-two votes against the Wilmot Proviso, which would have forbidden slavery in any territory acquired as the result of the Mexican War. As late as May 1860, he was still siding with the slaveholding interests in the Senate. Politically, he had little choice, especially since he was constantly courting support from fellow Southern lawmakers for his Homestead Act. It was more than politics, though. Johnson saw no evil in slavery, only in slaveowners.

"Damn the Negroes," he once roared when someone charged him with being a proponent of racial equality. "I am fighting those traitorous aristocrats, their masters." In October 1864 before a gathering in Nashville, he railed again against the plantation owners, with extra zest: "Why, pass any day along the sidewalks of High Street where these aristocrats more particularly dwell—these aristocrats whose sons are now in the bands of guerillas and cut-throats who prowl and rob and murder around our city—pass by their dwellings, I say, and you will see as many mulatto as Negro children, the former bearing an unmistakable resemblance to their aristocratic owners."

Johnson had half the equation down: the sins of those who held human flesh in bondage. He couldn't grasp the other side of it: the mothers of those mixed-race children, the black women and girls condemned to sexual as well as physical degradation. Nor could he ever move beyond viewing slaves in economic, not human terms, or get around the hard lump of his own mudsill rage. Again, imagination, empathy, failed him. Huck Finn learned from his time with Jim on the river. That's why Twain's novel endures. Huck is smarter, more humane at the end of his journey than he is when he undertakes it. Not so, Johnson. He, too, had been indentured, as an apprentice, not as property. Like slaves the South over, he had fled what he considered a cruel master and lived with a price on his head. Had he not fled, Johnson almost certainly would have remained in Raleigh, a struggling tailor or tailor's apprentice, part of the debt-peonage society that held poor Southern whites in check almost as surely as slavery held blacks in check. Yet Johnson never could make the leap that Huck completed, from his own struggle and escape, to the struggles and attempted escapes of the African Americans around him. That was Johnson's failing, to be sure, but it was a failing broadly shared—a national flaw and a local one, a failure of humanity as well as a failure of individual human beings. Maybe, finally, it's the difference between fiction and history.

"Suppose the Negro is set free and we have less cotton; we will raise more wool, hemp, flax, and silk," Johnson railed in that same October 1864 speech in Nashville. "Whether we attain perfection in the raising of cotton or not, I think we ought to stimulate the cultivation of hemp; for we ought to have more of it and a far better material, a stronger fiber, with which to make a stronger rope. For, not to be malicious or malignant, I am free to say that I believe many who were driven into this Rebellion are repentant; but I say of the leaders, the instigators, the conscious, intelligent traitors, they ought to be hung."

Abolition was about the slaveholders, not the slaves, and that's why Johnson finally came down in favor of it. The continuation of slavery would mean the slaveholders had won, and that prospect, above all else, Johnson couldn't stand, especially when it came to Tennessee. This was his theme in the fall of 1861 as he stumped through Kentucky for the Union: "But whatever [the Rebel leaders] may do—though they may ravage our State and make desolate our homes, though they convert the caves of our mountains into sepulchers and turn our valleys and plains into graveyards, there is still one thing they cannot do—they never can, while God reigns, make East Tennessee a land of slaves."

As for the increasingly hot-blooded rivalry between the slave states and the free ones, Johnson's answer was a pox on both houses. "I would chain Massachusetts and South Carolina together, and I would transport them to some island in the Arctic Ocean, the colder the better, till they cool off and come to their senses." Johnson made that snippet of a speech on the floor of Congress, to the approval of neither camp.

On the far harder question of what to do with the slaves, he had only vague solutions. Back in 1845, when he was still serving his first term in the House, Johnson advocated the admission of Texas to the Union in part because the state "in the end may prove to be the gateway out of which the sable sons of Africa are to pass from bondage to freedom." Who knows what he really meant? Perhaps he had in mind a buffer province along the Rio Grande in which millions of freed slaves might contend with the Native American population for whatever sustenance could be had—water first and foremost—while offering a human barrier against Mexican adventurism. Perhaps the slaves would find their freedom over the river, in some mystical Mexico where they would be welcomed as suffering brothers. Most likely, Johnson was dreaming, the easy way out of slavery.

Lincoln had basically the same dream, only bolder: colonization, African repatriation. He laid it out for a crowd at Springfield, Illinois, on June 26, 1857, in the aftermath of the Supreme Court's Dred Scott decision.

I have said that the separation of the races is the only perfect preventive of amalgamation. I have no right to say all the members of the Republican party are in favor of this, nor to say that as a party they are in favor of it. There is nothing in their platform directly on the subject. But I can say a very large proportion of its members are for it, and that the chief plank in their platform—opposition to the spread of slavery—is most favorable to that separation.

Such separation, if ever effected at all, must be effected by colonization; and no political party, as such, is now doing anything directly for colonization. Party operations at present only favor or retard colonization incidentally. The enterprise is a difficult one; but "when there is a will there is a way"; and what colonization needs most is a hearty will. Will springs from the two elements of moral sense and self-interest. Let us be brought to believe it is morally right, and, at the same time, favorable to, or, at least, not against, our interest, to transfer the African to his native clime, and we shall find a way to do it, however great the task may be. The children of Israel, to such numbers as to include four hundred thousand fighting men, went out of Egyptian bondage in a body.

West Texas, Mexico, Liberia—you can dress it up in all the biblical raiment you want. It's still the deus ex machina solution to slavery. Load up the ships, or the cattle cars. The idea of freedom *in situ*, of the slaves simply being manumitted in place and absorbed somehow into the general population, baffled Lincoln as much as it terrified Andrew Johnson and most other white Southerners, whether they were proslavery or antislavery, planter or mudsill.

Lincoln finally was able to cross the divide. The contribution of blacks to the war effort influenced his thinking. The Emancipation Proclamation, so much a political document when Lincoln issued it, seemed to blossom into a moral imperative in his mind. Lincoln grew in compassion rather than shrank from it as the horrors of battle mounted. Finally, he seems able to have envisioned a biracial America, or at least to have entertained its possibility.

Johnson eventually embraced the language of abolition and emancipation, but only because he had run out of options. Five days before he first rose in the Senate to denounce secession, Johnson had proposed measures that would have rotated the presidency and vice presidency between slaveholding and nonslaveholding regions and balanced the Supreme Court along the same lines. At heart, he was always proslavery *and* pro-Union, a viable position in the late 1850s for a politician who aspired to the presidency, as Johnson certainly did, but a position that had disappeared completely by 1861. Proslavery or pro-Union. Go or stay. That was the only choice left after Fort Sumter. "I am for my Government with or without slavery," Johnson told a crowd in Franklin, Kentucky, on August 22, 1863, "but if either the Government or slavery must perish, I say give me the Government and let the Negroes go." In fact, substitute "Union" for "Government," and the language is strikingly similar to the words Lincoln used in his famous written reply to Horace Greeley of exactly a year—to the day—earlier: "If I could save the Union without freeing *any* slave I would do it, and if I could save it by freeing *all* the slaves I would do it; and if I could save it by freeing some and leaving others alone I would also do that. What I do about slavery, and the colored race, I do because I believe it helps to save the Union; and what I forbear, I forbear because I do *not* believe it would help to save the Union."

In Nashville, a week after he had delivered his Franklin, Kentucky, speech, Johnson decried slavery as a "cancer on our society." Before long, he had joined Lincoln and Stanton's campaign, which he had resisted earlier, to recruit ex-slaves in Tennessee to the Union army. (Lincoln assured Johnson in a March 26, 1863, letter that as "an eminent citizen of a slave State and . . . a slaveholder," his endorsement of raising a black fighting force would go a long way toward making it happen.)

Having declared himself for emancipation, Johnson leapt in wholeheartedly. In one memorably overblown moment during the 1864 campaign, he even promised a crowd of former slaves that "I will indeed be your Moses, and lead you through the Red Sea of war and bondage to a fairer state of liberty and peace." One suspects, however, that the Red Sea this newly converted emancipationist had in mind was still the parched scrub of West Texas. Indeed, within weeks of the Moses speech, Francis Blair Sr. would write Johnson, suggesting that he make specific what he had only hinted at twenty years earlier: that a portion of Texas along the Rio Grande be set aside as a voluntary refuge for freedmen, where they might form "Negro Occupational forces" against Indian and Mexican and French aggression, much as the Romans had used armed settlers to secure their frontiers two millennia earlier, and much indeed as the Israelis would use settlers in Gaza nearly a century and a half later. "The policy," Blair assured Johnson, was "pregnant with revolution."

By the fall of 1864, freeing the slaves might have become good politics, but for Johnson emancipation still conjured a nightmare of epic scope. "If you liberate the Negro, what will be the next step?" Johnson once asked. "What will we do with two million Negroes in our midst? ... Blood, rape and rapine will be our portion. You can't get rid of the Negro except by holding him in slavery."

It was a horrifying piece of logic. Because we've kept the slaves in bondage, never provided more than a handful with formal education, given them no experience in civil institutions, no participation in the body politic, we can't let them go. And yet the closer one was to the problem, the more insoluble it seemed. On the eve of the Civil War, when Johnson was proposing to tow Massachusetts up to the Arctic Circle to cool off, the Bay State had a population of 1.2 million people, of which less than 1 percent was black. The 1860 U.S. Census barely registered any African Americans at all in New Hampshire, Vermont, and Maine. Meanwhile, three out of every five human beings in South Carolina were enslaved; Mississippi had 83,000 more blacks than whites within its borders. Just shy of half of all Virginians were black. Even in Tennessee, where the eastern mountains and hills were hardly conducive to slave crops, a quarter of the population was black. Wondering whether blood, rape, and rapine were to be the South's portion should the slaves be set free might smack of the grossest ignorance. Or blood, rape, and rapine might seem, and undoubtedly did in certain abolitionist circles, a fitting punishment for having inflicted the primal sin of slavery on the land. But to be uneasy and fearful about the social and civil fallout from the inevitable collapse of a labor system that was unsustainable economically and morally—even the Russian czars had given up on slavery by 1861—is also only human. With slavery, you were damned if you did, damned if you didn't. At least that's how many in the South saw the matter on the eve of the Civil War. The slaves themselves had no say in the matter.

Even Hinton Rowan Helper couldn't reconcile the realization of his abolitionist dreams with the reality of what he had helped to create. A little more than a decade after the publication of *Compendium of the Im-*

pending Crisis, Helper authored a hideously racist book titled *Nojoque, a Question for a Continent,* in which he proposed forcibly expelling all blacks, with those who refused to leave being "quickly fosssilized in bulk beneath the subsoil of America." With Helper, as with Johnson, it was ultimately the degradation of the white race that mattered, not the subjugation of the black one.

None of that is exculpatory—of Johnson's redneck ignorance, of Lincoln's earlier bafflement, even of the Founding Fathers for ignoring their own self-evident truth that all men are created equal, or of those liberal-minded Boston abolitionists whose fortunes had been built two generations earlier on the slave trade across the Atlantic. History happens in the moment; judgments are rendered in hindsight.

Johnson made his deepest mark not as a legislator, not as a political theorist or philosopher, but as an orator and debater. God alone knows how many times he must have repeated to himself those speeches by learned statesmen from the book he'd kept since he fled Selby the Tailor. Clearly, they shaped him. Oratory was Johnson's way up in politics. Debate awakened and honed an intellect that must have been screaming for release

Oliver Temple, the Whig candidate whom Johnson defeated in the 1847 House race, heard Johnson speak often, in Greeneville and across the state. To his ear, Johnson's "marked deficiencies" as a orator "were language and information—elegant language, exact and precise, in which to present his ideas, and wide range of knowledge for argument and reflection, for adornment and illustration." Johnson lacked discipline and "nice taste." He "had a habit of pandering to the passions of the people," and "was naturally cynical and morose [as] was only too evident from his gloomy countenance.... Having no reverence for the prestige of distinguished names, upon all subjects he thought for himself," Temple wrote in *Notable Men of Tennessee.* "He was an iconoclast of the most pronounced type, pulling down and breaking to pieces as suited his own haughty will." His intellect fell below the first class of the na-

tion—Hamilton, Webster, Clay, Calhoun, and Lincoln—although not
far below. Johnson deserved to be ranked with men like William Seward
and Salmon Chase, "the first men in the second class of his day." In fact,
the college-educated Temple never seems able to make up his mind
whether he admires the Greeneville tailor or simply marvels that a
mudsill could accomplish so much.

On the subject of Johnson's oratorical powers, though, Temple was
a true believer.

> At his first appearance in public life, his speeches were strong
> and sensational. His facts were presented in a bold and vigorous
> manner. There was in them that salt of bitterness, that impres-
> sive personality, which characterized him in so marked a degree
> in after life. Even then he gained victories over every antagonist.
> His delivery, if not elegant, was at least easy, natural, and pleas-
> ing. His flow of language was wonderful considering he was un-
> educated and inexperienced as a speaker. There was nothing
> violent or spasmodic in his manner. His voice was good and
> pleasant. In the course of time it became one of great compass
> and power.

Temple was twelve or thirteen at the time Johnson first began to
gain wide notice; Johnson was just twice his age, already mayor of
Greeneville, fully literate for maybe half a decade. "Few men of this day,"
Temple writes, "so impressed themselves upon my young mind." It's easy
to see why. Johnson had none of Temple's advantages, yet by age thirty
he was known throughout the state.

In 1840, Johnson stumped the length and breadth of Tennessee for
the incumbent Democratic president, Martin Van Buren. The cause
was hopeless. Van Buren had been Andrew Jackson's handpicked successor, but the Panic of 1837 and his own tightfisted ways had doomed
his administration. On the Whig side, William Henry Harrison—Old
Tippecanoe—still carried the reputation as a war hero from his 1811

suppression of a Shawnee uprising in what was then Indiana Territory. For good measure, and to appeal to the proslavery vote, Harrison ran with his fellow Virginian John Tyler. In the end, Harrison carried Tennessee by more than 12,000 votes out of about 108,000 cast, and the nation by nearly 150,000 votes, a 6 percent edge in the popular vote that translated into a landslide in the electoral college, where Harrison won 234 of the 294 votes cast.

For Andy Johnson, though, the 1840 election was a triumph as even Temple, a Harrison-Tyler supporter, acknowledges: "In all the encounters of this canvass, Johnson sustained himself as an adroit debater and skillful speaker. Indeed, it was one of his peculiarities that he was always equal to any demands on his powers. He never made an absolute failure. Put him against an inferior and he would triumph; put him against a superior and he would acquit himself with credit.... In a long series of debates," Temple writes later, "I'm not sure he ever met his match." William Seward, part of Temple's "second class" of the brightest men of his age, couldn't have agreed more: Andy Johnson was the best stumper in America. And by mid-nineteenth century, stumping might have been the most indispensable of all political skills.

Political back-and-forth is at least as old as Greece, and undoubtedly some of those debates took place on the platforms provided by felled trees. "Stumping," though, is a uniquely American usage. *The Morris Dictionary of Word and Phrase Origins* traces the roots back to a 1716 memoir by Ann Maury in which she recounts going down to the Saponey Indian town in Virginia and there seeing a great stump at the center where the headman stood to deliver pronouncements. By the Revolutionary War, George Washington was doing the same thing. "Upon a stump he placed himself, Great Washington, did he," as one popular song of the day put it. Soon, stumping was expected of those who sought political office—a raucous town meeting, social event, traveling road show, and political debate all rolled into one. In the 1854 Tennessee gubernatorial campaign, Johnson and M.P. Gentry debated each other a staggering sixty times over nearly three months, back and forth across the state until just about everyone who wanted to hear them had a chance to do so, often more than once.

These were not the tepid, scripted affairs debates have become in our time. Stumpers confronted each directly, without a famous news broadcaster to moderate the debate, and the crowd came primed for action. Sometimes too primed—politicians were known to fuel their partisans with whiskey. The stumpers of the mid-nineteenth century had to make it up on the fly. They were expected to inform, to exhort, to rally the troops, to show a little emotion, a little humor. Entertain and instruct—a lesson straight from Aristotle's *Poetics*. The most famous image of stumping comes from the painter George Caleb Bingham, better known for his Western pastoral canvases such as *Fur Traders Descending the Missouri*. The candidate in Bingham's *Stump Speaking*, which dates from the mid-1850s, looks more like a Pentacostal preacher than anything we'd recognize as a politician today, and like a Pentacostal preacher, stumpers needed endurance. In the summer and fall of 1858, in perhaps the most famous U.S. Senate campaign of all time, Lincoln and Stephen Douglas engaged in seven debates across Illinois before huge crowds—as many as 15,000 to 20,000 for the first debate in Ottawa, Illinois, a town with a permanent population of 7,000—for a total of twenty-one hours of speechifying. The unexpurgated text of the debates alone runs to nearly 370 pages.

That's what Andrew Johnson excelled at. He could lay out a proposition and craft rebuttals and rejoinders while he caught his breath. He had a warehouse of allusions, enough demagoguery to stir the juices, the salt of bitterness to keep things interesting, a healthy disrespect for authority if it ran counter to his own instincts and beliefs, and the stamina to stay at it all day and night if need be. (Johnson, in fact, sounds like the perfect candidate to host a political shout show—a mid-nineteenth century Rush Limbaugh or Bill O'Reilly, only with less staged bluster.) What Johnson wanted was a cause worthy of his oratorical powers, and on December 18, 1860, he found it.

CHAPTER 3

Triumph & Disgrace

To say that America was an unsettled place in mid-December 1860 is a gross understatement. Abraham Lincoln had been elected president six weeks earlier with slightly less than 40 percent of the vote, and only because the Democratic opposition had split into Northern and Southern factions, the former backing Lincoln's old sparring partner Stephen Douglas, the latter behind the incumbent vice president, John Breckinridge. Douglas finished second in the popular vote, but fourth in the electoral college, with third place going to John Bell, an ex-senator from Tennessee running as a Constitutional Unionist. Not since 1824, when John Quincy Adams collected two-thirds of the votes Andy Jackson had received yet won the presidency in the House of Representatives, had a president claimed the office with so little support. Yet a fractured 1860 outcome was only to be expected: America was a fractured place.

To many in the South and to the South's supporters in the rest of the nation, Lincoln's election had been the point of no return. On December 18, the day Andrew Johnson first married his voice to the cause that would make him famous in the North and infamous throughout Dixie, members of the South Carolina state legislature and delegates to the South Carolina Sovereign Convention arrived in Charleston to begin finalizing their crusade for secession. There they were greeted by a fifteen-gun salute provided by the Marion Artillery—one round for every state expected to join the new Confederacy. That same day, the eighteenth, the *New York Times* ran a lengthy conjecture from a correspondent in Baltimore on whether Maryland would stick with the Union or bolt to the Confederacy. "Identity of institutions, the joint ownership of the Potomac, and other interests, serve still more closely to link our fate with that of Virginia," the correspondent wrote. "On the Slavery question, many entertain the belief, that as a matter of State policy it would be well if it did not exist among us. But it does exist, and ... the late Presidential vote shows how very few are they who would support a policy adverse to it." Maryland's agriculture, he continued, is "best promoted by slave labor." Its climate is uniquely "adapted to the negro," as witness the 90,000 free blacks then living in the state. Perhaps most critical was the fact that the state's chief trading partners—North Carolina, Tennessee, Kentucky, and the western territories—were all reached via the Chesapeake Bay, "the mouth of which is held by Virginia.... If that State declares for dissolution and a Southern Confederacy, so likewise will Maryland. No argument advocating a contrary policy would here be heeded."

The *Times* correspondent had numbers on his side. In the election just past, Lincoln had won 2,294 votes in Maryland, a little more than 2 percent of all votes cast. The proslavery Breckenridge ticket polled 42,482 votes, more than eighteen times Lincoln's tally. Across the Mason-Dixon Line in Pennsylvania, Lincoln drew 56 percent of the vote. Maryland clearly did more than tilt South; it fell into Dixie. Had Maryland actually gone to the Confederacy, the Union's capital would have been seventy-five miles inside Confederate lines, an impossible situation. Both shores of the Chesapeake Bay, the Potomac on all sides, the C&O Canal westward, the rail yards of Baltimore—all would have been surrounded by the Confederacy, not to mention the Treasury, the Washington Navy Yard, the Capitol, and White House, along with the founding documents of the shattered American nation.

In the end, Lincoln essentially made Maryland's choice for it. On April 19, 1861, a Baltimore mob attacked 600 Pennsylvania troops transiting south through the city, killing four soldiers and a dozen rioters—

the first fatalities of the war. By June, Federal troops had seized the city and the state. The final stanza of what became the Maryland state song still contains the memorable line "Huzza! she spurns the Northern scum!"; Maryland, though, was sticking with the Union, like it or not.

A compromise capital that compromised strongly in the South's favor, Washington was no Union stalwart, either. In 1850, Congress finally outlawed trading in human chattel in the District of Columbia. Until then, Washington had been what the American Antislavery Society called the "slave market of America." Two of the larger slave pens—one at Seventh and E streets Northwest, another at Eighth Street Southwest—were within easy walking distance of the Capitol and White House. Had Washingtonians had the rights and means of self-determination in the early 1860s, it's not a stretch to think they might have aligned with the Confederacy. The local *Star* newspaper was estimating that by mid-1862, some 600 Washingtonians, including members of some of the city's most prominent families, were serving in the Confederate army. Other city luminaries simply lit out for Europe rather than be forced to take sides. W.W. Corcoran—Washington's most prominent banker and benefactor of the city's first major art gallery—shipped $1.25 million in gold to a London bank before sailing for Paris. Jefferson Davis might have set himself up on Pennsylvania Avenue instead of in Richmond. He had already spent more than a decade in Washington, as a senator and war secretary. The city was a second home to him.

"There seems to be no one, neither at the North nor at the South, brave or good enough to surrender party for mankind," the Baltimore correspondent had lamented in the pages of the *New York Times* that day. "If our public men would dare only follow what is right, public approbation would, in the end, follow them, and the Union would be preserved; but madness and imbecility rule the hour."

This, then, was the backdrop on the eighteenth of December, 1860, when Andrew Johnson rose to speak on the floor of the Senate and became, in effect, the public man the *Times* writer longed for. Considering who Johnson was and where he came from, remembering that he had spent that fall stumping in Tennessee for the Breckenridge-led Democratic ticket, what he had to say was remarkable. "No state has the right to secede from this Union without the consent of the other states which ratified the compact. . . . If the doctrine of Secession is to be carried out upon the mere whim of a state, this government is at an end. It is no stronger than a rope of sand; its own weight will crumble it to pieces and it cannot exist. If a state may secede why, as Madison asks, may not other states combine and eject a state from the Union?"

The Senate adjourned for the day before Johnson could conclude, but the delay didn't dampen his ardor.

> What then is the issue? It is this and only this: We are mad because Mr. Lincoln had been elected President and we have not got our man. If we had got our man, we should not be for breaking up the Union, but as Mr. Lincoln was elected, we are for breaking up the Union. I say, no, let us show ourselves men and men of courage. . . . Though I fought against Lincoln, I love my country. I love the Constitution. Let us therefore rally around the altar of our Constitution and swear that it and the Union shall be saved as "Old Hickory" Jackson did in 1832. Senators, my blood, my existence, I would give to save this Union.

The *New York Herald* reported that Johnson was shunned by his fellow Southern senators as he left the floor. Other reports say that insults followed him along Pennsylvania Avenue as he walked to his rooms at the St. Charles Hotel, at the corner of Third Street. Johnson was hanged and burned in effigy in Lynchburg, Memphis, and elsewhere. North Carolina governor John Ellis labeled him a "traitor to his section" for the speech. Another North Carolinian, Senator Thomas Lanier Clingman, later contended that Johnson's speech had brought on the war.

On the pro-Union side, Johnson became an instant hero. He was still for Union *and* slavery, still in search of some middle ground that would preserve both, still ready to support a constitutional amendment that would have made slavery a permanent institution in the land. The speech wasn't as radical as it was made out to be. Yet as so often happened with Johnson's public utterances, his inflated rhetoric had upped the emotional content. To the *Chicago Tribune*, Johnson had struck the "the first really stunning blow at the treason of the seceding States."

Whatever the ultimate effect of his December 1860 speech, having taken his stand, Andy Johnson had no intention of backing away from it. As Oliver Temple noted, once Johnson had determined the rightness of something, a team of oxen couldn't budge him. On February 5 and 6, 1861—with Lincoln's inauguration now only a month away—Johnson again took to the Senate floor to excoriate secessionists and abolitionists alike, warning that Tennessee would run with blood if she were forced out of the Union, and urging his colleagues to let the common sense of the people prevail. It was an old theme with Johnson: The people, *his* people, the mechanics and artisans and honest laborers, know best.

Back home, Johnson's February speech had an immediate impact. A referendum on whether to call a state convention to consider secession failed by almost 9,000 votes, of nearly 128,000 votes that were cast. Just about everyone agreed that Johnson's stand for the Union had swung the outcome. Elsewhere, the Tennessee senator was again labeled a traitor to the South, again praised in the usual Northern newspapers. On March 2, Senator Joseph Lane of Oregon, a native Virginian and noted general who had distinguished himself in the Mexican War, attacked Johnson in strikingly personal terms.

Johnson, Lane informed their mutual colleagues, was "triumphantly ignorant and exultingly stupid" and had "never had a correct idea in his head." His December 18 speech "has so encouraged the North and the Black Republicans it has prevented peace and peaceful Secession.... Would you forcibly hold the South in the Union, put her in the same relation to the Union that Ireland occupies to England, Greece to Turkey, Italy to Austria, Poland to Russia, the Netherlands to Spain?" "Like Esau," Lane concluded, "Andrew Johnson has sold his birthright!"

Who knows what it was that finally got to Johnson. The "triumphantly ignorant"? The "exultingly stupid"? That crack about selling his birthright? Perhaps, as Johnson saw it, the time for half measures was over. South Carolina had seceded while Johnson was still finishing his December speech. The state had claimed the Federal camp at Fort Moultrie as its own property and forced the Union garrison there to retreat to Fort Sumter. South Carolina's guns had fired nearly two months earlier on the *Star of the West*, an unarmed merchant ship being used to reinforce Fort Sumter. Now, Charleston was beefing up its arsenal: A shipment of heavy-caliber Dahlgren guns was soon to arrive from Richmond. The Palmetto State had nearly 200 tons of gunpowder in reserve. The wheels, in short, were just about off the Union, and Lincoln was to be inaugurated president in forty-eight hours. Whatever the reason, or combination of reasons, in his response to Lane's attack, Johnson laid everything on the table.

He started his reply calmly enough, even citing William Cowper's 1782 poem "Conversation": "A moral, sensible, and well-bred man / Will not affront me; and no other can." If affront had not been taken, though, it was soon to be given. "Sir," he said, reportedly extending two fingers directly at Lane,

> have we reached a point of time in which we dare not speak of treason? Our forefathers talked about it; they spoke of it in the Constitution of the country; they have defined what treason is.... Treason shall consist only in levying war against the United States, and adhering to and giving aid and comfort to their enemies. [Note still the plural use of "United States."] Who is it that has been engaged in conspiracies? Who is it that has been engaged in making war upon the United States? Who is it that has fired upon our flag? Who is it that has given in-

structions to take your arsenals, to take your forts, to take your dockyards, to seize your custom-houses and rob your treasuries? Show me who has been engaged in these conspiracies; show me who has been sitting in these nightly and secret conclaves plotting the overthrow of the government...and I will show you a traitor!

The March 4, 1861, *New York Times* is full of Washington news and innuendo. The capital was thronged on the night of March 3, the eve of Lincoln's inauguration. "There are more people in town than there ever were before on a similar occasion. Hundreds are roaming about the streets, carpet-bags in hand, seeking some place to 'put up.' It is a noticeable fact that scarce a Southern face is to be seen."

Of particular concern to authorities was a report that as many as 700 "plug-uglies" had only recently left Baltimore for Washington. (The phrase "plug ugly," originally applied solely to Baltimore gangs, derives from the uglifying effect of being punched or "plugged," one too many times in the snout.) "It is believed," the *Times* reported, "that their purpose is not to make a demonstration against Mr. Lincoln but, if anything, to create a disturbance, and plunder private persons, and commit depredations upon the citizens." In fact, the same plug-uglies had disrupted Washington city elections in 1857 and again in 1858.

There was also a report that an unnamed Alabaman from Montgomery had traveled incognito to the capital on behalf of the fledgling Confederacy. "This gentleman is instructed, immediately after the inauguration, to present his credentials as Ambassador of the Southern Confederacy, and ask for recognition by the United States." Edwin Stanton had been worrying for months about a full-fledged putsch by Rebel sympathizers prepared to seize the Capitol rather than let Lincoln take the oath of office there.

Of all the front-page news that day, though, nothing jumped off the page like the item five inches down in the third column from the left, under the banner A SCENE IN THE SENATE:

The senate, on Saturday, presented a scene of deep interest. There has been little like it in the history of the country. While it disgraces the Senate and insulted the Senators outrageously, it gave evidence of a feeling deep and strong for the Union. The speech of Senator Lane was the inciting cause of the exciting scene, and is denounced in bitter terms on all sides. The reply of Andy Johnson in his castigation of Lane eclipsed all his former efforts. His name is in every mouth to-day, and he is freely applauded as the greatest man of the age. The peroration of his speech was most eloquent, and as he closed, the galleries, where the people all along had maintained a breathless silence, burst forth with uproarious and long-continued applause, and three rousing cheers were given for the Union, followed by "three for Andy Johnson!" The Senators were, of course, indignant, and the galleries at once cleared. The proceedings will mark one of the most important pages of our history.

The report was partisan. Lane didn't have a chance in the pages of the *Times*. The nation also had become such a riven place that the "greatest man of the age" could be "great" only to a part of the populace. Still, the mudsill tailor had come into his own; his name was on every tongue.

Within a span of only a few months, Johnson had become quite possibly the most polarizing figure in the nation. He was in Lynchburg on his way south to Tennessee in April 1861 when an angry mob boarded his railroad car and one of its members attempted to give Johnson's nose a yank. He might have succeeded if Johnson hadn't pulled a pistol and backed the crowd off. In Knoxville, when he finally did arrive, Johnson made a speech that Oliver Temple, who had been listening to him orate for nearly three decades, later wrote "turned my heart—all hearts—... toward him as never before. It seemed as if his lips had been touched by a live coal off the very altar of patriotism." (And this, it's worth repeating, is from someone who seems to have fundamentally disliked Johnson.)

Throughout the spring of 1861, Johnson worked tirelessly and fearlessly to keep Tennessee in the Union. There was hardly a stump in the eastern mountains and even into the middle part of the state that he didn't climb on to decry the "hell-born and hell-bound" secessionists and to warn that if Tennessee voted for disunion its people would be "handed over to the Confederacy like sheep in the shambles, bound hand and foot, to be disposed of as Jefferson Davis and his cohorts may think proper." Momentum seemed to be all in Johnson's favor. Then Lincoln issued a call for the states to provide 75,000 troops to suppress the insurrection, and for the majority of Tennessee voters, that was one step too far. On June 7, Johnson barely escaped what appears to have been a plot to assassinate him as he traveled to Knoxville by train. (He went to Greeneville instead, by buggy.) The next day, the eighth, the middle and western parts of the state voted overwhelmingly to join the Confederacy, the last state to do so. Just as overwhelmingly, the eastern part of the state—Andy Johnson's state, the old one of Franklin—voted against secession.

Thus Tennessee came to reflect the nation: divided against itself. And Johnson became, in a sense, the embodiment of its contradictions: a Southern crusader for the Northern-backed preservation of the Union, a slave owner dead set against the plantation aristocracy, a senator whose state had deserted him.

On July 22, still in the Senate despite the fact that Tennessee no longer considered itself part of the Union, Johnson introduced a series of resolutions that read in part: "This war is not prosecuted upon our part in any spirit of oppression, nor for any purpose of conquest or subjugation; nor for the purpose of over-throwing or interfering with the rights or established institutions of those states, but to defend and maintain the supremacy of the Constitution and all laws made in the pursuance thereof, and to preserve the Union, with all the dignity, equality and rights of the several states unimpaired, and as soon as these objects are accomplished the war ought to cease." The language was statesmanlike. No thundering talk of traitors or hemp ropes—only of reconciliation. The Senate passed his resolutions five days later by an overwhelming vote.

Johnson held forth again in the Senate on July 27 for three hours in support of granting Lincoln special war powers. Writing after the war, Alexander Stephens, the Confederate vice president, called it the most effective speech "ever delivered by any man on any occasion," a speech that invigorated the North as none other had—high praise from someone whom Johnson was later to see committed to prison. By July 27, the North needed invigorating. Five days earlier, not a half day's ride from where Andrew Johnson had been speaking on the Senate floor, the Union army had been routed at the First Battle of Bull Run—"one of the most severe and sanguinary ever fought on this Continent," according to the *New York Times*. Nearly four years of slaughter lay ahead.

In the months after Bull Run, the fighting went no better for the Federals in Tennessee than it did for them anywhere else. In theory the eastern part of the state had remained loyal. In practice, it was Confederate territory. The gaps and passes of the Smokies—the critical land route between Virginia and the West—were all in Rebel hands. Then, in February 1862, Union forces under Ulysses Grant and Commodore A.H. Foote captured Rebel forts on the Tennessee and Cumberland rivers; General D.C. Buell took Nashville; and Andrew Johnson, who had served the state as representative, senator, and governor, was sent south from Washington by Lincoln to become Tennessee's military governor: judge and jury, civil chief executive, tax man, and autocrat all melded into one. It was the role of a lifetime, and Johnson played it to the hilt. Thomas Scott, Edwin Stanton's assistant secretary of war, sent his boss a warning that Johnson was quite likely a dead man if he set foot in Tennessee. The pro-Confederacy newspapers of the state agreed: Hanging was too good for the turncoat.

Johnson arrived in Nashville in the second week of March 1862, took over the deserted State House where he had presided in better times less than a decade earlier, and set about bending the recalcitrants to his will. To those who would reconsider the error of their ways, he offered an open hand. To those who wouldn't, he gave little quarter. The *Nashville Times*, he simply shut down. He dismissed city officials who refused to take an oath of allegiance to the Union and replaced them with new officials more ready to accommodate his iron rule. When a secessionist judge was elected with nearly 60 percent of the vote, Johnson commissioned him, then had him arrested and replaced by the man he had defeated. Ministers who had been preaching the Confederate cause from the pulpit, he had tossed in jail. How else to keep them from, in Johnson's words, "corrupting the female mind... [and] changing them into fanatics." No visitors were to be admitted to their cells, no special favors granted them.

The war inflicted terrible hardships on the soldiers in the field and on those they left behind. To support the wives and children of the poor mechanics lured into the armies of this "unholy and nefarious rebellion," Johnson levied an onerous tax on wealthy secessionists, the grandees on their sprawling plantations. To the Rebel raiders who were to roam freely through the state for much of the war—Nathan Bedford Forrest and John Hunt Morgan, most notably—the military governor promised ancient justice: an eye for an eye, a tooth for a tooth. Johnson had little use for the clergy, but that didn't mean he hadn't read the Old Testament.

There are rare glimpses of almost Churchillian humor. Robert Winston tells the tale of an immensely large woman—the wife of a wealthy Nashville secessionist—who petitioned the military governor for permission to visit her husband, then being held in a Yankee prison. Johnson granted the pass, then refused her a second pass to return home when the visit was through. Go, was the message; we don't want you back. Not surprisingly, the woman protested, threatening to take Johnson over her knee and spank him. "Madam," came the reply, "it would take the whole Union army to spank you." The laughs, though, were few. Shiloh, Stones River, Chickamauga, the Battle Above the Clouds at Chattanooga, Murfreesboro—Tennessee was a killing field. By comparison, Alabama and Mississippi, even Sherman's famous march to the sea through Georgia, were mop-up operations. Only Virginia saw fighting at the same level.

Early on, the Confederate courts had declared that Johnson, as an "alien enemy," had forfeited all "property rights and credits." In April 1862, Rebel forces in control of Greeneville acted on the decree, seizing Johnson's house and other holdings and giving Eliza and her youngest son, Frank, thirty-six hours to leave town. Both too sick with consumption to travel far, Eliza and Frank spent the summer on the farm of her daughter, Mary Stover. Expelled again by the Confederates, she and Frank, accompanied now by Charles Johnson and both Stovers, set out to join Johnson in Nashville only to have John Hunt Morgan refuse them permission to cross his lines. They finally arrived in Nashville in October of that year.

So frail was Eliza's health that two months later, shortly after the siege of Nashville was broken, she left to seek a cure in Vevay, a small town on the Ohio River in southeastern Indiana. Johnson had commandeered a handsome Nashville house for his family—the home of Lizinka Campbell Brown, who in May 1863 married the Confederate general Richard Ewell—but a war capital stretched to the limit of its resources was no place for a sick wife. Still, Johnson worried about Eliza constantly after she left; about their oldest daughter, Martha, who had stayed behind in Greeneville; about young Frank, who was sent to Louisville to school; about his two drink-addicted sons, one soon to be dead. There followed another of those dark, dark letters that bubble up episodically in the Johnson correspondence. "The Confederates went to my home while my wife was sick; my child, eight years old, consumed with consumption. They turned her and the child into the streets, converted my house, built with my hands, into a hospital and barracks. My servants they confiscated. It was with much suffering my wife and little boy were able to reach the house of a relative, many miles distant. Call you this Southern rights? If so, God preserve me from another such affliction."

He told the story time and again from his beloved stump, along with accounts of Tennesseans "now in the dungeons of Alabama, bound in irons and fed on rotten meat and diseased bones," held by secessionists "ready for a return to a monarchy and the establishment of an aristocracy that should control the masses." By his words as much as by armed force, Johnson intended to force his state back into the Union fold.

Through most of the fall of 1862, Nashville was essentially surrounded and under siege. On November 5, Confederate forces seemed finally ready to break through. By then, Johnson had turned the state capitol into a heavily defended citadel, dubbed Fortress Johnson by the locals. Constructed atop a hill only three years earlier out of massive limestone blocks, the capitol served the purpose well. Watching the deteriorating situation around the city from the capitol's cupola that early November day, Johnson is said to have thundered out to his staff, "I am no military man, but anyone who talks of surrender I will shoot!" Were another person speaking, the story might be apocryphal. The words, though, sound too much like Johnson to be fiction. Here was a time and place when the nation really did want the most obstinate man in America in charge of things.

Samuel Glenn, a reporter for the *New York Herald*, spent that fall in Nashville, trapped with everyone else, a Johnson watcher by profession as well as necessity. "The coolness and calmness of the Governor amid these trying scenes are beyond all praise," Glenn wrote in his diary. "He does all he can to preserve order; but notwithstanding this, midnight assassinations are frequent. There were six murders one night recently." In Nashville in 1862 as in Fallujah and Baghdad in 2006, it was almost impossible to tell enemy from friend. Elsewhere in his diaries, Glenn writes of Johnson's "working twelve or fourteen hours a day ... sleeping on a bed of revolvers and bayonets." On what was to become the touchy issue of Johnson's abstemiousness under pressure—or lack of same—Glenn reports that the governor "is drinking about as much stimulant as a clergyman at a sacrament."

Thus, Johnson went on for the better part of three years, through siege and sickness, amid an often-hostile populace, always in danger of being assassinated. Lincoln knew the details well. So did Edwin

Stanton, the flinty war secretary who would become Johnson's nemesis in the years to come. "In one of the darkest hours of the great struggle for national existence against the rebellious foes, the Government called you from the Senate, and from the comparatively safe and easy duties of civil life, to place you in front of the enemy, and in a position of personal toil and danger, perhaps more hazardous than was encountered by any other citizen or military officer of the United States," Stanton wrote Johnson on March third, once the hostilities were nearly ended. "With patriotic promptness, you assumed the post, and maintained it under circumstances of unparalleled trials.... You so long and so gallantly per-illed [sic] all that is dear to man on earth." In politics, praise so fulsome is always suspect. Johnson was to be sworn in as vice president on the day after those words were written. The record, however, bears Stanton out. Conditions in Nashville were appalling. For most of the war, east-ern Tennessee was a no-man's-land. Even after John Morgan was finally tracked down and killed in early September 1864—by Johnson's per-sonal bodyguard, led by his protégé, Brigadier General A. C. Gillem—enemy troops posed a constant threat. Yet Andy Johnson never flinched, never backed down, even when dead mules clogged the streets and rats roamed the city. "A position of personal toil and danger, perhaps more hazardous than was encountered by any other citizen or military officer of the United States": Even allowing for a rare outbreak of hyperbole on Stanton's part, the words are worth a second reading. The man and the moment were made for one another, the last time Johnson would have that luxury.

For Lincoln, the political war dragged on alongside the real one, and with just as much frustration. No American president had been re-turned to office since Andrew Jackson's reelection in 1832. Martin Van Buren's 1840 defeat had marked the last time a sitting president had even been renominated by his own party. Technically, Lincoln would not break the jinx. In 1860 he had run as the candidate of the Republi-can Party, founded only six years earlier. In 1864, he was nominated by the National Union Party, whose name was a semantic confection meant to broaden the Republicans' appeal while also masking almost three years of battlefield disappointments.

Labels aside, though, the nomination was Lincoln's for the asking. Always an astute politician, Lincoln controlled the party's levers at the state level. What he lacked in charisma—that came later, after his murder—he atoned for with practical necessity. A war was on, no time to change horses, at least for the party faithful. Moreover, the biggest dissidents within the Republican ranks already had bolted. Angered at the president's ten percent plan—offering reentry to the Union to any breakaway state once a tenth of its citizens had sworn loyalty to the federal government and renounced slavery—the Radicals grew enraged when Lincoln killed by pocket veto the Wade-Davis resolution, which would have upped Lincoln's loyalty threshold to half the male citizens of each state and required an "iron-clad oath" of loyalty. In May 1864, dissident Republicans staged their own early convention in Cleveland and nominated John C. Frémont, the party's presidential candidate eight years earlier.

For the rest of the party, Lincoln was the nominee by default if nothing else. Success in the general election to be held in November was another matter entirely. The spring offensives against Richmond and Atlanta, meant to bring the enemy to its knees and assure victory by the symbolic Fourth of July, had become mired instead in body counts: nearly 100,000 Union casualties over the two months heading up to Independence Day, almost two-thirds the tally for the first three years of the war, with virtually nothing to show for it. Richmond held. Atlanta stood. The war, so it seemed, could go on forever. One month into the Richmond and Atlanta campaigns, at about the moment when public perception in the North of the war's progress was tipping toward despair, the National Unionists met in Baltimore, put their rubber stamp on Lincoln's renomination, and dumped the incumbent vice president, Hannibal Hamlin, in favor of the military governor of Tennessee, Andrew Johnson.

For Lincoln hagiographers—which is to say for the bulk of Lincoln biographers—Johnson's selection is at best confounding. How could he do it? How could Lincoln allow the conventioneers to choose a man who would show up drunk for his own inauguration and nearly get himself booted out of office? The easy answer is that Lincoln didn't, that his hands are clean. According to John Nicolay and John Hay, Lincoln's private secretaries and coauthors of a ten-volume life of Lincoln that was for years the standard, the president left the choosing to the convention: his running mate, the party's platform, even the matter of his own selection. The president, the implication went, was not one to interfere with the workings of democracy.

More complex answers tend to make Johnson's selection a projection of the wrinkles in Lincoln's own psyche. In *We Are Lincoln Men*, David Herbert Donald acknowledges Lincoln's complicity in the matter, if only through his silence, but argues that the president was ill-served by his inherent incapacity to form broad, deep, and lasting friendships: "No matter what one says about Johnson's honesty and his bravery in standing up for the Union when his state joined the Confederacy, he was a terrible choice," Donald argues. "Trusted, disinterested friends who looked into Johnson's record as a senator and reviewed his conduct as the controversial, embattled Union military governor of conquered Tennessee could have given the President warning signals." Like so many other presidents, Donald contends, Lincoln just didn't give much thought to his running mate or to the vice presidency itself—that "bucket of warm piss," as John Nance Garner once called it. (Having spent two terms as Franklin Roosevelt's first veep, "Cactus Jack" Garner knew the bucket all too well. In later recountings, "piss" was gentrified to "spit".)

Others contend that Johnson was simply a last-minute political calculation, one of those Spiro Agnews or Geraldine Ferraros or Dan Quayles who periodically surface in American electoral life when a ticket needs balancing, only to disappear once the tour of duty has passed or the vote been lost. Whether it was politics as usual, or neglect, or the absence of friends, or allegiance to some code of impartial purity, the important thing to traditional Lincoln scholars has been that he not be tainted by the choice, that as much as possible Johnson be seen as an immaculate selection.

All of which might be fine were it not so far-fetched. Abraham Lincoln cared deeply about his reelection. He plotted it constantly, fretted over it, despaired for victory as the voting date grew nearer. If Lincoln failed in his quest for reelection, if the War Republicans were thrown out of office, then the White House must fall into the hands of the Peace Democrats—the Copperheads. At the worst, the North would accept Confederate independence, and the Union would be lost. At best, slavery would be preserved, the Southern aristocrats upheld. Either way, four years of unparalleled bloodshed would be for naught. Whether Lincoln cared more for God's judgment or history's, he didn't intend to let that happen, and Johnson was a key part of his strategy; not for governing after the election—the office really was a bucket of warm piss—but for winning the right to continue governing at all.

Johnson was a political calculation. All vice presidents are. Hannibal Hamlin of Maine brought almost nothing to the table. Lincoln polled 62 percent of the popular vote in Maine in 1860. Four years later, he wasn't going to lose it, with or without Hamlin on the ticket. (And he didn't. Lincoln won 59 percent of the Maine vote in 1864.) Daniel Dickinson, also considered for the post, might have shored up New York State, which he had served as senator and was currently serving as attorney general, and New York did need help. Lincoln's conscription and the bounty system for getting out of military duty were deeply unpopular in New York City. In mid-July 1863, draft riots killed or injured more than a thousand New Yorkers and inflicted more than a million dollars in damages on the city. So sharp was the memory still in November 1864 that Lincoln carried the state by a mere 7,000 votes. Lincoln, however, already had a prominent New Yorker in his cabinet, Secretary of State William Seward. Either Dickinson would have overbalanced the ticket in favor of the Empire State, or Seward, a trusted adviser, would have had to go to make room for him. A third possibility, Union general Benjamin Butler, had taken himself out of the running before the convention met.

Johnson solved the dilemma. He was a War Democrat, a front-line civilian combatant whose resume was already bulging at the seams. Johnson made the National Union Party a union in more than just name. He'd spent his public life cultivating laborers, mechanics, the common man as his political base. "Tennessee" Johnson's nomination would also send a message across the Atlantic, to England and France, that the South was not united and that intervening in its behalf would be a bad bet. As for the Radical Republicans who had bolted to John C. Frémont, what man in public life had spoken more pointedly, more dramatically than Johnson about hanging the traitors who had brought on the war?

All running mates are ultimately marriages of convenience. Politics is about winning far more than friendships. Yet Lincoln and Johnson weren't strangers to one another. They'd served in the House together, on different sides of the aisle, for one term back in the late 1840s. They had a common heritage of childhood poverty and educational and social disadvantages. "Gawks, rail-splitters, and tailors," the Copperhead papers would jeer once the ticket was set. ("Gawk," an awkward person or simpleton, is derived from a rural English expression for "left-handed.") Johnson had campaigned for the Democratic presidential candidate four years earlier, not for Lincoln. In the interim, though, the two men had come to agree on critical issues including the ten-percent plan. Johnson admired Lincoln for his unwillingness to compromise with the Rebels. Lincoln praised Johnson for his steadfastness under duress in Nashville and for the raw energy with which he pursued his duties as military governor. In all, Johnson might have raised as many as twenty-five regiments in Tennessee, vital troops in a strategically critical region.

Inevitably, Johnson came to the ticket with baggage. He had created a swarm of enemies in Nashville: Union generals who disliked his meddling and constant agitation for action, residents on both sides of the battle who thought his rule too harsh. Yet Lincoln didn't mind prodding a recalcitrant general himself, and from the beginning of Johnson's tenure, the president seems to have respected his judgment. Lincoln yielded readily to Johnson's December 1862 request that Tennessee be exempted along with other Southern regions from the soon-to-be-issued Emancipation Proclamation. Extending the proclamation to Tennessee would offend slave owners loyal to the Union, Johnson had argued, and it wouldn't gain the Union any traction with the vast major-ity of the mountain yeomanry who had rallied to Johnson's side. They fought against the planter class, the aristocrats—the ones who wouldn't have had the mountain men to their tables at the point of a gun—not to free the slaves. The situation was too precarious; too much hung in the balance to take such a risk. For Lincoln, that was argument enough.

Stylistically, the two men were vastly different yet with common traits. Lincoln brooded and joked. Johnson brooded and fulminated. At heart, both were private men, especially for their calling. They had lost sons during the war and seen their wives strained to the breaking point. Both had given everything for and staked everything on the preserva-tion of the Union.

Earlier that spring, Lincoln had sent General Dan Sickles, who had lost a leg at Gettysburg, to Nashville with instructions to vet Johnson for the vice presidency. A Tammany Hall operative—beholden to the New York City political machine that traced its roots back to before the Revolution—Sickles knew politicians through and through, and he knew something, too, about volatile men. He himself had shot and murdered the son of Francis Scott Key a dozen years earlier, allegedly because he was having an affair with Sickles's wife. When Sickles re-ported back that Johnson had exercised his authority within reasonable restraints given the war, Lincoln's subsequent course of action must have seemed clear. Rather than marvel that the nation's most revered presi-dent should allow what would later become its most disgraced one to share the ballot with him, we would do better to wonder how Lincoln, at that point, could have chosen anyone else.

Not that Johnson's selection seemed to make a difference. So long as

Richmond held and Atlanta blocked Sherman's march to the sea, Christ or Pericles or the ghost of George Washington himself couldn't have done the ticket much good. In mid-July 1864, Lincoln called for half a million more volunteers to finish the war off and began setting up a draft board to make up for the inevitable shortfall. Three weeks later, in an August ninth letter to Lincoln, Horace Greeley, editor of the Republican *New York Tribune*, excoriated the president for a policy that seemed to be built solely on negatives: "No truce! No armistice! No negotiation! No mediation! Nothing but [Confederate] surrender at discretion! I never heard of such fatuity before.... If this impression be not removed we shall be beaten out of sight next November."

On the Democratic side, the pressure to pursue peace, almost at any cost, was relentless. The president "prefers to tear a half million more white men from their homes," said the *New York World*, "...to continue a war for the abolition of slavery rather than entertain a proposition for the return of the seceded states with their old rights." The *World* had already allied itself with General George B. McClellan, soon to be named Lincoln's Democratic opponent in the November election. Republicans had their deep doubts, too. "What is all this struggling and fighting for?" wrote Sarah Butler, the wife of the same General Butler whom Lincoln had considered for the vice presidency. "This ruin and death to thousands of families?... What advancement of mankind to compensate for the present horrible calamities?"

Lincoln shared in the despair. "This morning, as for some days past, it seems exceedingly probable that this Administration will not be reelected," he wrote in an August twenty-third memorandum to his cabinet. "Then it will be my duty to so co-operate with the President elect, as to save the Union between the election and the inauguration; as he will have secured his election on such ground that he can not possibly save it afterwards." Lincoln asked the cabinet to endorse the memo's contents without ever reading the words. Instead, he sealed it in an envelope to be opened after the election.

Two days after his memo, Lincoln met with the Republican

National Committee in what his secretary John Nicolay described as "almost the condition of a disastrous panic." Another six days on, the Democrats officially made George McClellan their candidate on a platform demanding that "immediate efforts be made for a cessation of hostilities." McClellan was neither a war hero nor a particularly effective campaigner—Lincoln had removed him as the Union general-in-chief two years earlier for his inaction in the field. Nor was he willing to endorse the peace-at-any-price sentiments of the most radical wing of his own party. Nonetheless, at the moment he was nominated, a betting man might have laid a fortune on his likely success. Then, four days later, on September third, came news from William Tecumseh Sherman that Atlanta had fallen. That changed everything.

The war wasn't over—far from it. Richmond would hold out for seven more months against improbable odds. At last, though, the Union war machine had crossed the mountaintop and started down the backside, and nearly everyone, Northerner and Southerner, liberal and conservative, abolitionist and proslavery, knew it. Sheridan's army was rampaging through the Shenandoah Valley, laying waste to vital supplies and foodstuffs. John C. Frémont caught the drift of things and abandoned his rump candidacy. There would be no third-party candidate to siphon vital votes from Lincoln and spoil the party, nor would there be any suing for peace. Nothing short of surrender would end the hostilities, and only one side of the conflict was going to do that.

As surely as they had seemed bound for victory at the polls before September third, George McClellan and the Democrats suddenly looked almost silly. "I know Mr. McClellan well," Johnson told a Louisville, Kentucky, crowd in mid-October.

He falls far below mediocrity; a very nice little gentleman. When you try to grip him, he is so small you can't find him; he is so little there's no place to whip him on.... Talk now about failure, when Gen. Sherman has penetrated rebeldom's heart, and holds it in his grasp? Mr. Lincoln has proved himself a patriot above all party. Whatever he has done has been to defend and preserve the Constitution and the Government.... Re-elect Mr. Lincoln and this infernal rebellion is well nigh at an end. It will carry terror and dismay into the traitors' camps. It will appall Jeff Davis himself. Our armies will be encouraged and inspired, and our nation will be redeemed and regenerated.

The speech was vintage Johnson oratory: humorous in a crude way, disrespectful in the same manner, an ad hominem attack, and with enough juice to bring the crowd to its feet.

Best of all, the vice-presidential candidate had events on his side. A month later, on November eighth, Lincoln and Johnson outpolled McClellan and his running mate, George Pendleton, by more than 400,000 votes, a 55-45 romp in the popular tally. In Pendleton's home state of Ohio, where Johnson had campaigned most actively, the Lincoln ticket won over 56 percent of the vote, a 60,000-vote edge. Only Massachusetts gave the ticket a greater margin in the popular count. In the Electoral College, the vote translated to a landslide, 212 votes to 21, and the winning didn't stop there. The Republicans/National Unionists picked up enough new seats in the House to give the party an advantage of better than three to one, the first in four decades.

Like the war itself, the election had been won in the trenches: More than three out of four Union soldiers who voted cast their ballots for Lincoln and Johnson, the railsplitter and the mudsill tailor, the Republican and the Democrat, the Great Emancipator and the one-time slave owner. Surely, this was one of the most singular tickets in the history of American presidential elections, coming at one of the nation's most crucial moments: strange bedfellows for strained times.

On March 4, 1865, four years later almost to the day and at the very place where he had been acclaimed the "greatest man of his age," Andrew Johnson was sworn in as vice president of the United States and disgraced himself with a drunken oration.

Again, there are the easy answers as to why. Never sanitary during the height of the war, public-health conditions in Nashville deteriorated steadily as the conflict ebbed. The battle for the city that raged through November and into December 1864—the last serious effort by the Confederate army to turn the tide of the war—left Nashville relatively free for the first time in three and a half years, but it also filled the place with Union soldiers and their camp followers, as well as with ex-slaves desperate for refuge. By early 1865, Nashville had swelled to about 100,000 people, six times what it had been only five years before, a population that would have made it the tenth largest American city at the start of the war. "There were many cheap and dirty eating joints, filthy flop houses, barrelhouses (disreputable saloons), brothels, and slums swarming with rats," one history of the city recounts. "A request by the Nashville Academy of Medicine to the city authorities to appoint a Board of Health with the powers and funds to clean up the city was ignored until a plague of Asiatic cholera broke out in the city."

Johnson, who remained on duty in Nashville until late February 1865, avoided the cholera, but he was weakened: from the political campaign; from his three-year struggle as military governor; from the year before that when he had stood alone among all his Southern colleagues in the battle to prevent disunion; and from all the loss and suffering he had been witness to, including the loss of his son and son-in-law and the afflictions of his wife and youngest son. He was fifty-seven by then—not old, although he had ridden the last part of his life hard. Almost certainly, as the time neared for his own inauguration, Johnson was suffering from typhoid fever. He wrote to William Hickey, the chief clerk of the Senate, where the swearing in was to take place, to ask if he could have the oath of office administered in Nashville and to learn if any other vice presidents had failed to appear for their own ceremony. Hickey's reply reached Johnson at the start of February. In fact, six vice presidents had been no-shows at their inaugurals, including John Adams for his second term under George Washington.

Had the decision been left to him, Johnson would have been the seventh one not to attend his own swearing in. Lincoln, though, had other plans. He wrote Johnson on January twenty-fourth, urging him to attend if at all possible. "It is [the Cabinet's] unanimous conclusion That it is unsafe for you not to be here on the 4th of March. Be sure to reach here by that time." Unsafe? Perhaps Lincoln meant that a show of strength and unity was vital—Republican and Democrat side-by-side, the war front united in the war's closing act for the nation and Europe to see. Three days later, John W. Forney, the secretary of the Senate, added his own strong encouragement. "The interests of the country demand your presence. You are in fact the representative of the Democratic element without which neither Abraham Lincoln nor yourself could have been chosen."

Whatever Lincoln's reasoning and however accurate Forney's assessment, Johnson acceded to the request. In mid-February he agreed to speak on "Southern reconstruction" before a group called the American Union Commission in New York City sometime before his inauguration. A week later, on the twenty-second, Johnson reneged on the engagement. He was too sick to make the trip. Still, he set out from Nashville for Washington. On the twenty-seventh, he stopped en route in Cincinnati and delivered a speech that the local *Gazette* found wanting in strength and clarity. "Johnson seemed somewhat the worse for the wear and tear of the past year or two," the reporter noted. The vice-president-elect finally arrived in Washington on March 1 and moved into his suite of rooms at the Kirkwood House.

And with that, the story of Johnson's drunkenness gets considerably more complicated. Perhaps Johnson was self-medicating for his typhoid and simply overdid it. Brandy and whiskey were common proofs against all sorts of ailments in the middle of the nineteenth century, and in the nation's capital in those days a tumbler of either was almost as easy to come by as a glass of clean drinking water. Kidwell & Son, just two blocks west of Kirkwood House, advertised itself as "Manufacturing Chemists and Pharmaceutists; Dealers in English, French, and American Drugs, Chemicals, & Perfumery, Patent Medicines, Surgical Instruments, Fancy Articles, & Medicated Waters, Also, Brandies, Wines, & Liquors." Perhaps Johnson was weak-kneed from the typhoid fever or from overindulging the night before and tried to revive himself with a little hair of the dog. Could Hannibal Hamlin, who provided Johnson with his lethal bracers, have poured with a heavy hand, intentionally or even subconsciously? Hamlin had, after all, been dumped from the ticket in favor of the Tennessean, and he had obliged Johnson's request for a drink by sending across the street for a bottle.

Or perhaps Johnson realized at the last moment what a bad bargain he had made in accepting the nomination as vice president. Since early 1862 he had been in charge, in almost constant motion, planning and directing. For the year before that, he had been one of the pivotal men in America—the fate of the entire Union seemingly resting on his shoulders. Johnson was ambitious; the vice presidency would satisfy that longing. He was also not one for sitting around, and now he faced the prospect of four years of doing little more than that. He'd spent almost two decades in Washington, more than enough time to realize how passive his new post was likely to be. Why not a little drink at the outset? And another?

A modern account by the Senate Historical Office of the lead-up to Johnson's inaugural embarrassment favors the hair-of-the-dog theory: "The night before his March 4, 1865, inauguration, [Johnson] fortified himself with whiskey at a party hosted by his old friend, Secretary of the Senate John W. Forney. The next morning, hung over . . . Johnson proceeded to the Capitol office of Vice President Hannibal Hamlin, where he complained of feeling weak and asked for a tumbler of whiskey. Drinking it straight, he quickly consumed two more."

Outside, the day was wet and raw, typical of early March weather in the capital; the streets, rutted and muddy. Inside, the Senate chamber was stifling hot and stuffed to overflowing with lawmakers from both houses, Supreme Court justices, leading military officers, foreign ambassadors decked out in full regalia, and other luminaries. The visitors' gallery was packed, too, mostly with women who wouldn't be quiet. Johnson walked in arm in arm with Hamlin, more from custom than from any immediate need of support, but the whiskey would soon undo him.

The departing vice president spoke first, a few dignified remarks, barely audible above the general din from the visitors' gallery. By the time Johnson rose to follow him, he was already red in the face and unsteady on his feet. Speaking without notes—a dire omen, in retrospect—and in a voice that seemed to rise and fall with little logic or reason, the incumbent vice president proceeded to lecture senators, cabinet members, and justices alike on the fount of power in a democratic society. "In fact, you Mr. Secretary Stanton, and you ... Mr. Chief Justice Chase, owe what you are or will ever be, to the people." They must have cringed one by one as Johnson singled them out, or those whose names he could remember. Partway through his harangue, Johnson bent over and asked John Forney, the Senate secretary, "Who is the Secretary of the Navy?" The new vice president then insulted the diplomats in attendance en masse: "You ... with all your fine feathers and geegaws ..."

Sober, Johnson couldn't stop talking about his simple origins. Drunk, standing atop the biggest stump he'd ever had, all those years of struggling up off the mudsill and all the slights and insults along the way must suddenly have loomed larger than ever: "Humble as I am, plebeian as I may be ..." Inevitably, too, Johnson's abiding anger, his class rage, bubbled beneath the surface of everything: "Today one who claims no high descent, one who comes from the ranks of the people, stands, by the choice of a free constituency, in the second place of this Government. There may be those to whom such things are not pleasing ..."

And so on he went, lauding the common man ("the popular heart"), praising Tennessee's role in the war ("She has bent the tyrant's rod, she has broken the yoke of slavery"), and generally overreaching every inch of the way, one of those inebriated volcanoes that most of us would go miles out of our way to avoid. Alas, no one could. For his very worst moment, Andy Johnson chose a captive crowd on a national, even international stage. On the Republican side of the Senate, Charles Sumner, the

Massachusetts Radical, reacted to the rant with a sarcastic smile, then covered his face with his hands and lowered his head to his desk. Gideon Welles, the navy secretary whose name had eluded the new vice president, whispered to war secretary Edwin Stanton, who was sitting on his right, "The man is either drunk or crazy." Stanton, by most accounts, looked almost terrified as Johnson raved on, sometimes shaking his fist, other times stabbing at the air with a finger. William Dennison, the postmaster general, flushed red and went ghostly pale. Attorney General James Speed kept his eyes closed, as if that might make the spectacle disappear. In the press gallery, one correspondent simply shut his note pad, too disgusted to continue recording the moment. Awaiting his own inauguration, President Lincoln sat with his head bowed, an expression of "unutterable sorrow" on his face, according to one source, while Hannibal Hamlin tugged at Johnson's coattails, trying to get his successor to cut short his remarks. After Johnson finally quieted and took the oath of office, he held his lips to the Bible on which he had been sworn in, saying loud enough for everyone to hear, "I kiss this book in the face of my nation of the United States"—one last bit of gibberish. The vice president's one actual duty that day was to swear in the new senators, but he had already given more than enough proof that he wasn't up to the challenge. After a brief, muddled effort, Johnson turned the task over to a Senate clerk.

Never has a vice presidency gotten off to a less promising start. Never perhaps has any American politician more thoroughly embarrassed himself in plain view of the public. And never certainly has any inauguration ceremony moved more rapidly from the ludicrous to the sublime because not many minutes later, outdoors on the steps of the Capitol, Lincoln (after instructing the marshal in charge not to let Johnson speak again) delivered one of the great public addresses in American history, the one that ends so memorably: "With malice toward none, with charity for all, with firmness in the right as God gives us to see the right, let us strive on to finish the work we are in, to bind up the nation's wounds, to care for him who shall have borne the battle and for his widow and his orphan, to do all which may achieve and cherish a just and lasting peace among ourselves and with all nations."

"The inauguration went off very well," Michigan senator Zachariah Chandler wrote home to his wife afterward, "except that the Vice President Elect was too drunk to perform his duties & disgraced himself & the Senate by making a drunken foolish speech. I was never so mortified in my life; had I been able to find a hole, I would have dropped through it out of sight." In wildly partisan times, it helps to know who is speaking. Zachariah Chandler was by then in his second term in the Senate, a Radical Republican through and through. Lincoln was too tame for his tastes—indeed Lincoln's "malice toward none... charity for all" was precisely what the Radical Republicans didn't want to hear. Although of different political parties, Chandler and Johnson knew each other well and agreed on most matters. Before Johnson went off to Tennessee to become military governor, he and Chandler had served together on the Joint Committee on the Conduct of the War, created by Congress to goad the administration and its generals into a more aggressive stance on the battlefield. If Chandler found the vice president's swearing in mortifying, we can safely assume that nearly everyone else did, too, with the exception of those who were glad to see Johnson make a fool of himself.

The war-republican papers, the pro-administration ones, either ignored the story, softened its edges, or painted the uproar in partisan tones. Handed a wonderfully juicy tale right in its own backyard, the *Washington Evening Star* kept a dignified silence. Johnson was inaugurated. He spoke briefly. That was it. After publishing a highly sanitized version of the speech on March 5, the *New York Times* waited two weeks to address in the most delicate terms the ensuing hullabaloo. "There may be differences of opinion as to the timeliness and good taste of some of the topics which [Johnson] introduced on that occasion,—but few will venture, we presume, to question publicly the justice of the sentiments which he expressed. Still less will any basis be found in the speech for the unmeasured and intemperate vituperation of the Vice-President for which it was made the occasion [*sic*]."

The secession and Copperhead journals showed no such restraint. Johnson had carried the fight to them for four years. They must have been almost giddy with revenge. "All eyes were turned to Mr. Johnson as he started, rather than rose, from his chair, and, with gesticulations and shrieks, strangely and weirdly intermingled with audible stage whispers, began to address the brilliant auditory around and above him. Such oratory it was never my fortune to hear before, and I hope never to hear again." So began a widely reprinted dispatch to the *Times* of London, one that grew more acid with each paragraph. Johnson "disgraced not only the dignity of his official position, but even the honest working classes from whom he sprang. His behavior was that of an illiterate, vulgar, and drunken rowdy. . . . Mr. Johnson was so proud of the dignity into which fate had thrust him that he boasted of it in the language of a clown and with the manners of a costermonger. He pitched his voice as if he had been addressing a large multitude in the open air, and alternately whispered and roared in a manner that would have been ludicrous had it not been disgusting."

Imagine sitting in Cleveland or Boston or Philadelphia and reading those words. What kind of monster would they conjure up? The London *Times* correspondent wasn't through. He had one paragraph left to go, and one unidentified Democratic senator—a "moderate opponent of the Government"—still to quote: "'The country is disgraced,' he said, 'and I pray God for the health and long life of Abraham Lincoln. I never prayed for him before, nor knew how valuable his life was to this country. Should he die within the next four years, which calamity may Heaven in its mercy avert, we should have Andrew Johnson for President, and sink to a lower depth of degradation than was ever reached by any nation since the Roman Emperor made his horse a consul.'"

Like many unattributed quotes, then and now, it sounds a little too manicured to be entirely true. The point, though, is taken: It was a buffoon's performance never to be entirely lived down. In *The Age of Hate*, George Fort Milton cites a commemorative verse that was soon making the rounds of the capital:

> *At Washington the other day,*
> *There was a brilliant display,*
> *For some were drunk*
> *And some were gay*
> *At the Inauguration.*
>
> *O, was it not a glorious sight,*
> *To see the crowd of black and white,*
> *As well as Andy Johnson tight*
> *At the Inauguration.*

The Senate remained in special session until March 11 of that year, but except for a few minutes on March 6, the Senate's new president was nowhere to be seen. One account suggests that Johnson was not allowed to preside over the body he had just insulted. That seems unlikely and unnecessary—Johnson had no desire to be there himself. There was talk among the senators about asking the new vice president to resign his post, and a resolution was even offered that would have banned whiskey from the Senate side of the Capitol. It failed. Why cut off your nose to spite your face?

The person least upset by the spectacle Johnson had made of himself seems to have been the one who had invited him inside the tent in the first place. Mrs. Lincoln was appalled, the cabinet mostly aghast. The president, however, appears hardly to have been fazed at all. On March 6, Lincoln praised his new vice president to Marcus L. Ward, a philanthropist and later New Jersey governor. When Comptroller of the Currency Hugh McCulloch raised the subject of Johnson's speech with Lincoln shortly after the event, the president replied, "I have known Andy Johnson for many years. He made a bad slip the other day, but you need not be scared; Andy ain't a drunkard." McCulloch, who was soon to be appointed secretary of the Treasury, would need some convincing.

As for Johnson, he did what politicians regularly do in such circumstances: made a very few token appearances, then pleaded sick, fled town, and set out to scour the historical record. With his friend and adviser Preston King, a former New York senator, Johnson holed up at Silver Spring, the thousand-acre estate of Francis Preston Blair Sr., over the District of Columbia line in Montgomery County, Maryland. Like Johnson, Blair was an Andy Jackson man. He'd come to the capital in 1830 to start up the *Washington Globe* as a mouthpiece for Old Hickory, and settled into the four-story stucco mansion on Pennsylvania Avenue, diagonally across from the White House, that bears his name and is still used for official state visitors. A quarter century later, out of the newspaper business and retired to the country, Blair and his son, Montgomery, had been among the founders of the Republican Party and had helped to secure Lincoln's nomination in 1860. Montgomery had served as Lincoln's first postmaster general, although he no longer held the post.

Johnson stayed at Silver Spring for a week, presumably too ill to undertake any duties. On March 9, though, he did rally long enough to write the Senate's official reporter, Richard Sutton: "I see from the 'Congressional Globe' that the proceedings of Saturday, the 4th ins't, have not as yet been published, and as I understand there has been some criticism upon the address delivered by me in the Senate Chamber, will you do me [*sic*] favor to preserve the original notes, and retain them in your possession, and furthermore, at your earliest convenience, bring me an accurate copy of your report of what I said on that occasion."

"Some criticism"? Johnson was capable of understatement after all.

Johnson or someone else edited the verbatim copy provided by Sutton down to three exceedingly lengthy and coherent paragraphs that appeared later that year in a puff book titled *Life, Speeches and Services of*

Andrew Johnson, with a brief, bland introduction that makes no mention of the circumstances. As delivered on the Senate floor, Johnson's inaugural address lasted seventeen endless minutes. The sanitized version can be read aloud in no more than six minutes, about the length that Johnson had been expected to speak that morning. There's no evidence, by the way, that Johnson ever apologized for his behavior or sought to excuse his actions. For him, the best defense was always a good offense.

The new vice president did go back on public display. On April third, he spoke to a large crowd gathered in front of the Patent Office to celebrate the fall of Richmond. Later, he traveled to City Point, where he hoped to meet with Lincoln. That meeting didn't happen. A few days later, Johnson and King, along with the vice president's secretary, William Browning, went south to Richmond to have a look at the ruins of the former Confederate capital.

On the fourteenth of April, about three in the afternoon, Johnson finally got his meeting with Lincoln, the first since the inauguration debacle. Hans Trefousse writes that Johnson used the occasion to press for harsh treatment of the Southern traitors. That wasn't Lincoln's intent—his inaugural address had made that clear—but the get-together was cordial, with Lincoln pumping Johnson's hand vigorously and calling him Andy. Johnson for his part seemed relieved to have put the past behind him. Twenty hours later, Andrew Johnson—a latter-day Caligula in the *Times* of London dispatch—would be sworn in as president of the United States.

CHAPTER 4

Center Stage

*A*LITTLE AFTER MIDDAY on the Fourth of July, 1826—after the Declaration of Independence had been read aloud in the House of Representatives and following an hour-long oration by a local lawyer honoring the fiftieth birthday of the American nation—Secretary of War James Barbour ascended to the rostrum. He asked the distinguished assemblage to contribute to a fund that would help allay Thomas Jefferson's debts. Rains had ruined the fields at Monticello. Land prices were down. A friend had defaulted on a large loan. The cost of entertaining a constant stream of visitors had exhausted Jefferson's reserves. The need was pressing. President John Quincy Adams joined those who came forward afterward to pledge support. Two days later, Barbour informed the president that Jefferson had died at Monticello on the Fourth, just as the jubilee celebration was reaching its peak. It had taken that long for word to reach Washington, only 115 miles away.

On the eighth of July, Adams received separate letters from three family members in Quincy, Massachusetts, all bearing the news that his father, John Adams, the second president and Jefferson's longtime political adversary, was near death. The next day, the ninth, the president set out for Massachusetts by carriage just at sunrise. His traveling party was having breakfast at Waterloo, not far south of Baltimore, when the innkeeper told Adams that he needn't hurry. News had reached Baltimore only that morning: The senior Adams had also died on Independence Day, around five in the afternoon. To John Quincy Adams and virtually the entire nation, the passing of two Founding Fathers on such an auspicious day was proof of America's divine favor.

In the nearly forty years between that remarkable coincidence and Abraham Lincoln's assassination, the telegraph had changed everything. News of the attacks on the president and on William Seward arrived almost instantaneously throughout the North. By early morning on April 15, 1865, city streets were flooded with newspapers, special editions, constant updates. Church bells that one week earlier had rung in celebration at Richmond's fall and Lee's surrender now tolled the calamity to a waking population. Even while Lincoln clung to life, news of his death was being announced far and wide.

Yet if four decades had radically altered the speed of its transmission, time had not changed the way in which such news was received and understood. Once again, God had reached out and touched America. Again, he'd chosen a special day: Good Friday, the commemoration of Christ's own crucifixion. And again, he had made death his messenger. "We know and we trust we feel that Almighty Wisdom has some wise purpose in view in permitting this blow to fall upon the nation," the Lancaster, Pennsylvania, *Daily Express* editorialized in its April 15 edition. "What that purpose may be, time, perhaps eternity, only can reveal. It may be that Mr. Lincoln was too kind-hearted a man to finish the great work in which God has used him as the main instrument for the past four years. It may be that the nation needed even this terrible lesson to teach them that traitors, with their hands dripping with the innocent blood of our loyal brothers, are not to be taken to our bosoms with impunity and treated to a general amnesty until they have purged themselves of their guilt."

The lamb was gone. The lion was waiting. And God's hand was in it all. No wonder churches spilled over with worshippers the next day. In Cincinnati that Easter Sunday, churches were jammed "almost to suffocation," the local *Gazette* reported. Trinity Church in New York City was "never filled so full," lawyer George Templeton Strong noted in his diary.

"The crowd packed the aisles tight and even occupied the choir steps and the choir itself nearly to the chancel rails."

Ministers in the North and South had helped incite the populace to action: to free the slaves, to humble their owners, to defend hearth and home and honor. A nation of atheists might never have fought the war that a nation of believers had waged, might never have shed the blood. In the North, Black Easter—with Lincoln murdered, with Booth at large, with the pews crammed as almost never before —was no day to ease off the battle from the pulpit.

At that same Trinity Church in New York that had never been so filled, Reverend Francis Vinton took as his text a passage from the first book of Samuel that reads almost as a companion piece to the verses Andrew Johnson had chosen for his swearing in: "Then said Samuel, Bring ye hither to me Agag the king of the Amalekites. And Agag came unto him delicately. And Agag said, Surely the bitterness of death is past. And Samuel said, As thy sword hath made women childless, so shall thy mother be childless among women. And Samuel hewed Agag in pieces before the Lord in Gilgal." "In this stern spirit," Vinton concluded, "should the leaders of the rebellion be dealt with."

At the South Baptist Church in Hartford, Connecticut, that Easter morning, Reverend C. B. Crane made explicit to his parishioners the link between Christ and the newly martyred president. Lincoln's assassination was "the after-type of the tragedy which was accomplished on the first Good Friday, more than eighteen centuries ago, upon the eminence of Calvary in Judea.... Jesus Christ died for the world; Abraham Lincoln died for his country." From there, Reverend Crane went on to establish the guilty—most notably, John Wilkes Booth, "insane with revenge," and Jefferson Davis, who must now with Lincoln's blood on his hands "skulk through the world with...the mark of Cain upon his brow and the maledictions of futurity upon his memory forever"—before turning finally to Andrew Johnson and his role in this national morality play.

In Crane's telling, Johnson's part was one for which the vice president's recent history, especially his drunken spectacle six weeks earlier, had perfectly prepared him. Thus works the mysterious hand of the divine. "I believe that God purposes to bring final deliverance to the republic by the same Andrew Johnson in whom on the fourth day of last March we lost faith," Reverend Crane began.

> Do you not remember how we lost faith in Gen. Ulysses Grant at the bloody battle of Pittsburg Landing, and afterward during the siege of Vicksburg? But he was God's anointed man, and today we esteem him second to no captain whom the world has produced. Do you not remember how our confidence in Abraham Lincoln was shaken when he went from Springfield to Washington, making little speeches from the platform of the car all the way. Today we lament him as one of the greatest statesmen whom history celebrates.... And so my faith in God's using of Andrew Johnson for our national salvation is all the greater because the beginning of his more exalted career was so inauspicious.

Lincoln's tenderness, his "wonderful caution," the "humaneness" that had kept him from starving Rebel prisoners while the Rebels were starving Union ones—all these had "eminently fitted him for the conduct of the war" but not for wielding the "sword of retributive justice," Crane preached. Not so, Lincoln's successor. Andrew Johnson "appreciates treason. His sense of justice is paramount to his tender sensibilities." (And how nicely that is put.) Lincoln had been drifting toward pardoning Jefferson Davis, Robert E. Lee, and the other leading Rebels. Johnson, "a man of nerve," would bring the rebellion to a just end, not a private vengeance but the vengeance God intended for the South. "And so God has given [Johnson] to the nation when the nation needed him," Crane concluded. "The nation will understand ere long that the dark Providence of last Friday night was a merciful Providence. Andrew

Johnson is the Joshua whom God has appointed to consummate the work which our dead Moses so nobly commenced."

To a greater or lesser degree, bathed in religious sentiment or boiled down to the hard calculus of politics, the same general sentiment was everywhere. The *Chicago Tribune* of April 18 also invoked Moses and Joshua. Lincoln had led the American people "out of Egypt and across the Red Sea of civil war." Johnson would "drive out the Hittites and Amorites," that the people might enter Canaan and gain the Promised Land. In Boston that Easter Sunday, Reverend W. S. Studley told his congregation: "In dealing with traitors, Andrew Johnson's little finger will be thicker than Abraham Lincoln's loins." Like Crane, he meant it as a compliment. Ralph Waldo Emerson wondered in his journal "if it should turn out in the unfolding of the web, that [Lincoln] had reached the term; that the heroic deliverer could no longer serve us; that . . . what remained to be done required new and uncommitted hands?"

The Radical Republicans certainly thought so. From Benjamin Wade of Ohio and Massachusetts' Charles Sumner in the Senate to Pennsylvania's Thaddeus Stevens in the House, many could barely contain their glee that Lincoln was gone. The dead president had been far too soft for their tastes. "Johnson, we have faith in you," Wade told him. "By the gods, there will be no trouble *now* in running the government!" It was still Easter Sunday; Lincoln's body was barely cold. Sumner, who had wept at Lincoln's side as he lay dying (and smiled sarcastically at Johnson's drunken oration), went further: The assassination was a "judgment of the Lord" that had raised Johnson to the nation's highest office. Another of the Radicals, Representative George Julian of Indiana, wrote in his journal, "I believe that the Almighty continued Mr. Lincoln in office as long as he was useful, and then substituted a better man to finish the work."

For those most bent on vengeance against the South and for those newly turned to bloodlust by Lincoln's assassination, Andy Johnson had not simply succeeded to the White House; he had been providentially delivered unto it. "While everybody was shocked at the murder," Julian wrote, "the feeling was nearly universal that the accession of Johnson to the Presidency would prove a godsend to the country." Zachariah Chandler, who six weeks earlier during Johnson's inauguration debacle had looked in vain for a hole to crawl into, was of a similar mind: "Had Mr. Lincoln's policy been carried out, we should have had Jeff Davis, Toombs [Robert Toombs, the antebellum Georgia senator and later Confederate secretary of state and general], etc. back in the Senate at the next session of Congress, but now their chances to stretch hemp are better." "Thus in a moment the scepter of power has passed from a hand of flesh to a hand of iron," Senator James Doolittle of Wisconsin told a crowd in Racine in the wake of the assassination. Even Frederick Douglass, the nation's foremost black leader and no admirer of Johnson, perceived the hand of a benevolent providence at work in Lincoln's death. Speaking in Rochester, New York, on April 15, Douglass saw the assassination as a heaven-sent reminder not to be "in too much haste in the work of restoration . . . not to be in a hurry to clasp to our bosom that spirit which gave birth to Booth."

For many in the North, the question in those first days after the murder wasn't whether vengeance would prevail. Vengeance was a given, a necessary corrective to what had brought the war on in the first place—slavery, "that nurse of brutality," as one Massachusetts minister told his flock, "which has poisoned our moral life, deluged the land in blood, given us Libby Prison and Andersonville, and added this crowning horror to its crimes." The question was what form the vengeance would take, how broadly retribution would be spread, how deeply Reverend Crane's "sword of retributive justice" would cut.

On April twenty-third, from the pulpit of the South Presbyterian Church in Brooklyn, Rev. Samuel T. Spear provided an answer very much in the spirit of the times. "Upon a certain class [of Confederates], large enough to meet the demands of public justice, including high officers in the State and the Army, and by no means exempting Jefferson Davis or General Lee, I would, having first indicted, tried, and convicted them under law, and also confiscated their property, visit the extreme penalty of law;—that is to say, I would hang them by the neck till they are dead." A second class of traitors—"in some respects less criminal, yet deeply guilty and very dangerous to the public peace"—Spear proposed to expel from the country and confiscate their property for the common good. A third class, still less criminal yet guilty all the same, were to be disenfranchised, allowed to remain within the borders but forbidden from assuming any official duties under the government of these United States. "By these several methods ... I would make an utter end of the leading rebel-traitors. In this way I would vindicate the majesty of the law, and protect the masses of the common people, alike Northern and Southern. I would show the world, that this is a Government for the *people*, and not for the traitors."

As with his colleagues in Boston and Connecticut, as with Wade and Sumner and Julian on Capitol Hill, Reverend Spear had no space for the Christ of the New Testament in his theology of punishment. Turning the other cheek, malice toward none, charity for all, binding up the nation's wounds—that was Lincoln's way, and look what it had earned him. Had God shouted out the obvious truth from a burning bush at high noon on the front lawn of the White House, he couldn't have made himself much clearer. "Will you hang the foul wretch who shot the President, and leave that dark, broad background of treason whence he came, and in concert with whose spirit he committed the crime, untouched by the hand of public justice? Will you consign to death the assassin who strikes down the officer of law, and then welcome and excuse the greater assassin who hurls the shaft of destruction at the State?"

Treason, traitors, hanging by the neck—Johnson had been talking about these things for four years. Now the words were being shouted out from pulpits and on editorial pages. The time had arrived to see the work done and, in Lincoln's murder, so had the moment and the momentum to push the squeamish forward, or aside.

No president, indeed few leaders have ever been better served by a memorialist than Abraham Lincoln was by Walt Whitman. In three separate poems, Whitman captured the nation's sorrow, bade the dead president good-bye, and committed him to the pantheon of fallen heroes: the lesser known "Hushed Be the Camps To-day" ("Sing—as they close the doors of earth upon him—one verse, / For the heavy hearts of soldiers."); "O Captain! My Captain!," immediately and wildly popular ("It is some dream that on the deck, / You've fallen cold and dead."); and the unforgettable "When Lilacs Last in the Dooryard Bloom'd": "for the dead I loved so well, / For the sweetest, wisest soul of all my days and lands."

Andrew Johnson didn't inspire that kind of affection. He wasn't anyone's sweetest or wisest soul. Nor was he martyred. Johnson did have his own poet, though, a literary figure who knew perhaps better than any other man of letters in America the dark brooding spirits, the lone wolves, the iconoclasts; a man who understood obsessive behavior through and through: Herman Melville. In his poem "The Martyr," subtitled "Indicative of the passion of the people on the 15th of April, 1865," Melville, like Whitman, caught the spirit of the moment; but like the clergy thundering in their pulpits from one end of New England to the other, he also caught the expectation of what waited ahead:

> Good Friday was the day
> Of the prodigy and crime,
> When they killed him in his pity,
> When they killed him in his prime
> Of clemency and calm—
> When with yearning he was filled
> To redeem the evil-willed,
> And, though conqueror, be kind;
> But they killed him in his kindness,
> In their madness and their blindness,
> And they killed him from behind.
> There is sobbing of the strong,
> And a pall upon the land;

But the People in their weeping
Bare the iron hand:
Beware the People weeping
When they bare the iron hand.

He lieth in his blood—
The father in his face;
They have killed him, the Forgiver—
The Avenger takes his place,
The Avenger wisely stern,
Who in righteousness shall do
What the heavens call him to,
And the parricides remand;
For they killed him in his kindness,
In their madness and their blindness,
And his blood is on their hand.
There is sobbing of the strong,
And a pall upon the land;
But the People in their weeping
Bare the iron hand:
Beware the People weeping
When they bare the iron hand.

Andrew Johnson, the people's iron hand, took the presidential oath of office in a city under martial law. Roads, rail stations, the ports along the Potomac and Anacostia rivers had been sealed by order of Edwin Stanton. The secretary of war had effectively declared himself in control from the moment he realized Lincoln would not survive the morning. Stanton held the levers of power—the Union war machine, the telegraph lines into the capital. He was also thick with the Radical Republicans, whose cry for retributive justice had been newly elevated to something like a national, if not divine imperative by the president's assassination. What's more, Stanton seemed to have no doubt as to who stood behind Booth and his accomplices: the leading figures of the Confederate government, its top military leaders, and their co-conspirators named and unnamed.

A visitor to the capital, the Marquis de Chambrun, remarked later that in those first days the city's churches, newspapers, and public meetings all rang with the same message: revenge. So they did, and the taverns and the street corners, too; but the Marquis saw only one facet of a complicated whole. The District of Columbia in that opening scene of the Johnson administration had many backdrops: crime scene, secessionist hotbed, numbed capital, and home to a teeming population of black freedmen. What one observed depended on where one looked. In front of the White House, in those first hours of Johnson's presidency, "were several hundred colored people, mostly women and children, weeping and wailing their loss," Gideon Welles noted in his diary. "This crowd did not appear to diminish through the whole of that cold, wet day. They seemed not to know what was to be their fate since their great benefactor was dead, and their hopeless grief affected me more than almost anything else."

As many as 40,000 blacks had poured into the District over the four years of the war, primarily from Maryland and Virginia, equal to two-thirds of the city's population at the start of hostilities. At first, government and private philanthropy, including charity from established black families, managed to provide at least the rudiments of food, shelter, and sanitation for the "contrabands," as they were known. By the last winter of the war, numbers had utterly overwhelmed available resources. "Their sufferings are most heart rending," wrote one visitor to the slums that sprawled along the swampy margins of the Potomac. "The weather is cold; they have little or no wood. Snow covers the ground, and they have a scanty supply of rags called clothes. The hospital is very crowded with the sick. . . . Government gives them a very, *Very* small allowance of soup. Ninety gallons was given yesterday; but what is that to feed thousands of families. . . . The feeling against them, among many in this place, is bitter, malignant, devilish." The freedmen had come to Washington to seek the protection of the government and proximity to the president who had emancipated them. Now Lincoln was gone, replaced by an ex-slaveholder. Would the governmental protection crumble too? Little wonder so many wept in the rain in front of the White House as Abraham Lincoln's body lay inside.

The freedmen and their pitiable condition—and what they and their condition portended about the fate of blacks in America generally—were part of the capital Andrew Johnson inherited. So were the "seceshes," the Southern sympathizers, the one-time allies of the slaveholders, the soldiers and officers who had served in the Confederate army, taken the oath of loyalty, and either returned home again or come to Washington for the first time to be near the action. If Lincoln's murder was a disaster to them, it was most likely because they foresaw the iron hand that would follow. In her Pulitzer Prize–winning history of the capital, Constance McLaughlin Green speculates that if the Radicals in Congress had had their way, the District of Columbia would have been treated as conquered enemy territory—a Mississippi or South Carolina that just happened to be the seat of the Union government.

To forestall that possibility, the city fathers met on the very day Lincoln died and approved a $20,000 reward (about $236,000 in current dollars, and this from a budget already stretched thin by the war) for information leading to the arrest of the assassins. District residents took it on themselves to root out neighbors insufficiently grief stricken by the president's murder. On April 17, the Union League of Georgetown adopted a series of resolutions that read like a cross between the the McCarthy hearings of the 1950s and a user's manual for a Chinese reeducation camp from the days of the Cultural Revolution. Among the measures, published the next day in local newspapers:

+ *Resolved.* That while our hatred of traitors who risk their lives in battle for their crimes, is mingled with somewhat of admiration for their courage and endurance, worthy of a *better* cause, we have nothing but detestation and contempt for such as justify and wish well to the enemies of the country where they dwell; who add cowardice to the treason that festers in their hearts; and we earnestly ask them to "repent and do works meet for repentance," or to go where they belong.

⟡ *Resolved.* That impartial justice is in the body politic, what surgery is to the human body, a necessary, though painful remedy for evils that can not be otherwise cured. *Foul, gangrenous members MUST be removed, promptly and thoroughly,* that society may discharge its functions of *order,* and not die and be utterly dissolved.

⟡ *Resolved.* That all who are not *hearty* haters of Traitors and their nefarious designs, and who, by their associations, and words, and influence, do not take sides openly and thoroughly against the crimes of such, are themselves at heart only sneaking traitors, and should be treated as such by all decent people.

⟡ *Resolved.* That such is our confidence in the statesmanship, patriotism and fidelity of Andrew Johnson, now President of these United States, that we pledge to him our earnest support with the same cordiality with which it was given to his illustrious predecessor.

Between the freedmen and the Southern sympathizers, the vigilantes and those who were at heart only "sneaking traitors," were endless gradations. The capital had never been of one mind about Lincoln, about the war, about the Confederacy, about the wrong or right of slavery, about the wrong or right of secession, about whether the United States was singular "is" or plural "are," or about Andrew Johnson for that matter. In that, Washington was only the reflection of the North from which it drew its power. Throughout the Civil War, a second, parallel battle was being waged—between the accommodationist Copperheads and the war hawks, the Southern sympathizers and the abolitionists.

The fall of Richmond and Lee's surrender had rendered the second front, like the first one, moot. Support or oppose the war, it was almost over. Lincoln's assassination and Johnson's ascension redrew the battle lines even as they reopened old wounds.

The Mississippi River town of Dubuque, Iowa, suggests how the repercussions of the murder reached far into the heartland. On April 12, Dubuque's Copperhead newspaper, the *Herald*, rejoiced along with the townspeople at the news of Lee's surrender, then called on the president to give the South all the rights it had before the war. "Our faith, however, in Mr. Lincoln doing this we must acknowledge is small.... He will prove himself, we fear, instead of a wise and judicious statesman, nothing but a groveling Abolitionist, sacrificing the interests of a great and mighty nation and of millions of white men to an abstract question about a few niggers."

Three days later, with Lincoln dead, a Dubuque grocer named Morrill, doing business at Main and Eighth streets, proposed to lead a posse of right-minded citizens to tear down the offices of the *Herald*. Although he didn't, or he didn't succeed, others joined the fight. The Catholic bishop of Dubuque, who had condemned the assassination that Easter Sunday, had his barn burned to the ground three days later: Two Morgan horses were lost, as were a cow, a Newfoundland dog, carriages and sleighs, harnesses and hay—all gone. In a written notice, he blamed the "foul hand of some Southern secesh." On the twenty-second, the *Herald*, unmoved, editorialized against "fanatical priests [who] have been the curse of this country for the last fifteen years. Casting aside the work of their Master, they have entered fully into the service of the devil and have preached the country into a revolution and now they want to preach it into anarchy."

The *Herald* wasn't alone in anticipating the worst. Lincoln had just been carried from his deathbed to the White House when George Julian, the Indiana congressman and archradical Republican, wrote to his wife: "I fear we are on the verge of a new and more terrible war than ever." Who could ignore the possibility? The president was dead. The secretary of state had barely escaped the same fate. The vice president might have joined their ranks—dead or nearly so—if the plot had been more successful. The Rebel sympathies of the assassins and would-be assassins were well known; more direct connections to the Confederate leadership were widely suspected. America was on edge, exhausted from four years of battle, and at the moment of peace and release, the worst had happened. The parallel isn't exact, but imagine that all the terrible American assassinations of the 1960s—the Kennedy brothers, Martin Luther King Jr.—had taken place on the same night, and that the assassins were known to be Klansmen or war radicals or somehow associated with the Viet Cong and the North Vietnamese, or Mao's China, or the Soviet Union, and you'll have at least some inkling of the pitch and tenor of the times, and perhaps a better appreciation of the extreme reactions that followed.

In Brookfield, Massachusetts, a blacksmith who had exulted at Lincoln's death was given the choice of being tarred and feathered or immediately departing town, never to return again. He chose the latter. Elsewhere in the state, George Stone of Swampscott was tarred and feathered for the same reason—this time no choice was offered. The superintendent of the Middlesex Horse Railroad in Lowell narrowly escaped hanging for his own ill-timed outburst of joy. He was given fifteen minutes to leave town forever. In New York City, a youth living with his family on East Fourteenth Street announced at the dinner table, "I am going to follow Abraham Lincoln, and I will die under this roof before to-morrow night," then rose from the table, went upstairs, and slit his own throat. Thus, the *New York Herald* opined, "The influence which the present national calamity exercises over persons of a morbid temperament has been fearfully exemplified."

Public discourse was off the rails. Vigilante committees seemed to materialize from thin air. Hardly a minister stepped in the pulpit without his hair being on fire. Newspapers led the way, though. Every town of any size had two of them, one for the war and one against it, one a

Lincoln paper and one a Copperhead paper, one lamenting the assassination with tearful eyes and one lamenting it mostly because the moment called for an expression of grief.

Perhaps no city in the North reflects more starkly the divided attitude toward the war than Lancaster, Pennsylvania. Settled in the early 1700s largely by German immigrants and said to be the oldest inland city in the United States, Lancaster began the 1860s with a population of 17,603, the fifty-second largest city in the nation (ranked between Lawrence, Massachusetts, and Trenton, New Jersey). By April 1865, James Buchanan—Lincoln's predecessor, the fifteenth president of the United States—had retired to his estate, Wheatland, just to the west of Lancaster City. Another resident, Thaddeus Stevens, represented the region in Congress.

On the surface, Buchanan and Stevens would appear to have much in common. Both had practiced law in Lancaster. Both had come to the city from outside. Buchanan hailed from Mercersburg, more toward the south-central part of the state, near the Maryland border; Stevens was originally from Danville, Vermont. Both were bachelors, humorless, and fundamentally conservative. Both were also prosperous, although Stevens's ironworks at Chambersburg, Pennsylvania, north of Mercersburg, had been destroyed by Lee's forces during the Gettysburg campaign.

In fact, the two men couldn't have been much different. Like the Democratic Party that had nominated him for the presidency in 1856, Buchanan had Southern sympathies; he spent his term in office mostly mollycoddling the secessionists, hoping time would soften the issues and wear down the abolitionists' zeal. Stevens, a two-time Whig congressman in the late 1840s and early 1850s, had returned to the House in 1859 under the Republican banner. He spent much of that first year bitterly excoriating Buchanan from the House floor. Politically, Buchanan and Stevens were the war's alpha and omega: the failed politics of appeasement that had preceded the war and perhaps brought it on, and the as-yet-untested politics of retribution that the Radicals hoped to win Johnson over to, or force on him.

Buchanan—still Pennsylvania's only president—was interred upon his death in June 1868 at the Woodward Hill Cemetery, then Lancaster's finest burial ground, reserved exclusively for white residents. Two months later, Stevens was buried in a small in-town cemetery used by blacks so that, as his tombstone puts it, "I might be enabled to illustrate in my death the principles which I have advocated throughout a long life." It was commonly assumed among the local citizenry that Stevens's black housekeeper, Lydia Smith, was also his mistress.

By war's end, Lancaster's fewer than 20,000 residents were supporting two daily newspapers and one weekly. The Democratic daily, the *Intelligencer*, had once referred to Stevens as a "pestiferous political demagogue." The *Intelligencer* also took special note of his domestic arrangements: "Nobody doubts that Thaddeus Stevens has always been in favor of negro equality, and here, where his domestic arrangements are so well known, his practical recognition of his pet theory is perfectly well understood. . . . A personage, not of his race, a female of dusky hue, daily walks the streets of Lancaster when Mr. Stevens is at home. She has presided over his house for years. Even by his own party friends, she is constantly spoken of as Mrs. Stevens." To the Republican *Daily Express*, Buchanan's "last evil days of unfulfilled responsibility" in the presidency—the closing months of 1860 to March 1861, when his government sat idly by while the rebellion seized Union forts and armaments—had set the stage for all the brutal losses to follow. "Can there be a doubt that the cost of our Civil War, in blood and treasure, would have been at least half saved if our Government had been administered during the last six months of Mr. Buchanan's Administration, in the spirit and on the principles of Mr. Lincoln's?" It's a horrible accusation—hundreds of thousands of dead laid at Buchanan's feet.

The extremity was typical of the newspapers of the time, all across the nation. Modifiers got ransacked for worst possible connotations; scurrilous charges flew in every direction. Race-baiting, *ad hominem* attacks, the worst sorts of class snobbery were paraded out in print day after day. The process had been going on for the entire war, even before the war. General Joseph Lane of Oregon and others were its heralds in the U.S. Senate. The closing months of the conflict seemed to pile the stakes up even higher.

Throughout January and February 1865, the Lancaster *Intelligencer* complained bitterly about Lincoln's unwillingness to settle with Confederate leaders, describing his motives as "sinister and unworthy." Of Lincoln's second inaugural address—now carved in stone on the interior wall of the Lincoln Memorial—the *Intelligencer* found not a single good thing to say. Nothing "can give it dignity, or allay the deep disgust which has been everywhere excited by its perusal. It is blood-thirsty enough to have been the utterance of some painted Indian Chief, just starting out on a scalping expedition." Lincoln's new vice president elicited an even lower opinion. Neither Lincoln nor Johnson had ever managed to rise "superior to the vulgar associations which surrounded them in early life.... Just as the rapid boiling of a pot throws scum to the surface, so it seems political convulsions are sure to bring into positions of power, men whose proper positions would be the filthy purlieus of society." The election of the previous November had left the nation with "a buffoon for President, and a drunken boor for Vice President of the United States." The day before Lincoln was shot, the *Intelligencer* decried the president's "utter want of statesmanlike sagacity," the fact that "he has so long continued to be the mere blind puppet in the hands of impracticable fanatics."

On April 15, the day of Lincoln's death, the *Daily Express* fired back at its crosstown rival and at the dozens upon dozens of other overheated, Democratic-leaning journals that had declared open season on the executive branch. "This foul deed of double, perhaps triple murder, is the legitimate effect of the political morality of the times. The Copperhead press for the past two years have been boldly and shamefully setting at defiance the heavenly injunction of respecting our rulers.... In a word, a stranger from another planet hearing these stories talk and reading their organs, would very naturally suppose that the President of the United States was not fit to live, and that consequently to murder him would not be so heinous a crime!" John Wilkes Booth was still at large April 27 when the *Daily Express* printed two full columns of excerpts from its rival and then put a finer point on its argument. "The very best defense [Booth] could make against the awful crime of murdering the President of the United States, would be to produce a complete file of the *Lancaster Daily Intelligencer* and read to the court and jury the above articles—and many more like them which it contains."

Newspapers are untrustworthy guides to history. They get caught up in the heat of the moment, especially a moment as calamitous as an assassination. Circulation wars skew coverage. Advertisers are always watching and listening from the other side of the glass. The news gets written and edited by men and women working under deadline pressures. A fog still lies heavily over events when reporters start asking their questions. In our own time, virtually all serious newspapers work hard to keep a firewall between the editorial pages and the newsholes. Not so a hundred and forty years ago. Even eminent dailies like the *New York Times* bled their opinions all over the front page—regional papers even more so. Newspapers, however, do show what was exciting the popular imagination and how the fight to influence public opinion was being played out.

While the *Daily Express* was accusing the *Intelligencer* of everything short of pulling the trigger of Booth's derringer, the *Intelligencer* was busily spinning events to serve its own ends. On April 26, the paper reprinted in full, on the front page, the *Times* of London's description of Andy Johnson's inebriated performance at his inauguration, all the way down to the crack about the nation sinking to the level of Rome under Caligula. (The next day, the twenty-seventh, when news of the assassination finally reached London, the *Times* suggested that the best course of action Johnson could take was to resign "an office which no one ever seriously intended him to fill.") In May, beneath a front-page banner, NEGRO OUTRAGE, the *Intelligencer* told of a black soldier stationed in Shelbyville, Kentucky, who had murdered a deputy collector of internal revenue: "From every part of the South we hear of these negro outrages, and we have yet to see the first word of condemnation of them on the part of the Abolition press of the country. Step by step we are drifting to ultimate anarchy and ruin, as the Republicans seem determined to build up a negro aristocracy on the ruined wealth and misfortune of the South."

The *Daily Express* countered by rewriting history wholesale. On the third of May, 1865, the paper was pleased to inform its readers that Andy Johnson on the previous March fourth had been "under the influence, not of spiritous liquors, not either of a mere disturbing drug, intended only to disfigure him, but of a deadly poison, furtively insinuated into his drink with a view to take his life." Only Johnson's "powerful nature" kept him from succumbing to the "infernal draught." On May 6, the *Daily Express* even unveiled its own poet, James S. Thorn, ready to lionize the president and his newly restored reputation: "Another man, sprung from the people. / With ear bowed down, the nation's heart / He hears in each impulsive beating... / With Clay and Webster's dazzling skill / To win a listening Senate's wonder, / Another Washington, perchance, / Our nation's new adopted father."

Meanwhile, the dyspeptic, mule-headed, lifelong Democrat and former slaveholder whom Lincoln's death had thrust into the role of the "nation's new adopted father" was surprising just about everyone with his grace and dignity. Johnson made no inaugural address after his swearing in on April 15: The previous effort had been oratory enough, and the moment wasn't right. But he did address those in his rooms at Kirkwood House, saying that he sought their help and encouragement. "I shall ask and rely upon you and others in carrying the government through its present perils." As for what direction his administration might take, what policies it might pursue, "The message or declaration must be made by the acts as they transpire. The only assurance that I can now give of the future is by reference to the past." Indeed, he went on: "The course which I have taken in the past in connection with this rebellion must be regarded as a guarantee of the future.... The duties have been mine—the consequences are God's."

At noon that first day, Johnson met with the cabinet, minus the grievously injured Seward, at the office of secretary of the treasury, located next door to the White House. The new president was conciliatory to those who might doubt him. He wished to carry out Lincoln's policies, he assured one and all. To that end, he asked the cabinet members to stay on in their posts. Navy Secretary Gideon Welles noted in his diary that Johnson deported himself "admirably." The next day, Easter Sunday, with the pulpits aflame throughout the North, Johnson met with a delegation of Radical Republicans from the House and Senate. (This was the meeting when Wade famously crowed, "By the gods, there will no trouble now in running the government.")

The final meeting of the Thirty-eighth Congress had convened December 5, 1864, and remained in session until March 3, 1865, the day before the inauguration. Although the president extended the Senate by a week, the new Congress would not convene until December 4. The lengthy recess was typical of second sessions in those days—first ones tended to last about eight months—and Lincoln, for one, had been glad to see the lawmakers go. In the first of two lengthy papers Gideon Welles was to write on Lincoln and Johnson, the Navy secretary recalled Lincoln's comments on the matter at his last cabinet meeting, only hours before he was shot:

> We could do better; accomplish more without than with them. There were men in Congress who, if their motives were good, were nevertheless impracticable, and who possessed feelings of hate and vindictiveness in which he did not sympathize and could not participate. [The president] hoped there would be no persecution, no bloody work, after the war was over. None need expect he would take any part in hanging or killing those men, even the worst of them. Frighten them out of the country, open

the gates, let down the bars, scare them off, said he, throwing up
his hands is if scaring sheep. Enough lives have been sacrificed.

With Johnson in office, the Radicals had a second chance to do
more than scare the sheep away, and they had no intention of letting the
moment pass, or even of waiting until the dead president was in the
ground. To the Radicals' demand that Johnson appoint a new cabinet,
most notably with General Ben Butler filling in for Seward, the president seemed to turn a deaf ear. He'd already given assurances on that
front to the present officeholders. Yet he didn't send his visitors away
empty-handed. As he had with his small swearing-in party, Johnson assured his audience that his past was prologue. "Everybody knows...I
hold this: Robbery is a crime; rape is a crime; treason is a crime; and
crime must be punished. The law provides for it; the courts are open.
Treason must be made infamous and traitors punished." There wasn't a
man in the room—and they were all men, naturally—who didn't know
what Johnson had said eleven days before Lincoln's murder, on the steps
of the Patent Office, at a gathering celebrating the fall of Richmond:
"Since the world began, there never has been a rebellion of such gigantic proportions, so infamous in character, so diabolical in motive, so entirely disregardful of the laws of civilized war. It has introduced the most
savage mode of warfare ever practiced upon the earth."

The next day the Radicals were back, pressing for details on how
Johnson intended to deal with Jefferson Davis, Alexander Stephens,
Lee, and others. Instead of answering, Johnson asked Ben Wade what
he would do if he were president. Exile or hang perhaps a dozen of the
worst offenders, Wade answered, maybe "thirteen, just a baker's dozen."
According to one of the Radicals present at the meeting, George Julian,
Johnson remarked that it would be difficult to pick out such a small
number. Committee members told reporters waiting outside the Trea-
sury Department that they were "highly gratified with the tenor of the
President's conversation."

———

Andrew Johnson was president, commander in chief of the Army and Navy of the United States, possessor of the power—the Senate willing—to make treaties and appoint judges. On his shoulders fell the burden of determining the nature of the peace to come—a fateful decision for the nation then and still. Yet Johnson had no office space he could call his own, no official residence. Even had Eliza been up to the trip from Tennessee, Johnson would have had to house the new First Lady under a borrowed roof. Mary Todd Lincoln would stay in the White House until nearly the end of May 1865. Part of her delay undoubtedly was grief, part a deeper emotional distress, and part the practical difficulties of finding a place to settle—Springfield, Illinois, as it turned out, near her husband's grave—and transporting a household there. But part, too, could be attributed to a stubbornness born of suspicion. How was she to turn the presidential palace over to the man whom she believed was behind the assassination, the coup d'état?

For Johnson, there was no choice. He couldn't move in while Mrs. Lincoln still lived there. Nor could he work at the White House. There was no West Wing then, no Oval Office. They were added in 1909 and first occupied by William Howard Taft. Johnson would have been directing the nation's affairs while sharing space with a woman who despised and feared him. Not until June ninth, nearly two months after he had assumed the presidency, did Johnson move into the White House. Eliza and their daughter Martha Patterson and her children didn't join him for another ten days. In the interim, Johnson and his friend and adviser Preston King settled into a house located at Fifteenth and H streets that belonged to a wealthy Boston merchant and congressman, Samuel Hooper. Although Hooper was temporarily out of town, the house wasn't free—Johnson had to pay for food and the servants—and the arrangement didn't get any cheaper when the owner returned to Washington and began living as Johnson's guest.

For an office, Johnson might have used the secretary of state's chambers; Seward wasn't coming back to work anytime soon. According to Gideon Welles, though, Edwin Stanton wouldn't hear of it. Instead,

Johnson accepted the offer of Treasury Secretary Hugh McCulloch to use his newly redecorated reception room. Johnson would stay on there until May 24, laboring away in the anteroom of one of the men who reported to him. Still concerned about the new president's sobriety, the treasury secretary kept a close eye on him. Johnson labored nonstop, McCulloch reported. "He was there every morning before nine o'clock, and he rarely left before five. There was no liquor in his room. His luncheon, when he had one, was, like mine, a cup of tea and a cracker." Four months later, on August 15, the *New York Times* would worry that the president was working himself to death.

By the eighteenth of April, with Booth still at large, with the dimensions of the assassination plot still being explored, Johnson already seems to have dismissed whatever extra security had been assigned him. The *Washington Evening Star* of that day quoted one observer: "The old practice by our President of indifference to, or fearlessness of, personal harm seems to characterize Mr. Johnson; for with the merest apology of a guard, he drove out yesterday with Hon. Preston King. . . . We trust that the President will not indulge this fearlessness too far," the paper went on to editorialize, "and that in deference to the wishes of the nation—to whom he now belongs—he will allow such precautionary measures to be taken in his behalf as will discourage any would-be assassin." Andy Johnson was playing the part he knew best. If they (Booth, Atzerodt, whoever "they" might be) had it in mind to test him, he was ready to face them. Johnson was closing in on sixty by then but still ready for a fight.

What Johnson seems to have done most in those first days as president was meet with delegations, more than thirty of them in his first two weeks in office alone: citizens groups; local ministers; a Maine delegation headed by Hannibal Hamlin, who must have found the occasion strange; foreign diplomats; Perseverance Hose Company No. 5 of Philadelphia; six hundred female employees of the Treasury Department. An Illinois group headed by the governor came to see him on the eighteenth. On the twentieth, around eleven A.M., officers of the Navy and Marine Corps stopped by Johnson's temporary Treasury office to pay their respects. They were followed by delegations from Massachusetts and New Jersey, both led by their respective governors, and another composed of members of the New York Union League. Johnson thanked the New Yorkers and informed them that while he could not yet lay out a policy to govern the future of the South, the American people had clearly come to the conclusion that treason was the highest of crimes and therefore to be punished accordingly.

The next day, however, speaking to an Indiana delegation, Johnson seemed less certain about the public's full appreciation of the horrors of treason. "The time has arrived, my countrymen, when the American people should be educated and taught what is crime, and that treason is a crime, and the highest crime known to the law and the Constitution.... It is not promulgating anything that I have not heretofore said to say that traitors must be made odious, that treason must be made odious, that traitors must be punished and impoverished. They must not only be punished, but their social power must be destroyed."

On the morning of April 24, again at Treasury, Johnson met with a large gathering of what the *Washington Evening Star* described as "loyal refugees from the Southern States, principally from Virginia and North Carolina." They, too, called for retribution, according to the *Star*'s account. "It was folly to give sugar plums to tigers and hyenas; it was more than folly to show kindness to those who sought the death of the nation. By the blood of our martyred President, by the starved and mutilated of the rebel prisons, by the slain in this horrid war, they prayed that the administration might be a terror to evil doers." These were Johnson's own people—Southerners outcast from their homes. They shared his history and his blood.

The next day another Southerner, Mr. A. Barratti of Richmond, stopped by Treasury to present Johnson with a gift: a silver-plated tea service that had been used by Jefferson Davis. Barratti said he had purchased it at auction just before Davis and others fled the Confederate capital. The set was a perfect miniature of a locomotive and coal tender: a steam whistle to signal when the tea was ready, an elegant sugar caisson in the tender, racks for cigars, a music box hidden within the tender that played eight popular airs of the day. On the side of the locomotive was emblazoned "President Jefferson Davis." On its front, where the cowcatcher should be, were the Confederate banner and battle flag entwined with the flag of France—another Southern dream that had long since turned to ashes.

The same day, Johnson met with a delegation of black citizens, the National Equal Rights League, headed by its president, John Mercer Langston of Oberlin, Ohio. "The colored American asks but two things," Langston told the president. "He asks, after proving his devotion to his country by responding to her call in the hour of her sorest trial, and after demonstrating upon many hotly contested battlefields his manhood and valor, that he have first, complete emancipation, and secondly, full equality before American law." Johnson responded as he so frequently did in those early weeks in office, by making reference to his own past because in it, he told Langston, "you will find the guarantee of my future conduct toward your people.... I fear that leading colored men do not understand and appreciate the fact that they have friends on the south side of the line. They have, and they are as faithful and staunch as any north of the line."

Speaking two weeks later to a small audience of black preachers, including the president of the Washington-based National Theological Institute for Colored Ministers, Johnson again struck what seemed a conciliatory note. While he had owned slaves, he had never sold one (although he seems to have traded one). What's more, he had freed his slaves even though the Emancipation Proclamation did not include Tennessee in its purview. He then went on to lecture on the tendency of Negroes, like Mormons, to indulge in "open and notorious concubinage" and to warn that freedom does not mean being "taken care of in idleness and debauchery.... The correction of these things is necessary in commencing a reform in social condition, and in this there must be the force of example." He would do everything in his power, Johnson promised, to secure the protection of the freed slaves and to better their condition, and he trusted in God that the time might come when "all the colored people would be gathered together in one country best adapted to their condition, if it should appear they could not get along together with the whites."

What was he really saying? What did he really mean? What did his past record suggest about the treatment of the ex-slaves and about his plans for the South? Sifting the new president's words for clues became a leading sport of the day. "What is the great truth that confronts [Johnson] at the opening of his new career?" *Harper's Weekly* asked in its April 29, 1865, edition. "It is that the policy of his predecessor had been so approved by the mind and heart of the country, had so disarmed hostility and melted prejudice, that the spirit of that policy has almost the sanctity of prescription. That President Johnson will so regard it we have the fullest confidence."

Yet *Harper's* wasn't expressing its confidence in a very confident tone. Rather, the magazine seemed to be wishing hope would triumph over experience. Save for his single term as governor of Tennessee and his war duty in Nashville, Andy Johnson had been around Washington for twenty-two years. He had been a public man for virtually his entire adult life. Yet he seems to have been a mystery to just about everyone.

What time Johnson didn't devote to delegations must have been severely strained by correspondence. It poured in during the days after Lincoln's death—from citizen's groups, from armchair advisers, from every quarter. In a letter dated April 15, 1865, A. H. Adams from Nashville, Tennessee, presumed on his "fast acquaintance and friendship" with the new president to seek "the bestowal of patronage"—and this on the day of Lincoln's death. The first thought in his head must have been: What's in it for me? William F. Channing sent a telegram from Providence, Rhode Island, the same day, urging Johnson to complete Lincoln's work by declaring movingly that "the destruction of slavery everywhere under the United States flag had become a military necessity. Make us truly a free people by your first word as President and we will love and honor you as never a ruler was loved before." William Hemstreet (or Nemstreet—the scrawl of the telegraph operator is hard to read), a captain with the Eighteenth Missouri Volunteer Infantry, then on leave in New York City, wired on the fifteenth with a fervent wish undoubtedly inspired more by the absent president than the new and living one: "I pray to be assigned the most desperate duty in the extermination of traitors here or elsewhere." George W. Ashburn wrote from three rooms away—Ashburn occupied suite sixty-five at Kirkwood House—to tell the new president, "The hand of God is in the assassination. The country needs a more vigorous administration," and to warm him that "the Rebels will next Murder their own assassin to avoid detection." A Georgia loyalist, Ashburn had spent much of the war in Tennessee, supporting the Union cause. From Baltimore, an unidentified woman added her own warning within hours after Lincoln's death. "Oh! In Heaven's name & for the sake of our loved country heed the prayer of a loyal woman of Virginia, & take not a single step *without or even within* your own portals unattended by a strong guard. One President has fallen the victim to the demon of Revenge—Your firmness is so well known that you will be slain to avert the dreaded but just doom of traitors."

Over and around and winding through all these events were the services honoring the fallen Lincoln. On April 17, his casket was placed in the East Room of the White House on a platform fifteen feet high, supported by four pillars, under two massive chandeliers with black crepe decking the catafalque, walls, and windows. April 19, a national day of mourning, opened with rifles fired on the hour. At eleven A.M., a procession of sixty clergymen from across the nation began filing into the East Room. Governors, senators and congressmen, ranking bureaucrats, military officers, the diplomatic corps, members of the Union League and Christian Commission, leading merchants all followed behind. Six hundred tickets had been issued. The room was packed.

At noon, President Johnson entered the room, along with all his cabinet save Seward and a few of the cabinet members' wives. (The *Evening Star* reported that the estimated 600 mourners in the room included only seven women.) The president took his place opposite the main entrance to the East Room, with Preston King on his left and Hannibal Hamlin on his right. Stanton, who had been planning the service since the day after Lincoln died, was directly behind Johnson. Unable to mask his grief, Ulysses Grant stood near the head of the catafalque. Lincoln family members and intimates sat in a semicircle at its foot: the two surviving sons, Captain Robert Todd Lincoln, twenty-one years old, and Tad, nine years his junior; the president's two secretaries, John Nicolay and John Hay; cousins; and brothers-in-law to Mrs. Lincoln. A delegation of immediate relatives from Springfield had been expected, but train delays kept them from the service. Mrs. Lincoln wasn't there, either: She remained upstairs, suffering from nervous prostration and a fever.

"It was a cruel hand—the dark hand of the assassin—that smote our honored, wise, and noble President and filled the land with sorrow," Reverend Phineas D. Gurley told the crowd in his funeral eulogy. Yet the sorrow was only temporary. "Though weeping may endure for a night, joy comes in the morning. Thank God that in spite of this temporary darkness, the morning has begun to dawn, the morning of a brighter day than our country has ever before seen. That day will come, and the death of a hundred Presidents and Cabinets cannot prevent it." The message of hope, of a bright dawn ahead was lost on little Tad. The twelve-year-old sobbed throughout the service, clinging to his older brother's arm.

Afterward, the casket was carried to the Capitol in a hearse pulled by six gray horses. Lincoln's own horse followed riderless, led by its two grooms. Five thousand marchers took part in the procession down Pennsylvania Avenue, including the Twenty-second U.S. Colored

Troops, which Stanton had ordered up from Petersburg to take part, a gesture both appropriate and political. Thousands more spectators lined the route, an ocean of humanity, yet save for the footfalls of the marchers and the beat of muffled drums, the procession was virtually silent. Not until the hearse and the carriages with the pallbearers reached the Capitol steps did military bands strike up a dirge. Inside the Rotunda, Johnson and Grant, Nicolay and Hays, the physicians who had attended the late president in his last hours, and others—a smaller group this time—assembled once more for a brief service. And with that the official events concluded.

Lincoln remained in state at the Capitol for two days, while tens of thousands of Americans filed by in a final tribute—"one continuous stream of human beings going up the steps of the eastern portico," the *Evening Star* reported. Hundreds of thousands more mourners greeted the funeral train as it traveled its circuitous, 1,700-mile route toward Springfield, Illinois. The martyrdom was over; sainthood had begun. But Andrew Johnson was president now, not Lincoln, and fate had placed him at a remarkable crossroads.

A pair of illustrations by the New York City lithographers Kimmel & Forster provide an allegorical history of the Civil War. The first— "The Outbreak of the Rebellion in the United States 1861," printed in 1865—has Liberty standing at the center on a cracked pedestal, dressed in a flowing white robe and supporting an American flag with an eagle perched on the top of the staff. To her right, Justice holds a scale in one hand and points her sword at a hissing poisonous snake wrapped around a palmetto tree. Jefferson Davis stands at the base of the palmetto. In front of him, Rebel soldiers tear at an American flag. Still closer in the foreground, James Buchanan lies asleep, his head resting near Liberty's feet. Just to Liberty's right, Abraham Lincoln appears to be giving an address. His left hand raised, palm upward, Lincoln faces out toward Union soldiers and citizens. Gloom envelops the Confederate left of the illustration; on the Union right, sun rises on a bountiful pastoral scene. Battles can be dimly seen across the background. In the vivid foreground, a kneeling woman and two young girls grieve the death of an unknown soldier.

Kimmel & Forster returned to the subject a year later, in a companion illustration titled "The End of the Rebellion in the United States." Liberty still holds the American flag. This time, she's joined at center stage by Columbia, crowned with stars. Beneath their feet is a pedestal—whole, not cracked—decorated with the carved images of George Washington and Abraham Lincoln. In front of the pedestal, Justice, sword raised, leads a charge of Union infantrymen. The Confederates have the right side of the image this time: Jefferson Davis with a sack of money thrown over his shoulder; a weary Robert E. Lee holding up his sword in surrender; a sinister-looking John Wilkes Booth kneeling with pistol and knife. Behind them are ranks of dispirited troops. A palmetto leans in the background, about to topple, with a dead snake draping loosely from its trunk. A freed slave, not a grieving widow, has the foreground in this one, along with a black soldier holding a bayoneted rifle. Orderly ranks of Union infantrymen fill the background, led by generals Grant, Sherman, and Ben Butler. In front of the mounted Grant, behind the charging Lady Liberty, stands a stern-faced Andrew Johnson, slightly larger than life, more detailed than any other nonallegorical figure, by far the dominant human in the tableau. In both illustrations, among all the central figures shown in them, Andrew Johnson is the only one who stares directly out at the viewer: the people's president through and through. That's the way history looked on the ground in late April and May of 1865. Johnson's eye was on the people, and the people's eyes were all on him.

CHAPTER 5

"Bloody-Minded Tailor"

T HE DEFEATED CONFEDERACY was watching Andy Johnson with much the same uncertainty although surely with far more dread. Having lost a war it stood little chance of winning, having squandered its wealth and seen its fields ruined, its foodstocks devoured, and its already scant manufacturing capacity destroyed by four years of fighting waged almost entirely on its own soil, the South could only contemplate what wasn't to be, breed rumors, and wonder about what actually waited down the road. Apart from hunger and general deprivation, the one hard lump of reality most Southerners had to deal with in early May of 1865 was the Tennessee iconoclast and Old Testament thunderer whom murder had promoted to the presidency.

From a purely military perspective, the Southern rebellion had been near mass delusion from the moment the first shot was fired at Fort Sumter. "The Northern people not only greatly outnumber the whites of the South, but they are a mechanical people with manufactures of every kind, while you are only agriculturists—a sparse population covering a large extent of territory—and in all history no nation of mere agriculturists ever made successful war against a nation of mechanics." So William Tecumseh Sherman told a Louisiana friend in late December 1860, four days after South Carolina seceded from the Union. "You are bound to fail. Only in spirit and determination are you prepared for war. In all else you are totally unprepared, with a bad case to start with.... If your people would but stop and think, they must see that in the end you will surely fail."

Hinton Rowan Helper had devoted an entire book to showing how the North's economic vitality and diversity proved its moral superiority over the decadent slave system of the South. Andy Johnson had made a political career out of extolling the virtues of the "mechanical people"— the manual laborers and artisans—and decrying the vices of the decadent planters and would-be royalists. Consummate warrior that he was, Sherman applied the same evidence to the military theater. In truth, had he scripted the war himself from Manassas to Appomattox, Sherman couldn't have been more on the money. In the short term, the war was arguably a toss-up. In the long term, it was no contest.

The North had factories—86 percent of all the industrial establishments that existed at the start of the war were located in nonslave states. Although the South had wealth, by some measures vast wealth, its economy had been built on an inedible crop tended by a subjugated workforce. By mid-1863, the Union army was backed by thirty-eight arms manufacturers turning out 5,000 infantry rifles every day. The Confederacy had a theoretical capacity of about 300 rifles a day; a more realistic figure, though, was closer to 100. Most of the workmen skilled in armaments manufacture were off fighting the war, with a dwindling supply of weapons. In fact, there was little choice. The Union states had four times the white population of the secessionist states but only three times the fighting forces. In the North, enough able-bodied men remained behind to work the farms and forges. Not so the South, where shirking military duty dishonored even older boys and middle-aged men. The North had a seventeen-to-one advantage in the production of textile goods, a twenty-to-one edge in iron production, a thirty-eight-to-one advantage in coal production. From uniforms to musket barrels, the match-up was lopsided in the extreme. The Union made trains— steam engines, locomotives, and the rails they rode on—and it laid tracks, too. More than 70 percent of the 30,626 miles of railroad that existed in 1860 were in Northern and border states. The North had a more sophisticated system of trunk and feeder lines, more trained brakemen and more expert track repairers. It also had more expert track destroyers, and more than any other Union general, Sherman took full advantage of their destructive talents. By war's end, the Confederacy was littered with what became known as Sherman bow-ties—track sections so heated, bent, and twisted that they were almost impossible to put back into service again.

The North's advantage went far beyond its manufacturing capacity. South of the Potomac, the value of the Confederacy's currency was drifting from wildly inflated to utterly worthless, the only consolation being that there was nothing left to buy. The South had neither credit nor the means to secure it from European lenders. Sherman and the others had put tens of millions of dollars worth of cotton to the torch, the only collateral the South had left. The Union by contrast was awash in cash. Stoked by the voracious appetite of combat, the economy boomed. Wages in the North rose by 43 percent during the war years—a boon to those who avoided service but not such a blessing to veterans who returned home at war's end to find that the cost of living had more than doubled in their absence. Municipal coffers swelled as the fighting raged. More than two dozen Northern cities built street railways during the war. On the battlefront, mass killing; on the home front, philanthropy and good works: Vassar, Swarthmore, Cornell, and a dozen other colleges and universities all got their start between April 1861 and April 1865.

The North simply had more of almost everything that mattered. Union horses outnumbered Confederate ones by almost four to one—one reason those famous Rebel cavalry charges tended to lose their spunk as the war wore on. (Mules were about the only meaningful war-related statistical category in which the Confederacy had a lead—good for hauling but not much for storming a position.) The Union's teeming wheat crops and cornfields and its plentiful hog farms gave it a huge advantage over the South. Domestically, there was more to eat, especially since the fighting and foraging took place mostly on Southern soil. Just as important, drought-plagued Europe needed bread far more immediately than it needed bales of cotton. At the start of the war, the four major salt-producing states of the Confederacy—Virginia, Kentucky, Florida, and Texas—were turning out a little over 2.35 million bushels of salt annually. New York, Ohio, and Pennsylvania alone produced more than five times that, a gap that widened dramatically as Union Navy units methodically destroyed Southern salt works and the naval blockade kept imported salt from Southern ports. Without salt, meat went uncured. Uncured, it couldn't be transported far or kept long. For an army traveling on its stomach in the 1860s, an absence of salt spelled disaster.

Of all the advantages the Federals enjoyed, the telegraph might have been the greatest. About 90 percent of the roughly 50,000 miles of telegraph wire ran through Union states and the territories they controlled. (The railroad disparity inevitably affected the telegraph one since the primary use of the telegraph before the war was to connect railroad stations and systems.) During the course of the war, the North added another 15,389 miles to its total, including a twenty-mile stretch of submarine line across the Chesapeake Bay. Edwin Stanton's Military Telegraph Department, the nerve center of Union communications during the war, transmitted something on the order of 6.5 million dispatches, nearly 5,000 a day. Never before had an army's widely dispersed field generals been in such close communication with each other and with their headquarters. Meanwhile, the private telegraph companies the Confederacy depended on managed to string about a thousand miles of new line, an average of 250 miles a year, barely enough to reach from Richmond to the South Carolina state line. Even then, there was almost no wire left for repairs when the lines were down or severed, as they frequently were.

That superior Union telegraph system is what carried news of Lincoln's assassination and Johnson's ascension almost instantaneously to every little nook and cranny of the North. It was virtually real-time information, unheard of in the world hitherto. And it was the absence of any working system—and the tight hand exercised by Edwin Stanton over what telegraphic traffic did head south—that kept the dying Confederacy almost completely in the dark about perhaps the most dramatic event in American history, one that would profoundly shape its destiny.

Before the war, Joseph Addison Waddell had been the owner and editor of the *Staunton Spectator*, in the heart of Virginia's Shenandoah Valley. Too old to join the fight, Waddell served as a clerk in the local quartermaster's office, but he never lost his newspaperman's eye for detail or the slightly jaundiced perspective that seems to go with the job. Like all journalists, Waddell had a need to know and the long-standing habit of recording his observations, yet by mid-April of 1865, his diary makes clear, Waddell knew almost nothing of events around him. On the day Lincoln was shot, Waddell confided to his journal his own mixed feelings about the war just ending.

> While I felt an intense indignation against the North, the Confederacy never enlisted my affections or compliance. I never ceased to deplore the disruption, and never could have loved my country and government as I loved the old United States. Yet our cause seemed to be the cause of state rights and involved the question whether or no the people should choose a government for themselves, or have one imposed upon them. With our fall every vestige of State rights has disappeared, and we are at the mercy of a consolidated despotism. What the conqueror will do with us we know not.... Notwithstanding my strong local attachments, I feel that it would be a relief to get to some new and foreign country.

"What a termination!" Waddell laments in the same journal entry. Looting had become commonplace—the people of Staunton and Augusta County were grabbing everything they could from the Confederate storehouses. The next day, the fifteenth, Waddell joined the mob: "This morning, I removed an ambulance [a wagon for transporting the wounded] from a late Government stable but wish now that I had not touched it. I do not like to be mixed up with the scramble for spoils. The whole affair disgusted me."

As elsewhere in the South, gossip and speculation were rampant throughout the Shenandoah Valley. France, England, and Spain were all about to sign on with the South. Lincoln had been assassinated. A Yankee army was working its way up the valley, paroling Rebel soldiers as it went. Something for everyone yet empty calories all around, or so it seemed. "Have felt very dull and listless all day," Waddell wrote on the nineteenth.

> Could not work in the garden, and begin to despair of making a living by bodily labor.—Don't know how we are to subsist— I have not a cent of money, and no prospect of getting any. Cant buy anything to eat or to wear. Confederate notes are of course, entirely worthless, so far as relates to purchases. Some persons have been giving as much as $1 specie for $300 C. S. treasury notes, getting the latter to square off their accounts.

The assassination rumor was back in town again on the evening of April 20: "There is a general regret in our community, as Vice President Johnson is a much worse man than Lincoln." That same day came word that Joseph Johnston's North Carolina army had defeated Sherman and that Nathan Bedford Forrest had seized Knoxville. "All very ridiculous," Waddell wrote, and the more absurd because while rumors of renewed success flew this way and that, order of any sort was collapsing in front of his eyes. "We are now in a condition of anarchy. Bands of soldiers are prowling about taking off all cattle, sheep, horses etc. they suspect of being public property."

On April 22, Waddell finally learned that Lincoln was indeed dead. It had taken a week for definitive word to reach Staunton, 158 miles west of Washington. "Rumor says that some persons at the North attribute the murder to the 'Knights of the Golden Circle'; while others attribute it to the ultra Abolitionists who are disaffected on account of Lincoln's supposed leniency to the South. Vice President Andrew Johnson has sworn in as President of the United States, and has made several speeches in which he announced a vengeance against 'traitors.'"

So it would continue for days and days—snippets of fact caught in a swirl of myth and speculation. "Rumors of momentous events came in rounds to-day," Waddell wrote on the evening of April 25.

> ...A gentleman arrive[d] from Charlottesville with a report that Andrew Johnson, Lincoln's successor, had been killed, and that Washington, Philadelphia and New York were in flames. Finally, it was reported by some one who came up the Valley, that Grant had been killed, that fighting was going on in Washington city, and that all the troops had been removed from Winchester. We know not what to think of all this. It is not more strange than the intelligence of Lincoln's death, which we did not believe, but can it be that society is broken up, and the whole country in a state of chaos! That assassination, heretofore unknown amongst us, has become a common event!... We have no mails, no newspapers, and no regular communication with the world.

The Civil War was a letter-writer's war, a diarist's war, a memoirist's war. Education had undergone a revolution in the new nation in the three decades before fighting broke out. In 1830, only about one in three white children between the ages of five and nineteen attended school. That figure crossed the 50 percent mark in 1850 and kept on climbing. By the start of hostilities, the public-education movement had brought schools to near backwaters throughout the North and Midwest. (State-funded education in the South didn't take root until the end of the century.)

New production techniques cut down on printing costs, and

textbook publishing boomed, along with newspapers and magazines. Once relatively rare, pens, paper, and writing pads were being mass produced by midcentury. Although higher education was still rarified air—only about one in twenty people attended college before the Civil War—intellectual aspiration was everywhere. The so-called lyceum movement swept across the northern tier of America like some high-minded brush fire. Imported from Scotland and France and patterned on the ancient Greeks—Aristotle taught near the temple of Apollo Lyceus—the movement had instituted thousands of lecture series by the 1840s, although, again, rarely in the South, where the planters discouraged learning among poor whites as well as blacks.

The lyceums, in turn, encouraged libraries and gave even greater impetus to the idea of universal schooling. They also helped provide a living for writers and thinkers. Many of Ralph Waldo Emerson's books were compilations of lectures delivered on the lyceum circuit before large and enthusiastic audiences filled with blue-collar workers out to better themselves. The 1860 U.S. Census estimated that nine in ten adult white Americans were literate—an astounding literacy in a nation still being carved out of a wilderness; higher than in Scotland, Germany, England, and France. The best estimates are that about 5 percent of slaves were literate as well by the time of the Civil War, an amazing number given the slave codes that made it a crime to teach Southern blacks even basic education skills. (The Alabama slavery code of 1833, for example, provided a fine of not less than $250 and not more than $500 for any white person who attempted to teach a black, slave or free, to spell, read, or write.) As the bullets whizzed around them, as soldiers tromped through their towns, this new army of writers took up their pens.

By and large, though, all the Southern diarists could do by the spring of 1865 was what Joseph Waddell had been doing: stumble through their pages from day to day in a fog of rumor and despair, hemmed in by ever-dwindling resources, uncertain if the good news was as good as it sounded or the bad news as dire. The war was over, or maybe it wasn't. The time for sacrifice had come and gone, or maybe it was just beginning in earnest. They were citizens of a nation crumbling beneath their feet or one rising from its own ashes. Or maybe they were citizens still of the nation that wouldn't let them go, that had waged war to preserve the status quo. Theirs was a compass with few fixed points.

"The South lies prostrate—their foot is on us—there is no help," a seventeen-year-old Columbia, South Carolina, diarist named Emma Florence LeConte lamented on April 20. "During this short time we breathe, but—O who could have believed who has watched this four years' struggle that it could have ended like this!... Is all this blood spilled in vain—will it not cry from the ground on the day we yield to these Yankees! *We* give up to the *Yankees!* How *can* it be? How can they talk about it?"

The next day, the miserable LeConte finally had something to celebrate: "Hurrah! Old Abe Lincoln has been assassinated!" Upon hearing the news, LeConte writes, "I actually *flew* home and for the first time in oh, so long I was trembling and my heart beating with excitement." Then came the realization of what waited ahead. "Andy Johnson will succeed him—the rail-splitter will be succeeded by the drunken ass. Such are the successors of Washington and Jefferson—such are to rule the South." From Virginia to Georgia, from the Carolinas to the Mississippi and beyond, the very mention of Johnson's name seemed to give everyone the hives.

To the Virginian Belle Boyd and thousands of others, Lincoln's murder was a "heavy calamity.... Not that Mr. Lincoln was [the South's] friend: on the contrary, every man and woman in the South, and every child born within the last four years, regarded him as the official head and personal embodiment of all their enemies. But, by the removal of the Commander-in-Chief of the great army and navy with which they were contending, a far more vindictive and unrelenting man is invested with the supreme power of the nation."

One of the great female characters of the war—acquitted of killing a Union soldier near the start of the war on the grounds of justifiable homicide, and later twice arrested as a Confederate spy and twice released—Boyd wrote in her memoir of "the horror everywhere felt at the idea of being 'ruled with a rod of iron' by such an unprincipled demagogue as Andrew Johnson!" Like Mary Todd Lincoln, she also followed the logic of the crime to its illogical conclusion. "It is usual in cases of murder to look for the criminal among those who expect to be benefited by the crime. In the death of Lincoln his immediate successor in office alone receives 'the benefit of his dying.'" Johnson was still in his first year as president when Boyd's memoir, with its outrageous allegation, was published by Saunders, Otley, & Co. of London.

Had they been in Selma, Alabama, on April 21, Belle Boyd and Emma LeConte could have celebrated together. On the twentieth, the *Chattanooga Rebel*—by then being published in Selma—had informed its readers of the deaths of Seward and Lincoln, "that political mountebank and professional joker, whom Nature intended for the ring of a circus." On the twenty-first, the *Rebel* added Andrew Johnson and Edwin Stanton to the bloody toll: "murdered by a mob which has obtained and holds possession of the capital of the nation." Other cities had been sacked as well; a great popular revolt was impending. "While their armies are devastating our land, their own down-trodden populace, infuriated by tyranny and driven to despair by want, bursts the bonds of law, and a reign of terror and of ruin is established."

France, it was said, had finally joined the Confederacy. Emma LeConte charted the progress of this new ally, or the rumored progress of the rumored new ally, in her diary: "Now the French fleet was at New Orleans—now at Beaufort—now at Georgetown, and finally it was confidently stated that the ubiquitous fleet had defeated the Yankees at Hampton Roads." In fact, no rumor was more persistent than the French one as the real fighting ground to a close. The phantom fleet kept working its way up the coast—to Hampton Roads, to the Chesapeake, to the Potomac, until it seemed only a matter of days before French warships would be docking at the Washington waterfront and French sailors and marines routing the enemy at its seat.

Perhaps the second most persistent rumor revised events at Appomattox. In Louisiana, diarist Sarah L. Wadley consoled herself on May third with the news that General Lee had surrendered only himself and his rear guard, some 4,000 men in all. The rest had escaped Grant to join Joe Johnston, and the combined force had inflicted a terrible defeat on the hated Sherman: 8,000 "well prisoners," untold numbers of sick and wounded ones, seventy cannons seized. A day earlier, a newspaper in Jackson, Mississippi, relying on a doctor who had showed up in town with two-and-a-half-week-old copies of some Georgia newspapers, reported that Lee and Johnston had whipped Grant decisively on the battlefield with 100,000 Union soldiers lost. As for that speech Lee supposedly made to his troops after the alleged surrender at Appomattox—the one urging them to beat their swords into plowshares—"It bears the stamp of forgery on its face." Imagine: The French fleet engaged at last! Sherman routed! Grant crippled! Lee riding Traveler once again at the head of his Army of Northern Virginia! Johnson and Stanton both dead, along with Lincoln and Seward!

In Savannah, a correspondent for the *Cincinnati Commercial* reported in mid-April that nearly every woman to be seen on the streets was wearing black—"love's sackcloth and ashes for the lost"—and all the men had long faces and sorrowful miens. The children, however, still gaily sang their favorite song:

> *Jeff Davis rides a very fine horse,*
> *And Lincoln rides a mule.*
> *Jeff Davis is a gentleman,*
> *And Lincoln is a fool.*

By the time that story ran in the *Galveston* (Texas) *Weekly News*, Lincoln had been dead a week. One wonders what those Georgians might have taught their children to sing about Andy Johnson had they known their fate was now in his hands.

In that same issue, the *Galveston Weekly* reprinted an appeal to the

"Women of Alabama and Mississippi" from a Mobile newspaper, the *Army Argus and Crisis*. Like "the mothers of ancient Israel, of Sparta and of Rome," the women of the Confederacy were to urge their sons, brothers, and husbands to do their duty. "Know then, that more than one-third of the whole number of soldiers whose names are on the rolls are not in the army with their brethren, ready to defend you and to beat back the foe; but they are absent without leave, loafing, skulking, or hiding from duty! Know further, that this state of things would be simply impossible, if public opinion at home did not tolerate this shameless desertion of duty. Never would these straggling soldiers remain a single week at home, in the criminal desertion of their flag, if the women of the country would take the matter in hand."

A week after that, the paper was reporting that the good ladies of Galveston were still coming forward with riches to swell the Confederate treasury. From Mrs. Sessums: a silver card case, a silver cup, a silver ladle, two gold chains, two cuff pins. From Mrs. Mohl: a gold watch and gold chain, a jet cross and gold chain, a gold ring. "All articles received will be receipted for and turned over to the C.S. Depository here," the *Weekly* assured readers.

It all sounds insane. Lee had left the battlefield. Johnston was soon to do so. The men they had commanded were starving by the end. On April 4, five days before he surrendered his army, Lee had sent an appeal for food to the citizens of Amelia County, Virginia, sustenance for "the brave soldiers who have battled for your liberty for four years. We require meat, beef, cattle, sheep, hogs, flour, meal, corn, and provender in any quantity that can be spared." Lee had 30,000 hungry men to feed; promised provisions had not arrived from Richmond. The next day, his foraging wagons returned from the countryside empty. Even for the sainted Lee, there was nothing left in the fields, no livestock in the pastures or barns, no grain in the silos. Down in North Carolina, Johnston's army was deserting at the rate of nearly a thousand soldiers a day: heading home to see if anything or anyone was left.

The Confederacy was bled dry. Its Congress had disbanded. Its president was on the run, zigzagging his way through the Carolinas. What treasury the Confederacy still had was traveling parallel with Jefferson Davis: gold and specie to back up worthless currency. In the closing volume of his Civil War narrative, Shelby Foote tells the haunting story of the last time a Georgia slave saw his master, a man who had lost three sons in the war: "He was a-setting in a wicker chair in the yard looking out over a small field of cotton and corn," the ex-slave recalled. "There was four crosses in the graveyard on the side lawn where he was setting. The fourth one was his wife." That's what four years of fighting had left so much of the South with: their dead, and if they were lucky a small patch of corn—although the odds in this case are that it was field rather than sweet corn.

Yet what is war but controlled insanity? Anyone who had looked at the South's prospects rationally from day one would have seen exactly what William Tecumseh Sherman saw: that it was bound to fail.

All across the increasingly despondent and sometimes delusional South, people waited for the new president to send a sign, some indication of whether his actions would match his reputation and the vengeful tone of his public statements. Beginning in the last week of April 1865, Andy Johnson sent three of them, each seemingly clearer than its predecessor. The first involved the great Sherman himself.

In the days just after Lincoln's murder, rumor had swept Washington that elements of Sherman's army camped 275 miles southwest, near Raleigh, North Carolina, had slaughtered 400 Rebel captives in revenge of Booth's treachery. The story fit the spirit of the moment. It fulfilled expectations. Hadn't the preachers called for retribution from the burning pulpits of Black Easter? Like Andrew Johnson, Sherman seemed its ideal instrument, the avenging angel of the field. Look what he had done to Atlanta and Columbia, South Carolina. In fact, Sherman didn't even know about Lincoln's assassination until Monday morning, the seventeenth.

To alert his most important general still in action to the dire events in Washington—and to suggest to Sherman that he might himself be a target of future assassination attempts—Stanton sent a ciphered message via a steamer bound for Morehead City, on the North Carolina coast. From there, the message was telegraphed to Raleigh, where it arrived just as Sherman was boarding a train for Durham Station. Sherman waited half an hour for the message to be decoded; then swearing the telegraph operator to secrecy, he set off for Durham, and on by horse to Hillsboro to begin negotiating the surrender of the Confederacy's last significant army, under General Joseph Johnston.

In Hillsboro, Sherman showed Johnston the telegram as soon as the two generals were alone. "[I] watched him closely," Sherman recalled. "The perspiration came out in large drops on his forehead, and he did not attempt to conceal his distress. He denounced the act as a disgrace to the age, and hoped I did not charge it to the Confederate Government. I told him I could not believe that he or General Lee, or the officers of the Confederate army, could possibly be privy to acts of assassination; but I would not say as much for Jeff. Davis . . . and men of that stripe."

Back in Washington, the same thought seemed to be going through everyone's mind. Lee, Johnston, Forrest, and the other generals were surely traitors—they'd waged war against the nation of their birth— but they would never stoop to assassination. Davis was another matter. Though he was a West Point graduate, though he had served as a U.S. senator and secretary of war in the Pierce administration only eight years earlier, the Confederate president was devil enough to stoop to such a heinous act.

Later that day in Raleigh, Sherman posted news of the assassination for his troops to read. "Thus it seems that our enemy, despairing of meeting us in open, manly warfare, begins to resort to the assassin's tools," the notice concluded. "We have met every phase which this war has assumed, and must now be prepared for it in its last and worst shape, that of assassins and guerrillas; but woe onto the people who seek to expend their wild passions in such a manner, for there is but one dread result!"

Sherman and Johnston concluded their documents of surrender on the evening of April 18. By then, the two had been joined by the Confederate secretary of war, John Breckinridge. Sherman met with him reluctantly—as a military man, his brief didn't extend to civilian officials—but Johnston reminded his Union counterpart that the war secretary was also a commissioned general. What's more, Sherman had already shown that he was quite capable of crossing the line into political affairs. On January 15, in Savannah, having swept his army to the sea, Sherman issued Special Field Order 15, appropriating some 400,000 acres of abandoned rice plantations along the Georgia and South Carolina coasts and turning them over in forty-acre parcels to African Americans to settle. The order was only temporary; he didn't have the authority to issue anything permanent. Arguably, the order had a military purpose, too. Sherman's army by then was dragging behind it a second ragtag force of emancipated slaves. The settlement plan would free him of that weight. To sweeten the kitty, he offered a mule with each parcel, from his own stock of beasts worn and broken by the long march to the sea.

Sherman's "forty acres and a mule"—the origin of the phrase—was more than just field expediency. He had clearly crept up to the edge of civilian policy. Four months later, in Hillsboro, North Carolina, Sherman went careening over the top. At Appomattox, Grant had accepted Lee's surrender and sent his Army of Northern Virginia home on parole. Of necessity, it was a separate peace. Grant couldn't place demands on armies he had yet to surround, as he had Lee's; and Lee wouldn't and couldn't speak for more than his own command. At Hillsboro, encouraged by Johnston, Sherman went a quantum leap further. Johnston would disband his army and disperse its men to their various state capitals, "there to deposit their arms and public property in the state arsenals," and all Confederate armies still extant would do the same. In return, Andrew Johnson would invite back into the Union all state governments once their leaders had sworn loyalty to the United States, federal courts would be reestablished across the South, and all citizens of the late Confederacy would see "their political rights and franchises, as well as their rights of person and property, as defined by the Constitution," restored in full.

That, basically, was it. The soldiers could return home and live in peace and quiet, so long as they "abstain from acts of armed hostility, and obey the laws in force at the place of their residence." No mention of emancipation, other than to comment that Johnston and Breckinridge both thought slavery dead. No provision for the rights of the newly freed blacks. Not a whisper of black suffrage. Sherman, the scourge of the Old South, was out to save it, or so the terms suggested.

On the morning of the nineteenth, Sherman sent the seven-paragraph document north by courier to Grant with a cover message noting that, if approved, the agreement "will produce peace from the Potomac to the Rio Grande" and asking that President Johnson endorse the terms and place Sherman in charge of executing them. Lincoln might have done just that. The late president had never been inclined to give the store away. He had, however, advised "letting 'em up easy," and Sherman had taken "easy" to the absolute edge. Lincoln, however, had been providentially delivered by Booth's derringer from the better angels of his own nature, or so the preachers were proclaiming. His casket was making its way north toward New York City by the time the cabinet met on April 21 to consider Sherman's terms, and there wasn't a sympathetic ear in the room.

To Attorney General Speed, Sherman's usurpation of civilian authority suggested the opening salvo of a coup d'état. Gideon Welles recalled Speed's conjuring up images of Sherman "at the head of his victorious legions," marching next on the national capital. Although Welles described Edwin Stanton as even more exercised than Speed, the war secretary took a longer view: Sherman's capitulation to Southern interests was a bold-faced bid for Copperhead support for the 1868 Democratic nomination for president. Welles wrote that Speed was under Stanton's sway—as was much of the cabinet to a lesser degree—and that Stanton was subject to "jealousies and wild vagaries . . . [he seemed] to have a mortal fear of the generals and their armies, although courting and flattering them."

"I think we have permitted ourselves amid great excitements and stirring events to be hurried into unjust and ungenerous suspicions by the erroneous statements of the Secretary of War," Welles noted on April 25, still in the thick of the Sherman uproar. The historical record is one-sided—Welles left his elegant diaries behind; Stanton, nothing comparable to refute him with. Yet Welles wasn't alone in his assessment. Stanton was "a dyspeptic," wrote Interior Secretary John Usher, who served in his post from early 1863 until the middle of May 1865, "and because of that his temper was irascible and unequable." Sherman's brother, a Republican senator from Ohio and Stanton's Washington neighbor, thought the war secretary had been unnerved by Lincoln's assassination and its night of terror—a dangerous additive to an already volatile personality.

In this company, Andrew Johnson must have seemed, as he so rarely did, the picture of calm. Yet Sherman's terms were clearly unacceptable to Johnson, too. The president had been promising a grim justice to the traitors. Sherman wanted to send them home unscathed by anything other than the four years they had just lived through. Johnson had also vowed in his first cabinet meeting to carry on existing policy wherever possible, and Grant had set that precedent two weeks earlier when he struck his peace terms with Lee at Appomattox. Sherman had gone completely off the template. Nor did public opinion, or at least the opinion reaching the president, augur well for the gentle peace being proposed.

"Almost unanimous against the Sherman armistice," John W. Forney, the secretary of the Senate and publisher of newspapers in Philadelphia and Washington, wired Johnson on April 24. "Feeling tremendous." Two days later, after he had criticized the Sherman peace terms before a large crowd in New York City's Union Square, the historian George Bancroft wrote Johnson to say that his remarks had been met with "unanimous support." In a letter from Knoxville, Johnson's

friend Sam Milligan wrote that "Sherman has at last verified your opinion of him," a reference to Johnson's complaints early in the war that
Sherman was proceeding too cautiously against the enemy. "Even the
soldiers here are loud in his abuse," Milligan went on. "He must have
been crazy."

With the full support of the cabinet, the new president rejected
Sherman's terms. Grant himself went south to deliver the news: Johnston gets what Lee got, nothing more, and in fact, Johnston accepted
those terms on April 26, much to the disgust of his own president, Jeff
Davis. Attorney General Speed fretted the whole time Grant was gone
that Sherman might make a prisoner of him, the first hostilities of his
government in exile. More practical, Stanton launched a smear campaign against Sherman that is remarkable even today for its rancor. In
two official war bulletins issued by his office, the war secretary stopped
inches short of calling the conqueror of Atlanta a traitor to the Union
cause and a gross incompetent in the bargain. "General Meade, Sheridan, and Wright are acting under orders to pay no regard to any truce of
General Sherman's respecting hostilities," the bulletin for April 26 reads
in part. Elsewhere, the bulletin notes that while Sherman cools his
heels, the Confederate treasury, estimated at between $6 million and
$13 million, was "moving south from Goldsboro [N.C.], by wagons, as
fast as possible." The next day, Stanton and his aides went back on message: "Generals Canby and Thomas were instructed some days ago that
Sherman's arrangement with Johnston was disapproved by the President, and they were ordered to disregard it." By then, mention of Johnson's disapproval was gratuitous. Everyone knew.

Newspapers favorable to the administration jumped on the cause:
JEFF DAVIS AVAILING HIMSELF OF THE ARMISTICE TO SKEDADDLE! ran a
headline in the April 27 Washington Evening Star. HE IS RUNNING OFF
THIRTEEN MILLION OF SPECIE IN WAGONS! As Sherman would later
note, transporting that much money in gold would have required no
fewer than fifteen and perhaps as many as thirty-two six-mule teams,
hard for his 80,000-man army to miss, especially since they had been in

and around the Goldsboro area for more than a month, beginning in late March. In fact, Davis had at best a fortieth of that, and the noose was tightening, not loosening.

Accuracy wasn't the point. General Henry Slocum, who had been with Sherman at Atlanta and was the first to wire Stanton that the city had fallen, later remarked that the last property he ever saw Sherman's men burn was a wagonload of New York City newspapers pillorying their commander. They watched the blaze, Slocum recalled, "with keener satisfaction than I had felt over the destruction of any property since the day we left Atlanta."

Sherman, not surprisingly, would never forgive Stanton for the insult. He and Johnston, who carried on a feud with Jefferson Davis to the end of both their lives, were much alike in their ability to hold a grudge through thick and thin. Although Johnson was quick to make enemies, he escaped Sherman's eternal enmity, and indeed there's no evidence that he colluded with Stanton in the smear campaign. If anything, he was still inclined to give the war secretary his head, and Stanton was always one for using all the authority he could get.

On May 13, two and a half weeks after he had struck his watered-down peace with Johnston, Sherman traveled to Washington and met with the new president, who assured him he had known nothing of the two war bulletins until he'd read them the next morning in the newspapers. Johnson was "extremely cordial to me," Sherman wrote in his *Memoirs*, as were nearly all the members of the cabinet. Although Grant offered to act as an intermediary with Stanton, Sherman wanted nothing to do with it. Still, he couldn't help noting of Stanton that "I found strong military guards around his house, as well as all the houses occupied by the cabinet and by the principal officers of Government; and a sense of insecurity pervaded Washington, for which no reason existed."

Yet even if he played no part in censuring Sherman—even if, as Welles suggests, he had been swayed by Stanton along with the rest of the high administration officials—Johnson couldn't walk away from the weight of the many harsh words he had been uttering in one forum or another for weeks on end. Peace had been offered on generous terms, and not only had the terms now been rejected, but Sherman, who had proposed them, had been dragged through the mud. Johnson was living up to his reputation. For the South, it was message one.

The second message to the South and the nation involved the man whose actions had handed Johnson the presidency.

John Wilkes Booth was not "in Washington secreted Beneath Ford's Theatre," as an anonymous woman of New York City wrote Johnson on April 20. ("He never left [the theatre] but droped [sic] through a Trap Door.") Nor did Johnson avail himself of the plan advanced in an April 18 letter by an Illinois farmer named Yarnall Cooper that the president appoint a "certain and fixed time" for Lincoln's assassin to come forward, then should he fail to do so, execute "on Each and Every day thereafter the number of Seven per day of Officers of the Rebel Army now in our custody and they of highest grade and to be continued and Inforced until his Surrender to Military Authority." Instead, Booth was run to ground by more conventional means—in the middle of the night of April 26, in a tobacco barn two miles outside Port Royal, Virginia, just off the Rappahannock River. Convinced that the assassin would not give himself up, Lieutenant Colonel E. J. Conger ordered the barn set afire. As the flames spread, Booth, holding a carbine in one hand and dispensing with a crutch in the other, began shuffling toward a door. Ten feet away, firing through a crack in the barn siding, his target lit by the fire within, Sergeant Boston Corbett hit Booth in the side of the neck with a shot from a .44 Colt revolver. The fatal round was fired at three fifteen A.M. Booth, the *Evening Star* informed readers later that day, died a few hours later "in great physical pain, and the torments of the damned upon his soul.... Thus miserably perished the most atrocious criminal that the world ever knew."

With Booth gone and with David Herold, who was discovered with him, hauled back to Washington with his legs tied together beneath the belly of a horse, the question became how to administer justice to

Booth's co-conspirators, the ones who had colluded in the murder of Lincoln and the planned assassinations of Seward, Johnson, and Grant. The president resolved that matter on May 1 when he ordered Herold, Lewis Powell, George Atzerodt, and five others, including Mary Surratt and Dr. Samuel Mudd, to stand trial in Washington before a military commission, "said trials [to] be conducted with all diligence consistent with the ends of justice ... without regard to hours."

If Gideon Welles is to be relied upon, such "diligence" wasn't nearly quick enough for the Radicals. Stanton wanted Booth's co-conspirators found guilty, hanged, and in the ground before Lincoln's funeral train had completed its journey and the late president was himself interred (May 4, as things turned out). Others, including Lincoln's first attorney general, Edward Bates, thought that a military commission of any sort, at any speed, was the wrong vehicle entirely. Guilty or not—and nobody questioned the matter—Booth's co-conspirators had acted as civilians and thus should be subject to civil law: their constitutional right to a fair and prompt trial by their peers. "If the offenders are done to death by that tribunal, however truly guilty," Bates complained, "they will pass for martyrs with half the world."

Maryland congressman Henry Winter Davis wrote Johnson on May 13 that the military commission was in conflict with "the express prohibition of the constitution; & not less in conflict with all our American usages and feelings respecting criminal proceedings. ... The only safety is to stop *now*, deliver the accused to the *law* and let the Courts of the United States satisfy the people that the prisoners are either guilty or innocent in law; for the people want justice and vengeance." Carl Schurz, a leading light of the large German American community, who had visited Johnson in Nashville during some of the worst of the fighting, wrote the same day, also urging the president to remand the case to civilian courts and the constitutional protections available there. "This is the most important State-trial this country ever had," Schurz wrote. "It will go far to determine the opinion of mankind as to the character of our government and institutions." Hanging over the whole affair, too, and behind the urgent advice being rendered to Johnson were the supposed abuses of justice perpetrated by Lincoln, Stanton, and others during the war: more military tribunals, writs of habeas corpus suspended, and so forth. The Copperhead press had painted the president as a wartime despot, a man who had put the Constitution on hold for the duration. Johnson had been similarly accused of operating more as a warlord than a military governor during his reign in Nashville. Perhaps the fighting itself was all the excuse needed then. Now, though, peace was at hand.

Against this advice and these concerns stood a 7,300-word legal opinion Johnson had ordered from Bates's replacement as attorney general, James Speed. In it, Speed (with Stanton undoubtedly whispering in his ear) rambles over a broad legal terrain, from Socrates, Caesar, and Cato, to the bushwackers, jayhawkers, bandits, and war rebels of the current conflict. Military courts, he argued, are necessary to prevent a harsher brand of justice from occurring. "War in its mildest form is horrible," Speed wrote, "but take away from the contending armies the ability and right to organize what is now known as a Bureau of Military Justice, they would soon become monster savages, unrestrained by any and all ideas of law and justice. Surely no lover of mankind, no one that respects law and order . . . would, in time of war, take away from the commanders the right to organize military tribunals of justice, and especially such tribunals for the protection of persons charged or suspected with being secret foes and participants in the hostilities." As for the portion of the Constitution that declares, "No person shall be deprived of his life, liberty or property without due process of law," it simply does not apply in this instance, Speed argued, nor can it. "Trials for offenses against the laws of war are not embraced or intended to be embraced in those provisions. If this is not so, then every man that kills another in battle is a murderer, for he deprived a 'person of life without that due process of law' contemplated by this provision; every man that holds another as a prisoner of war is liable for false imprisonment, as he does so without that same due process." The Founding Fathers, Speed concluded, could not possibly have intended to fling Constitutional guarantees "around offenders against the laws of war," and thus since Booth and the others had acted as "public enemies" and as secret agents of a government at war with the United States, "it would be as palpably wrong of the military to hand them over to the civil courts, as it would be wrong in a civil court to convict a man of murder who had, in time of war, killed another in battle."

Whatever its merit as legal theory—and the subject echoes resoundingly in our own times—Speed's argument seems to have convinced the new president. The military commission Johnson approved on May 1 meant that civilian protocols disappeared in the courtroom. Prisoners were led into the courtroom wearing heavy canvas hoods that covered their faces entirely. The male prisoners had their hands bound by iron bars, their ankles shackled to balls and chains. A soldier carried the ball on the walk to and from the prison cells where they were held. (Whether it was erring generals or alleged assassins, Stanton had a penchant for piling it on.) A harder case to make might still have been successful, but this one was easy, and at least in the instance of Powell, Herold, and Atzerodt, its conclusion was essentially foreordained. As in a morality play, the audience—and it was nationwide, by newspaper or by rumor—knew the outcome before the first witness took the stand. Not only would the terms of peace be harsh, justice would be sure and speedy: a terrible swift sword. Message two was delivered.

Message three was the most personal, or was taken that way, for it involved Johnson's counterpart, Jefferson Davis, a man nearly as polarizing as Johnson himself.

On the advice of Robert E. Lee, Davis and his cabinet had abandoned Richmond by train a little before midnight on April 2, 1865. The Army of Northern Virginia had held out as long as it could. The city was doomed. Davis had set up his government-in-exile in Danville, Virginia, on the North Carolina border, by April 3, when Richmond caught fire. He was still there at two thirty P.M. the next day when Abraham

Lincoln stepped off a barge tied up in the James River and set foot in the charred hulk of the Confederate capital, where he would stay for the better part of five days.

Even with Richmond fallen, Davis still held out hope that Lee and Johnston in North Carolina might somehow unite their forces, defeat Sherman, then turn back north to drive Grant out of Virginia. The Old Dominion was Lee's home. He had to have something up his sleeve to save it. Within weeks, rumor would have Lee doing just that. Hope, though, was one thing; prudence, another. On April 6, Davis sent the Confederate treasury south by train to Greensboro: $327,000 in gold bullion and coins—a fraction of what the Northern press kept contending (and less than two-thirds what Ezra Cornell gave away that same year to found the university named in his honor). It was all the would-be nation had left. Late on the evening of April 10, Davis and others followed the money to Greensboro. There, on the twelfth, the Confederate head of state learned beyond any doubt that Lee had surrendered his Army of Northern Virginia. The news left Davis weeping openly.

On the fifteenth, the day Lincoln died, the day Andy Johnson was sworn in as president of the United States, Jefferson Davis, Confederate War Secretary John Breckinridge, other members of the civilian government, and a motley assortment of wagons left Greensboro escorted by some 1,300 Confederate cavalry, headed west for Charlotte. Rail travel was done with; the tracks were destroyed. They would go the rest of the way on horseback, "a gloomy cavalcade as they toil along the Southern sandy roads under a Southern sky," as one Union newspaper put it.

Four days later on April 19, by now in Charlotte, Davis learned of the assassination and attempted assassinations for the first time in a telegram sent by Breckinridge, who had joined Johnston and Sherman to work out terms of surrender. When the wire was handed to him, Davis was addressing the local citizenry from the front steps of a modest house owned by Lewis F. Bates, superintendent of the Southern Express Company. (Grander homes were not so welcoming. George

Stoneman, one of the Union generals pursuing Davis, was said to have vowed to burn down any house that took him in.) "At the conclusion of his speech to the people, [Jefferson Davis] read this dispatch aloud," Bates testified on May 30 before the military commission trying the Lincoln conspirators, "and made this remark, 'If it were to be done, it were better it were done well.'" Whether Davis was intentionally echoing Macbeth's famous speech from act one—"If it were done when 'tis done, then 'twere well / It were done quickly"—is anyone's guess, but both men were talking about assassinations.

A day or two later, still in Charlotte, still under Bates's roof, and now rejoined by Breckinridge, Davis returned to the theme: "If it were to be done at all, it were better that it were well done," Bates recalled Davis saying again, "and if the same had been done to Andrew Johnson, the beast, and to Secretary Stanton, the job would then be complete."

Time never softened Davis's position. In a memoir published in 1890 shortly after his death, Davis would write of Lincoln: "For an enemy so relentless in the war for our subjugation, we could not be expected to mourn." Yet, he added, the assassination "could not be regarded otherwise than as a great misfortune to the South. [Lincoln] had power over the Northern people, and was without personal malignity toward the people of the South. . . . His successor was without power in the North, and [was] the embodiment of malignity toward the Southern people, perhaps the more so because he had betrayed and deserted them in the hour of their need."

On May 2, 1865, twenty-four hours after he had ordered the military trial for Powell, Atzerodt, and the others, Johnson issued a proclamation that put his official imprimatur on the most popular theory of who was ultimately behind the assassination.

Whereas it appears from evidence in the Bureau of Military Justice that the atrocious murder of the late President, Abraham Lincoln, and the attempted assassination of the Honorable William H. Seward, Secretary of State, were incited, concerted

and procured by and between Jefferson Davis, late of Richmond, Virginia, and Jacob Thompson, Clement C. Clay, Bev-
erly Tucker, George N. Sanders, William C. Cleary, and other
rebels and traitors against the Government of the United
States, harbored in Canada.

Now, therefore, to the end that justice may be done, I, Andrew Johnson, President of the United States, do offer and
promise for the arrest of said persons, or either of them, within
the limits of the United States, so that they can be brought to
trial, the following rewards.

For all the lesser inciters, co-conspirators, and procurers, Johnson
offered a reward of $25,000. (The sole exception was Cleary, a clerk to
Clement Clay, who commanded only $10,000.) Two days later, Tucker
and Sanders wrote to the president from Montreal that the proclamation was, in effect, a death warrant aimed at Jefferson Davis, since, if captured, he was almost certain to be executed, or so they assumed. "Your
proclamation is a living, burning lie, known to be such, by yourself and
all your surroundings, and all the hired perjurers in Christendom shall
not deter us from exhibiting to the civilized world, your hellish plot to
murder *our* Christian president."

For Davis, whom the proclamation was most meant to run to
ground, the reward was set at $100,000, about $1.18 million in current
dollars. The figure is high enough in its own right; considered as a per-
centage of total U.S. annual expenditures, it is staggering, even given the
wildly war-inflated budget of 1865. A reward today of similar proportions would be on the order of $150 million, six times the $25 million
being offered by the FBI as these words are written for information
leading directly to the apprehension or conviction of Osama bin Laden.

Part of the urgency involved good police work. Were Davis and the
others guilty as charged, they would have been willing participants in
the most heinous crime in American history up to that moment, one
that could have been still worse had Johnson, Seward, and Grant also

fallen. Part, too, must have been personal. Johnson hadn't become Davis's "beast" overnight. The two had been at each other's throats for two decades. But part of the urgency also was logistical. By May 2, when Johnson announced the reward, Jefferson Davis was about the last distant hope of the Confederacy; and the Trans-Mississippi, the last of the Confederate departments that wasn't defeated and occupied, was Davis's last viable refuge. With its president holed up across the Mississippi in the Ozarks, the swamps of Louisiana, or the vast sere expanses of Texas, who knew how long the South could hold out, what kind of rump campaign it might wage under Davis's command.

The Confederate newspapers talked longingly of such a last-ditch stand. "A nation of eight millions of freemen are capable of prosecuting a war of self-defense indefinitely for generations to come and are determined to do so, sooner than accept terms that would disgrace a nation of slaves," declared the *Galveston Weekly* in its April 26 edition. Davis himself wrote of the possibility in an April 24 letter to his wife, Varina. "It may be that with a devoted band of cavalry, I can force my way across the Mississippi. If nothing can be done there, then I can go to Mexico and have the world from which to choose a location."

Davis wasn't simply saving his skin, escaping Johnson and his oft-repeated threat to stretch Davis's neck. That wasn't the Confederate president's way any more than it was the way of the Union president. The two commanders in chief were alike if nothing else in their obstinacy, far more so than Lincoln and Davis had been alike. Even as he fled, Davis was never ready to abandon the battle until he had some assurance of terms that wouldn't beggar the South to the Union. Moreover, in Texas and Mexico, he was running to familiar ground. As a colonel, he'd distinguished himself almost two decades earlier at Monterrey and Buena Vista in the Mexican War. During the Civil War, Davis had shown himself to be a brilliant military tactician. Certainly he was ready to command a fighting force again, even if that meant darting through the sagebrush and attacking by night.

In the war councils of Washington—to Johnson, to Stanton, to

Grant—letting Jefferson Davis escape across the Mississippi was unthinkable, and not solely because he was the most wanted man in America now that Booth was dead. Davis would be hell to root out in Texas. Rebel soldiers were sure to join him. Even if the Union could be patched together again, rogue bands might harass America's southern and southwest border states for decades to come. The conflict would linger interminably in the "last and worst shape" that Sherman had foreseen, a war of assassins and guerillas.

Mexico offered in some ways a worse scenario still. The French had installed their Austrian puppet, Maximilian, on a throne in Mexico City. Let Davis cross not only the Mississippi but the Rio Grande, and France might finally agree to back the Confederacy, if only to protect its Mexican adventure. The French fleet would no longer be merely rumors, and its superiority to the Union Navy was unquestionable. With Northern ports now blockaded, an exhausted Northern Army would have to take up the fight again, against a fresh foe harbored by a hostile, not-quite-conquered people.

From the vantage point of the twenty-first century, it all seems completely far-fetched, fodder for alternative histories, not serious ones. Nothing short of divine intervention was going to breathe life back into the South. What's more, the French in Mexico already had their hands full with Benito Juárez and his rebel band. Still, the prospect alarmed Grant enough that he continued to advocate driving the French out of Mexico for months after the Confederacy officially ended.

In any event, Davis never got there, never even got close. In the early morning of May 10, the Confederate president finally ran out of road at an encampment outside Irwinville, Georgia, where he was visiting his wife and their children. Davis had been in flight for more than five weeks and still had two entire states to cross before he reached the Mississippi. By mistake, in his dark tent, he'd thrown on Varina's sleeveless overcoat once he realized the camp was surrounded. He'd also let her throw her shawl over his head and shoulders before he stepped outside with a maid and her pail, as if headed to the creek for water. The disguise worked not a lick, but the Northern press would never let Davis alone for it.

Davis, his wife, and family were taken to Macon, Georgia, where the soon-to-be–ex-president learned for the first time from the Union general James Wilson that he carried a $100,000 reward on his head for complicity in the assassination of Abraham Lincoln. "Fearing that I might never have another opportunity to give my opinion to A. Johnson, I told [General Wilson] there was one man in the United States who knew that proclamation to be false," Davis wrote in his memoir, unrepentant and unforgiving as ever. "He remarked that my expression indicated a particular person. I answered that I did, and the person was the one who signed it, for he at least knew that I preferred Lincoln to himself."

From Macon, the Davis family was placed on a train to Atlanta and then on to Augusta, where a river steamer carried them to Savannah. At Savannah, they boarded the side-wheeler *William P. Clyde* and started north by sea, along with other prominent captives hauled in from elsewhere, including Major General Joseph Wheeler and Alexander Stephens, Davis's diminutive vice president. On May 19, after three days at sea, the *Clyde* dropped anchor at the mouth of Hampton Roads, in the lower Chesapeake Bay, and there she sat for three more days in the shadow of the massive U.S. Fort Monroe. Built between 1819 and 1834, Monroe featured thirty-foot-thick granite walls. Second Lieutenant Robert E. Lee had once been stationed there for three years, during the final phase of construction.

On May 20, Stephens and the Confederate postmaster general John Reagan were transferred to a warship and taken off to Boston harbor. Wheeler and others left the next day for a fort near Philadelphia. Davis had steamed up the coast expecting to be delivered to the capital at Washington. On the twenty-second, he learned for certain that he was wrong. Davis said good-bye to his wife and children, who were forced to return to Savannah on the *Clyde*, and left by tug for the fort he'd been staring at for the past seventy-two hours. He would spend the next 720 days of his life imprisoned there. Though Davis had no chance of escape, though the fort was enclosed by a moat and surrounded by impenetrable walls, the commandant, Nelson Miles, ordered the Confederate president placed in shackles.

The shackles would last for less than a week—while the door was being replaced on Davis's cell—but the harsh treatment would go on for months. Davis's cell, he would later complain, was kept brightly lit day and night. Nor was Davis ever alone or allowed any newspapers or other reading matter or even let out to exercise. "Bitter tears have been shed by the gentle, and stern reproaches have been made by the magnanimous, on account of the needless torture to which I was subjected, and the heavy fetters riveted upon me," Davis would later write. In fact, Johnson had little to do with any of it. Treasury Secretary Hugh McCulloch recalled in his memoir that Johnson sent for him one day and asked him to go privately to Fort Monroe to investigate whether Davis was being abused. "'He was,' said the President, 'the head devil among the traitors, and he ought to be hung; but he should have a fair trail, and not be brutally treated while a prisoner.'"

Perhaps Johnson should have inquired sooner about Davis's condition. He'd been a prisoner for months before McCulloch was sent to check on him. Perhaps the president should have suspected that Stanton's War Department would impose the harshest conditions. Perhaps, too, the president could have done more about Davis's condition once McCulloch reported back to him. Conditions did improve in the fall. Still, almost a year after Davis was first imprisoned, when Varina was first allowed to see him (after passing through three lines of sentries and a guardroom), she found him emaciated and glassy eyed.

At the worst, Johnson's sins seem to have been ones of omission, not commission. Once again, though, he couldn't walk away from his inflated rhetoric. Jefferson Davis had been his arch-traitor; Johnson, Davis's beast. Now the one was in what amounted to a dungeon cell, waiting to see if he was to stretch hemp, as the other had so frequently promised. To the advocates of a punitive peace and to those who most feared it, the harsh treatment afforded the Confederate president must have been the clincher: first Sherman slapped down, then the military tribunal, then this.

Hang Jefferson Davis, and "YOUR LIFE SHALL BE FORFEIT," a Southerner who signed himself "Pro Patria et Preside" (for country and president) wrote Johnson on May 14. "Gaurded [*sic*] at every step as your craven life is, *it will not always be so.* . . . For that time I will watch and wait, WITH A RESOLVE AS FIRM & FIXED AS THE HEAVENS." To drive the point home, the anonymous writer drew a raised arm wielding a dagger over his nom de guerre. This was more than a week before the shackles went on, an indignity that seemed all the proof needed that the war was to end vengefully.

In Camden, South Carolina, the acid-tongued diarist and aristocrat Mary Boykin Chestnut recorded on June 4 that she had gone to visit the old family house, Kamchatka, a splendid three-story mansion wrapped in porches, where a preacher named Trapier was now living. "In those drawing rooms, where the children played 'Puss-in-Boots,' where we have so often danced and sung but never prayed before, Mr. Trapier held his prayer meeting. I do not think I ever did as much weeping—or as bitter—in the same space of time. I let myself go. It did me good. I cried with a will," Chestnut continued. "He prayed that we might have strength to stand up and bear our bitter disappointment, to look on our ruined homes and our desolated country and be strong. And he prayed for the man 'we elected to be our ruler and guide—that he might be given power from on high to bear all that a base and cowardly tyranny might heap upon him—that strength may be his to be true to himself, true to us, true to his own fame, true to his country, true to his God.' We knew they had put him in a dungeon and in chains. Men watch him, day and night. By orders of Andy, the bloody-minded tailor."

CHAPTER 6

Waiting Game

$\mathcal{A}$BRAHAM LINCOLN GAVE INDELIBLE EXPRESSION to our highest national ideals and left behind some of the defining documents of American history. His Emancipation Proclamation made concrete the aspirations of the oppressed and desperate, and began to lift the sin of slavery from the people who had allowed it to exist. Yet when it came to Reconstruction, Lincoln refused to tip his hand. To the extent that he had a plan, it seemed to be contained within his December 1863 Proclamation of Amnesty and Reconstruction, offering full pardon and the restoration of all rights to almost any Confederate willing to take a loyalty oath and accept emancipation. (The offer did not extend to high-ranking military officers and government officials.) Once 10 percent of voters in any seceded state—as measured by ballots cast in the 1860 presidential election—had sworn fealty, the loyalists could form a new state government, appoint senators and representatives to resume the abandoned seats in Washington (Congress willing), and generally start behaving as if Fort Sumter and Bull Run, Shiloh and Vicksburg, Antietam and Gettysburg, Chickamagua and Chattanooga had never happened.

As wartime policy and propaganda, Lincoln's ten-percent plan was a stroke of genius: a chance to divide and conquer, to isolate the diehards from the secessionists who never were all that committed, perhaps even to stack Lincoln's own deck for the 1864 presidential campaign since only the loyalists would be permitted to vote. At a more practical level, Lincoln's plan was folly warmed over, as he surely knew. Mississippi cast a total of about 69,000 votes in the 1860 election; Texas, 63,000; Arkansas, 54,000; Louisiana, 50,000; Florida, 13,000. Imagine a functioning Mississippi government built on fewer than 7,000 citizens who had all sworn allegiance to Washington and affirmed that slavery was dead; or a Florida one that rested on a mere 1,300. The government couldn't control its own state capital, much less the state itself. And what of South Carolina, which still had no popular vote for president? The Union-occupied areas of Arkansas and Louisiana did, in fact, set up ten-percent governments in fairly short order. Sections of Virginia and Tennessee followed, the latter at the urging of Andrew Johnson. They were governments in little more than name, yet Lincoln wouldn't be pinned down to anything more definitive, more workable. When Congress passed the Wade-Davis Bill on July 2, 1864, raising the loyalty threshold and toughening Lincoln's terms for returning to the Union, the president waited until lawmakers went out of session, then let the bill die by pocket veto. On July 8, in a proclamation on the matter, Lincoln explained that he was "unprepared, by a formal approval of this Bill, to be inflexibly committed to any single plan of restoration." Nor was he willing to see the puppet governments already established in Arkansas and Louisiana set aside in the wake of Wade-Davis.

In early August, the bill's sponsors—Benjamin Wade and Henry Winter Davis—fired back at Lincoln in the pages of the *New York Tribune*. The president's response "strides headlong toward the anarchy his Proclamation of the 8th of December inaugurated.... A more studied outrage on the legislative authority of the people has never been perpetrated." (Bear in mind that this criticism comes from members of Lincoln's own political party. Andrew Johnson, by contrast, wrote Lincoln from Nashville on July 13 to declare that his statement of July 8 was "just as it should have been ... real union men are satisfied with it.")

Nine months later, with Richmond captured and Lee's army dissolved, with Jefferson Davis and his government on the run, Lincoln was no more ready to be cornered into a hard-and-fast position. On

April 11, 1865, in what was to be his last speech, the president bobbed and weaved every which way, anything to avoid being pinned down. Reestablishing national authority, he allowed, is "fraught with great difficulty. Unlike the case of a war between independent nations, there is no authorized organ for us to treat with. No one man has authority to give up the rebellion for any other man. We simply must begin with, and mould from, disorganized and discordant elements. Nor is it a small additional embarrassment that we, the loyal people, differ among ourselves as to the mode, manner, and means of reconstruction."

Lincoln argued that in his December 1863 proclamation, he had "distinctly stated that this was not the only plan which might possibly be acceptable; and I also distinctly protested that the Executive claimed no right to say when, or whether members should be admitted to seats in Congress from such States." The proclamation, he said, had been "distinctly approved" by every member of the cabinet and had been received warmly by Congress. As for the constitutionally critical issue of whether the seceded states had ever left the Union, Lincoln had "purposely forborne any public expression upon it." For four years, the states had been "out of their proper practical relation with the Union." Everyone knew that. The challenge now was to get them back into the Union again on a proper footing. "Finding themselves safely at home, it would be utterly immaterial whether [the states] had ever been abroad." In that single statement lies perhaps more wiggle room than Andrew Johnson permitted himself in a lifetime of public pronouncements.

Lincoln had freed the slaves. He had no intention of going back on that. In his July 1864 rejection of the Wade-Davis measure, he called for a constitutional amendment to embed emancipation in the ultimate law of the land. But amending the Constitution takes time, and the Emancipation Proclamation had freed only the slaves in the Deep South, the out-and-out combatant states. Four slave states—Delaware, Kentucky, Maryland, and Missouri—had never left the Union. A part of a fifth one, what became West Virginia in June 1863, likewise lay outside the jurisdiction of the proclamation, as did various Tidewater counties of Virginia, twelve parishes of Louisiana including New Orleans, and, thanks to Andy Johnson, all Tennessee. Thus, their slaves were unaffected by the decree. And what had Lincoln freed the slaves for? The ten-percent solution imposed emancipation as a condition of reentry, of reunion with the Union. It required the restored states to provide for the freedmen's education, but it also allowed states to impose on the ex-slaves temporary measures consistent "with their present condition as a laboring, landless and homeless class." What did that mean? What types of temporary measures might even a loyalist Mississippi government be likely to impose? Wendell Phillips, the Boston abolitionist crusader, complained that the amnesty proclamation "frees the slave and ignores the negro."

On the issue of black suffrage—increasingly, the litmus test for Radical Republicans as the war wound to a close and its outcome became inevitable—Lincoln seemed to disappear behind benign words. "I would myself prefer that [suffrage] were now conferred on the very intelligent, and on those who serve our cause as soldiers," he said in that last speech of April 11. Here, too, his sentiments are couched in rhetoric common in Washington today. "I myself would prefer . . . I distinctly stated . . . distinctly protested . . . distinctly approved . . ." (Give a politician three *distinctlys*, and you know he wants to remain fuzzy.) History elevates such evasions to statesmanship. In fact, they were practical politics in the extreme.

Lincoln did direct cabinet members to turn their attention "to the great question now before us" at what proved to be his last meeting with them, on April fourteenth. Even then, though, he refused to take a firm stand on the time-sensitive issue of what to do with the rebellion leaders, according to Treasury Secretary Hugh McCulloch. "Mr. Lincoln merely remarked in his humorous manner, 'I am a good deal like the Irishman who had joined a temperance society, but thought that he might take a drink now and then if he drank unbeknown to himself.

A good many people think that all the big Confederates ought to be arrested and tried as traitors. Perhaps they ought to be; but I should be right glad if they would get out of the country unbeknown to me'"

The abracadabra solution: *Poof!* Davis, Stephens, Lee, and the others disappear. Problem solved. This wasn't so much bold leadership as it was deft footwork. Looking at it from 140 years since, the iconic Lincoln so towers over the pragmatic one that we sometimes forget what a masterful politician he was. Now you see him; now you don't.

How refreshing, by contrast, Andy Johnson must have seemed in those opening weeks of his administration, at least to the Radicals. Here was a stationary target, a man who knew exactly where he stood on the Confederate military and civilian leadership. The new president had been calling them traitors ad nauseum, to every delegation that came crowding into his Treasury Department offices, and they crowded in on him by the dozens.

From that position came Johnson's other positions, in a clear and logical sequence. If their leaders were traitors, so was it treasonous for the states themselves to attempt to depart the Union. So much for letting Virginia, South Carolina, Georgia, and the others up easy. Like people, political entities must be made to feel the pain of their transgressions. To be sure, Stanton had been nudging Johnson in this direction ever since Lincoln's murder. Sherman's censure, the military tribunal instead of a civil one, shackles for Jefferson Davis—they all had the war secretary's stamp on them. But Stanton was merely pushing Johnson toward where he already wanted to go. A hundred flaming preachers couldn't be wrong about the new president. Even on the issue of black suffrage, Johnson seemed to be coming around, according to Charles Sumner, the Massachusetts senator and card-carrying Radical Republican who practically lived in the Tennessean's back pocket during those first weeks of his presidency.

And yet what one heard from Andy Johnson was not always what one got. Hugh McCulloch, who would prove one of the most astute of Johnson's observers, commented on it in his memoir. Born in Kennebunk, Maine, and educated at Bowdoin College, McCulloch had moved to Fort Wayne, Indiana, as a young man and eventually climbed the ranks, becoming president of the State Bank of Indiana and U.S. Comptroller of the Currency, then ascending to the cabinet not many weeks before Lincoln's death. McCulloch was, by nature, a social conservative, a man of moderate habits, one reason he had been so alarmed by Johnson's drunken vice-presidential oration. What's more, since he had to share office space with Johnson until Mary Todd Lincoln vacated the White House, McCulloch had the best seat in the capital for observing the new president. "It was there," McCulloch would later write of their shared quarters, "that [Johnson] made the speeches which startled the country by the bitterness of their tone—their almost savage denunciations of secessionists as traitors who merited the traitor's doom. So intemperate were some of these speeches, that I should have attributed them to the use of stimulants if I had not known them to be the speeches of a sober man, who could not overcome the habit of denunciatory declamation which he had formed in his bitter contests in Tennessee."

Johnson had stump speaking in his blood. Even now that fate had elevated him to the highest office in the land, at one of the gravest moments in national history, he couldn't resist the high drama, the histrionics, the over-the-top-ness of it all. Give Johnson an audience, and he was off and running, hellfiring and brimstoning every inch of the way. "If [Johnson] had been smitten with dumbness when he was elected Vice-President, he would have escaped a world of trouble," McCulloch wrote with beautiful understatement. "From that time onward he never made an offhand public speech by which he did not suffer in public estimation."

True as that was, there was more to Johnson than his intemperate fulminating; and McCulloch, who stuck by Johnson to the end of his term and ended up admiring him despite their opposite personalities, knew it. "There was a marked difference," he went on, "between his carefully prepared papers and his offhand speeches. The former were well written and dignified; the latter were inconsiderate, retaliatory, and in a style which could only be tolerated in the heat of a political campaign." Like a lot of people who fly off the handle too easily and play to the mob's passions too readily, Johnson also tended to work himself up to a fine fit of vituperation, then wind down toward something more moderate as the rage wore off. The froth always seemed to lead the news accounts of Johnson's off-the-cuff talks; the meat and potatoes were buried down in the bottom paragraphs.

Johnson's April 18 remarks to a group of Illinois citizens suggest the pattern. The president opens with the usual thanks for the kind words of encouragement. His heart is heavy with loss. "Perhaps the best reply I could make, and the one most readily appropriate to your kind assurance of confidence, would be to receive them in silence." (Little chance of that.) Then the fuse begins to light. By the halfway point, Johnson is in full throttle and the crowd along with him. Lincoln's assassination was "barbarous" and "diabolical," and "springs not alone from a solitary individual, of ever so desperate wickedness." As for treason, "the people must understand that it is the blackest of crimes, and will be surely punished." "Applause," the newspapers report, "applause ... applause." And then, almost as rapidly, the steam goes out of Johnson. The show is done. Time to get down to business, which is in effect no business, or at least no particular insight into what lies ahead. "In regard to my future course, I will now make no professions, no pledges ... As events occur and it becomes necessary for me to act, I shall dispose of each as it arises, deferring any declaration or message until it can be written paragraph for paragraph in the lists of events as they transpire."

The new president was back at it again on April 21, speaking to the Indiana delegation that had called on him at the Treasury Department. The opening paragraphs in the *Evening Star's* account were filled with talk of revenge, as if Johnson were specifically seeking to refute the healing message of his predecessor's Second Inaugural Address: "I know it is very easy to get up sympathy and sentiment where human blood is about to be shed, easy to acquire a reputation for leniency and kindness, but sometimes its effects and practical operations produce misery and woe to the mass of mankind.... Traitors must be made odious.... Their social power must be destroyed." It was old hat for Johnson, repeated in every forum, to Northerner and Southerner alike. The tone shocked even Radicals like Ben Wade. Grant worried that the South would think the president was speaking for the North generally—and was certain that he wasn't: "But for the assassination of Mr. Lincoln, I believe the great majority of the Northern people, and the soldiers unanimously, would have been in favor of a speedy reconstruction on terms that would be least humiliating to the people who had rebelled against their Government. They believed, I have no doubt, as I did, that besides being the mildest, it was the wisest, [*sic*] policy." To the secessionists who came to see him personally, seeking some glimmer of what a postwar South might be like, some morsel of hope that it might not be too unbearable, Johnson's words rained down like brimstone. "He uttered his denunciations with great vehemence," Grant wrote in his memoir, "and as they were accompanied with no assurances of safety, many Southerners were driven to a point almost beyond endurance."

What they heard was Melville's Avenger—the iron hand of the weeping people—but scroll down further in Johnson's remarks to that Indiana contingent, for example, and again one finds a markedly different tone. In its most extreme form, the Radical position called for a draconian remake of the South: territorial status, military rule, a black-based society to replace the white planter-based one. Johnson, while he was glad to rail at the leading traitors, wanted nothing to do with it. "Upon this idea of destroying States, my position has been heretofore well-known," he told the Indiana contingent. "Some are satisfied with the idea that States are to be lost in territorial and other divisions; are to lose their character as States. But their life breath has only been suspended, and it is a high constitutional obligation we have to secure each of these States in the possession and enjoyment of a republican form of Government.... I think the progress of this work must pass into the hands of its friends. If a State is to be nursed until it again gets strength, it must be nursed by its friends, not smothered by its enemies." Johnson was talking about the loyalist friends of the prostrate states, not the secessionist leaders. Yet the idea of the South, in effect, healing itself was heresy in Radical circles.

Lincoln was the lamb; Johnson, the lion. There seemed no question of that. As the first weeks of Johnson's presidency drew to a close, though, the lion was proving as elusive in some ways as his martyred predecessor. Would the ex-Confederacy run with the blood of its traitors? Would the Southern states see their full rights restored, or any rights? Would they even retain their status as states? Were the freedmen to be truly free—educated, granted suffrage, allowed to hold public office, and judged by their peers? What spoils belonged to the victor? Was the end of one war only the beginning of a longer, slower war of resistance? Johnson's inflamed words seemed to paint a South forced to its knees, a nation healed—if at all—at the end of a noose. In the margins of the president's public pronouncements, though, were words to comfort the despairing Mary Chestnut in Camden, South Carolina— words that must have driven Sumner, Wade, Stevens, and the rest of the Radicals to pure distraction. The simple fact was that no one knew which way Johnson would jump.

When he visited Sherman at Morehead City, North Carolina, in the first week of May 1865, Chief Justice Salmon P. Chase, who only three weeks earlier had sworn Johnson into office and who later would preside over his impeachment trial, painted a Washington still on the verge of spinning apart. Sherman took little at face value, but he and Salmon Chase had close ties. When Chase resigned his Senate seat in March 1861, after serving only two days, to become Lincoln's treasury secretary, he had been replaced in a special election by Sherman's brother, John, a fellow Ohioan and Republican. Sherman wrote that it was plain to him from his conversation with Chase that Lincoln's assassination "had stampeded the civil authorities ... and that they were then undecided as to the measures indispensably necessary to prevent anarchy at the

South." (And who should know better than Sherman, who was on the scene and had helped create the massive deprivation that fueled the anarchy?) As for the new president, Johnson was beset by "the wild pressure of every class of politicians to enforce on [him] their pet schemes," according to Chase.

That Washington reeled yet from Booth's and Powell's attacks; that Reconstruction was still up in the air; that some plan was necessary, and soon, to prevent the South from falling into chaos—these are indisputable. America and its capital were being taxed to do the near impossible: end a horrific civil war, right the primal wrong of slavery, and launch a lasting peace—all in the shadow of the most shocking crime in the nation's history. Such moments always bring forth the schemers and opportunists, the idealists and save-the-worlders. Washington had been full of them during the war, and they weren't about to go away now that peace was on the horizon and the terms of reunion still to be determined. Inevitably, Johnson was besieged by them, in delegations and in pairs and individually, in person and by mail.

Benjamin Butler, the Union general who was the Radicals' choice to replace William Seward as secretary of state, wrote Johnson on May third to suggest he issue an executive proclamation on agriculture, assuring Southern planters that no decision about the disposition of their lands would be enforced until after the fall. It was seed time, Butler argued. No man would plant what he wasn't assured of harvesting, and if the fields of the defeated Confederacy lay fallow through the summer, starvation would be widespread by Christmastime.

A week later, the president received a petition from "colored men of the State of North Carolina," reminding him that until 1835 free black men in the state could vote and asking him to restore that right, now that the war was at an end. "It seems to us that men who are willing on the field of danger to carry the muskets of republics, in the days of peace ought to be permitted to carry its ballots." They were submitting the matter to Johnson's "better judgment," they wrote, "...in the fond hope that the mantle of our murdered friend and father may have fallen upon your shoulders." A letter on the same subject arrived May 23 from A.D. Jones, of Ohio. "Having Searched Every page of History Relative to the Degradation of my Beloved Race, The Elevation of us as a People Scattered amongst the Whites as we are is I believe a matter of impossibility." Instead, Jones urges the president to enfranchise blacks in only a few Southern states, where they can concentrate their numbers and accrue real political power. Everyone had an opinion, however odd, on how Reconstruction should proceed.

Inevitably, too, each faction, each cabal worried that the other was ascendant, too close to the president's ear, too deep inside his pocket. Radical Republicans fretted that Johnson was spending too much time with Francis Blair and his son Montgomery, who had taken Johnson in at their estate, Silver Spring, after he disgraced himself on March 4. The Blairs had both been among the few present at Johnson's presidential oath-taking at Kirkwood House. As postmaster general, Montgomery had proven himself an ardent enemy of the Radical elements in Lincoln's cabinet. Even now, out of office, he led the conservative wing of the Republican Party, far more ready than the Radicals to accommodate the South and make peace with the Democrats, far less inclined to impose military rule and turn the antebellum social order entirely upside down. Woe to black suffrage if the Blairs got Johnson's ear, and woe to states' rights and the Constitution if the Radicals prevailed. For the most part, the battle lines were crystal clear. The target, though, was beyond everyone's aim.

Johnson was, first of all, incorruptible. It was the one absolute fact of the man. He had so few material wants to play to. "In appointments, money was not potent," Hugh McCulloch would later write. "Offices were not merchandise. The President never permitted himself to be placed under personal obligations to any one. He received no presents. The horses and carriage which were sent to him soon after he became President [by a group of New York City merchants] were promptly returned.... For him, fashionable watering-places had no attractions. Neither by him nor by any member of his Cabinet was recuperation sought at the seaside or in the mountains." He was a drudge, a workaholic, a man of little or no recreation. How can you corrupt someone who won't even accept a weekend in the mountains? Johnson was almost impossible to influence.

He did have great ambition. As people who start out so low in life often do, Johnson cared greatly for the world's opinion once his own massive exertions and his wife's tutelage had raised his star high enough to be admired. He had thin skin and took social slights hard. On the great issues of the day, though, he trusted and valued no man's opinion more highly than he trusted and valued his own. Oliver Temple had seen it early on in Tennessee: Johnson was his own touchstone. Once he found his ideological footing, he railed at will against his political enemies. He allowed himself to be pushed slightly here and there, especially in the whirlwind of those first weeks in the presidency. But Johnson ultimately sanctioned nothing, believed nothing until he had subjected it to the test of his own intellect, his own experience.

As military governor of Tennessee, he had an autocrat's powers and too often acted the part. Some of that was of necessity: Nashville had never been safe for Johnson or Unionists generally during the entire length of the war; governing there required a strong hand. But as with his speeches, so with his actions Andy Johnson couldn't seem to help going a step too far. The oaths he required of voters in his halting attempts to establish a functioning wartime government in Tennessee were so sweeping and thus so exclusionary that the elections turned farcical. The relatively few voters still eligible once the election was held were almost certain to pick the one candidate among many whom Johnson most approved of. This was not democracy in action, but this was war. Apart from being among the most obstinate presidents in American history, Johnson was also one of the least nuanced and most tone-deaf men ever to rise to the peak of public life.

Johnson prided himself on his self-reliance, and with good cause. No president had traveled a rougher road to the White House, not even Lincoln. If self-reliance is the ultimate American virtue, as Ralph Waldo

Emerson suggested, then Johnson was perhaps the ultimate American. Yet he seemed determined to carry that hallmark of the national character to its most extreme interpretation. One gets the impression that if Johnson could have ruled eastern Tennessee entirely on his own during the war years—without any company save for family, with only an army at his beck and call—he would have been happy to do so. Once Johnson had chewed a matter over thoroughly and made up his mind on it, what was the point of others except to stand up and applaud, or get out of the way?

Temple, who spent the war years in Nashville, writes that Johnson was fond of calling mass public meetings with himself as the featured speaker and frequent honoree. The military governor would dictate to his secretary a series of resolutions that were to be introduced at the meeting. The secretary then would pass them on to William Brownlow, the Fighting Parson of the Southern Highlands, a newspaper editor and fellow Tennessee Unionist who had once been Johnson's bitter political foe but who had joined him in Nashville against the common enemy. Brownlow, in turn, would rise up at the meetings and propose the resolutions as if they were his own inspiration. Temple recalls one such instance in especially acid tones: "When Mr. Johnson rose to speak, he said, as if he had known nothing that was to take place, that he had listened with great interest to the resolutions offered by his friend, Mr. Brownlow, and he took great pleasure in saying they met his hearty approval. No doubt the resolution which declared that the meeting had 'full confidence in the integrity and patriotism of Andrew Johnson, Military Governor of the State,' did meet with his hearty approval and gave him great pleasure!"

It all reads like a scene out of a comic opera about a tin-pot dictator. Nonetheless, the story goes to the nature of the president whom so many people were trying to sway in that first month after the assassination. Johnson listened. What he mostly heard, though, was his own voice echoing back at him. Not surprisingly, given his distrust of others' opinions and his distaste for consultation and collegiality, the new president, like the late one—though for different reasons—had few intimates. "He gave his confidence reluctantly—never without reserve," McCulloch writes. Oliver Temple cites two close friends, Sam Milligan and John Jones, both from the Greeneville area, both college educated, both men of unquestionable honesty. But Temple largely agrees with McCulloch: Johnson "was in a high degree unsociable, preferring solitude. Occasionally, he wanted, indeed seemed to require, a friend, a solitary person. But it was a hearer he needed; someone to listen while he discanted on some new idea. It was not personal, but mental sociability he desired; food for the mind, not for the heart." The one intimate Johnson did have on hand in Washington in April and May of 1865—Preston King—seems to have been even more gloomy, more borderline depressive than the new president. Named by Johnson to be collector of the port of New York, King leapt to this death from a ferryboat that November.

Johnson lost his father at age three, was apprenticed by his mother at age nine, ran away at fifteen, and was married by eighteen. His extreme self-reliance and solitary nature, perhaps even his feelings of abandonment, are hardly surprising. He was an autodidact, fearless, humorless, driven to succeed, loath to accept help, given to rhetorical overstatement, prone to internalize, and insecure despite his great accomplishments. None of it was a secret. Johnson was both a deeply private man and an open book. He'd struggled up from destitution, been apprenticed out, faced the worse the young nation had to offer—except the ultimate worst of slavery—and by dint of his own will aided by the hand of fate, had come out on top. Fighting his way up from the mudsill had shaped him, made him what he was.

This is the man everyone was trying to sway, the one whose ear everyone—senators, generals, association heads, the franchised and the disenfranchised, the rich and the poor—was seeking to bend. A daunting task on the face of it. There was, however, one more element central to Andy Johnson's personality, a trait that would finally prove fatal to his place in history. Johnson was one of those people who chews a matter

thoroughly; weighs the right and wrong from every angle; holds each detail, every argument up to the light for flaws; then makes up his mind on
a course of action and can't be budged a single inch off the mark he has
set. We've all known them: highly intelligent mule-heads.

Oliver Temple saw that, too. Johnson "was an investigator, a thinker,
and the reason for all things must appear. With slow mental processes,
he weighed and compared everything, omitting no element of consideration. His mind, too astute to be deceived, when it once rested in its
conclusions, could not be shaken." Richard G. White, a New Yorker
who wrote for the London *Spectator* during the war, captured this critical element of Johnson as well as anyone. The new president, White
wrote, was "a very original, very determined, it may be very dangerous,
but unquestionably very powerful man.... This is no feeble ruler, sure to
be a tool in the hands of his secretaries or the parties around him, any
more than it is a drunken rough elevated by an accident and incapable
of an idea, but a strong, self-reliant man, accustomed to rule, and to rule
in a revolution, with a policy as distinct as that of the oldest European
statesmen, and a will which, be that policy wise or rash, will assuredly
make resistance to it a most dangerous task."

Johnson, Richard White concluded, "is one of the most individual
men on the continent—a ruler who ... will borrow knowledge, but
accept advice only when it harmonizes with his own preconceived
convictions."

On May 8 and 9, the full cabinet, minus Secretary of State Seward, who
was still recovering from his wounds, met with the president to consider
how best to govern two of the defeated states, Virginia and North Carolina. Virginia was the easier issue. A loyal government of sorts already
existed there. The Union had cobbled the government together early in
the war so that Lincoln's appointee, Francis Harrison Pierpont, could
agree to the formation of West Virginia. Even at war's end, Pierpont's
practical authority was confined to not much more than the town of

Alexandria, just across the Potomac from the eastern reaches of Washington, D.C., and parts of some of the western counties from which the new state had been created. For the moment, though, that was good enough. On May 9, Johnson issued a proclamation declaring Pierpont the true governor of Virginia and his government the official authority of the Old Dominion. Actual power could come later.

A week later, in a foreshadowing of the struggle to come, Thaddeus Stevens wrote Johnson that, to force Pierpont "on the million inhabitants of Virginia as their governor and call it a republican form of government may provoke a smile, but can hardly satisfy the judgt. of a thinking people. Had you made him a military govr. it were easily understood." Far better, Stevens went on, to suspend further Reconstruction efforts until an extra session of Congress, which wasn't expected to return to Washington until December, could be called "than to allow many to think that the executive was approaching usurpation." If Stevens meant his letter as a warning shot, Johnson seems not to have heard it.

North Carolina presented the president and cabinet with more of a challenge and with much higher stakes. The Tar Heel State was to be the template on which the other temporary governments would be based, the beginning of a lasting Reconstruction. Its detail work—who was permitted to serve in office, who was allowed to vote—was likely to be replicated in Georgia and Mississippi and Alabama and the others to follow. At last, the postwar South was to get a first glimpse of its new face. Used to pushing things along, Stanton brought along draft language for what he considered the key issue, the sticking point of suffrage: "The loyal citizens of the United States, residing within the State of North Carolina on the second Tuesday of July next, may on that day, in the several precincts and customary places of holding elections, and between the usual hours, elect members of a State Convention to adopt a state constitution and republican form of State government in said state." Gideon Welles objected. Who exactly would be included among "loyal citizens"? The phrase was so vague as to be meaningless. His intention, the war secretary answered, was to include both negro and white men.

And thus the battle was joined. Stanton was backed by Attorney General James Speed and by Postmaster General William Dennison. Speed had been in Stanton's camp all along. Dennison was close to Chief Justice Salmon Chase, who had sent Lincoln two letters in the days before his assassination, urging him to support black suffrage. Siding with Welles were Treasury Secretary Hugh McCulloch and Interior Secretary John Usher.

Welles, who seemed to get ants in his pants whenever the war secretary opened his mouth, complained in his diary that Stanton had been newly converted to black suffrage, not for the noblest of reasons. "These were not his views a short time since. But aspiring politicians will, as the current now sets, generally take that road." As for his own views, Welles acknowledged that there "may be unjust prejudices against permitting colored people to enjoy the elective franchise, under any circumstances; but this is not, and should not be, a Federal question." Even if states could be compelled to grant a particular group the right to vote, Welles worried that, having been "enslaved mentally as well as physically," blacks were unprepared for "the discharge of the highest duties of citizenship." Like a "considerable portion of the foreign element which comes amongst us," black voters would end up "the tool of demagogues."

Welles's stance on the matter was a fairly conventional one in the early months of 1865—mainstream moderation, as opposed to the Stevens-Wade-Sumner brand of radicalism. The publisher and Senate secretary, John Forney, a Johnson ally who would later turn on him, wrote Lincoln on January 7, 1865, to say that "it will look very odd if the legislators from free states should endeavor to confer the right of suffrage upon the as yet illiterate negroes, just delivered from slavery, in the South, when, in nearly all the free states the negroes are wholly disenfranchised."

The generals who had liberated the South's slaves were no more ready than Welles or Forney to grant blacks ready access to the ballot box. Sherman was shocked in early May when Chase told him about the letters he had written Lincoln, urging black suffrage. "He was the first man, of any authority or any station, who ever informed me that the Government of the United States would insist on extending to the former slaves of the South the elective franchise." In his *Memoirs*, finished shortly before his death in 1885, Grant says of that April and May twenty years earlier: "I do not believe that the majority of the Northern people at that time were in favor of negro suffrage. They supposed that it would naturally follow the freedom of the negro, but that there would be a time of probation, in which the ex-slaves could prepare themselves for the privileges of citizenship before the full right would be conferred."

Where Andrew Johnson stood on the matter of extending the franchise to blacks, North or South, no one present at the cabinet meetings on May 8 and 9 could have said for sure. Johnson had declared himself for emancipation. He'd vowed the summer before to be the Moses who would lead blacks to some sort of Promised Land. His hatred of the big planters, the former slaveholders, was a matter of public record, extending back at least two decades. As for the war just ending, the one out of which Reconstruction was to emerge, it ranked among the darkest moments in human history. "Since the world began," he had told a crowd celebrating the fall of Richmond, back on April 3, "there never has been a rebellion of such gigantic proportions, so infamous in character, so diabolical in motive, so entirely disregardful of the laws of civilized war."

All that was basis for speculation. But so was Johnson's deep and public devotion to a Constitution that, in article 1, section 4, specifically reserved to the states the right to determine the "times, places, and manner of holding elections." There was the matter of timing, too. As historian Eric Foner has pointed out, no sooner had the cabinet discussion on black suffrage ended than Johnson extended his official recognition to the ten-percent state governments organized in the South during the

Lincoln years. The recognition was virtually without meaning. Whatever form Reconstruction would take, it was likely to sweep the just-
approved governments away in a heartbeat. Omen-watchers could note
that no ex-slave was entitled to vote in any of the ten-percent quasi-
states, but beyond this speculation, there was almost no hard ground to
stand on. The president who denounced rebel traitors wherever two or
more were gathered and stood so ready, or so it seemed, to stretch the
hemp was, on the subject of voting rights, silent as a sphinx.

Charles Sumner, who had worked so hard to bring the president
around to black suffrage, believed Johnson was on his side: "the sincere
friend of the negro and ready to act for him decisively." Sumner would
later say that Johnson had assured him "there is no difference between
us." Chief Justice Chase, an open advocate of extending the franchise to
blacks, visited Johnson in Sumner's company and came away believing
much the same as the Massachusetts senator. Ben Wade, a consistent
thorn in Lincoln's side, also refused to back away from his early enthusi-
asm for Johnson's presidency.

Frederick Douglass, among other black leaders, was nowhere near
so sanguine. When Johnson and Douglass met for the first time, back in
March at Lincoln's second inauguration, the great black orator was appalled at the grimace that came over Johnson's face. "Whatever else this
man may be, he is no friend of our race," Douglass told a friend. Johnson,
it's worth remembering, was drunk on that occasion, maybe not the best
time to take the measure of the man. Still, Douglass's comment was to
become a much-cited indictment of Johnson's character.

Three years later, after any semblance of comity had collapsed between
the executive and legislative branches, after Congress had denied Andy
Johnson the power even to remove his own cabinet members, Edwin
Stanton (the cabinet member most directly in question and the immediate *casus belli* between the president and the Radicals) would testify
that Johnson had dismissed the idea of black suffrage out of hand at the

May 9, 1865, debate: "The objection of the President to throwing the franchise open to the colored people appeared to be fixed."

Welles wrote afterward that no such thing had happened, that "Johnson forbore to express an opinion in the Cabinet meeting, gave the question much careful thought and consideration, and reserved his decision for some days." That, in fact, sounds more like the slow, deliberate grindings of Johnson's intellect. What matters most is that in one of the few times since Johnson had assumed the presidency, his war secretary had pushed, and the president hadn't budged. Space had opened up between them, which meant perhaps that space also could be found between Johnson's rhetoric and his intentions. And since the proceedings of the cabinet meeting were about as public as a private meeting can be, just about everyone noticed.

The Democratic *Intelligencer* of Lancaster, Pennsylvania, which two months earlier had called Johnson a "drunken boor" and only a few weeks before was comparing him to Caligula, suddenly found something to like, some reason to hope. "It is remarkable that while Johnson's speeches before the war and since, made in the Senate, are very bitter against treason and traitors, threatening the extreme penalties of the law, they contain nothing definite about slavery. And the same is equally true of all his remarks since his inauguration as Vice-President and President.... Let not the 'radicals' rejoice too soon." A Philadelphia paper, the *Ledger*, saw hope, too. Out of the fog of Johnson's endless denunciations and imprecations might, in fact, emerge a gentle peace, "a disposition ... to make the situation for our 'wayward sisters' as pleasant as possible." Better still, Johnson had the backbone to make the Radicals swallow his medicine. "Let those beware who attempt to oppose the policy of President Johnson. Mr. Lincoln has been credited with firmness, but in his successor's little finger there will be more of the Jacksonian firmness than there was in Lincoln's whole hand."

The *Intelligencer* was wrong about slavery. That wasn't on the table and never would be again in any serious way. The *Ledger* was over optimistic as well. One can hardly imagine the word "pleasant" escaping Johnson's lips. Both newspapers, however, correctly foresaw that Johnson would not cede authority or slink away in the face of other powerful personalities or institutions. Booth's action had left Johnson to craft the peace, and he would craft it on his own founding rock. "The truth is," Gideon Welles wrote in his diary entry for May 12, "[Reconstruction] is still in the hands of the President, who will shape it right."

Of any such rightness, Edwin Stanton and the Radicals no longer were quite so certain. Stevens and the others could demand a special session of Congress all they wanted. Lincoln wouldn't have called one, and Johnson wasn't about to do so, either. Until the House and Senate reconvened in December, the president had the playing field to himself—perhaps too much leeway under the pressing circumstances for a man already prone to headstrong action, and the beginning of a rift between the executive and legislative branches that would ultimately bring the government to near anarchy. The constitutional crisis was for later, though. For now, Johnson was in charge, Congress was in recess, the nation needed to be put back together in some form, and the president who would set that process rolling and who had once seemed so set in concrete was suddenly proving an increasingly unpredictable commodity. Stanton, however, was not without resources. He still controlled Lincoln's funeral procession—the train that would bear the corpse home to Springfield—and he had every intention of using that control to assure that whatever the fine details of Reconstruction, the peace itself would be made more punitive by the outrage that had landed Andrew Johnson in the White House.

At eleven P.M. on the night of April 26, 1865, the side-paddle wheeler *Sultana* left Memphis and headed across the rain-swollen Mississippi to Hopefield, Arkansas. The *Sultana* had begun her voyage on the twenty-first in New Orleans, carrying a hundred passengers and a crew of eighty-five as well as a hundred hogsheads of sugar; maybe 175 head of assorted livestock, including hogs and horses; ninety-seven cases of wine; and a ten-foot alligator in a cage, the ship's mascot. The 260-foot wooden steamer docked at Vicksburg on the twenty-fourth and began loading newly released prisoners of war who had been waiting at Camp Fisk for transportation north—perhaps as many as 2,000 of them, until the ship was packed with nearly six times its registered capacity. (The captain was being paid $5 for every enlisted man he carried north and $10 for every officer.) While repairmen patched the *Sultana's* leaky boilers, the crew pounded extra timbers into place to keep the upper decks from collapsing under the weight. Still, despite the crowding, the mood aboard the *Sultana* was jovial. "At last, all dangers and hardships were over," one of the ex-POWs would remember later, "and song and laughter would take the place of groans and tears of agony."

At Memphis, seventeen hours north of Vicksburg, the *Sultana* again had to tie up for boiler repairs. With those completed, she crossed to Hopefield and took on a thousand bushels of coal. One hour after leaving Hopefield, about two in the morning of April 27, just off a group of small Mississippi River islands known as Paddy's Hens and Chickens, the *Sultana's* boilers finally gave out for good, in an explosion that could be heard back in Memphis and a pillar of fire visible for miles around. As many as 500 men survived the explosion, but some 1,600 didn't, killed by the violent eruption of the boilers or burned beyond hope or drowned in a river that was miles outside its banks in the spring flooding. These were the sickest of the sick—Union soldiers held under horrible conditions at Cahaba in Alabama, and at Andersonville, Georgia.

It is a sign of how thoroughly the Lincoln funeral train dominated public attention that the *Sultana* explosion—the worst maritime disaster ever in U.S. waters—barely made a ripple in the nation's newspapers. Only four battles of the Civil War claimed more Union lives: the Wilderness, Spotsylvania, Gettysburg, and Antietam. Yet the *New York Times* didn't mention the explosion until two days afterward, and then in a one-paragraph story on page four. On April 30, "The Sultana Disaster" finally made page one of the *Times*, in a forty-seven word short in the bottom left corner. With very few exceptions, that pattern was repeated in newspapers throughout the country. The martyred president was being borne to his final resting place, and the nation's front pages had no space left. In Washington, the *Evening Star* reported the *Sultana* explosion on the first page of its April 29 edition, in a five-paragraph story tucked under a much longer, blow-by-blow account of the funeral train's passage through Buffalo; Wickliffe, Ohio; and then on to Cleveland.

None of America's four assassinated presidents has gone to his grave unmourned or unhonored. Shot at the old Baltimore and Potomac Railroad station in Washington on July 2, 1881, James Garfield was taken to the New Jersey shore to recover. When he finally died, after a ten-week struggle, Garfield was returned to the same Washington station and taken by procession down Pennsylvania Avenue to the Capitol, where he lay in state. William McKinley got similar treatment after he died of a gunshot wound received while visiting the Pan American Exposition in Buffalo, New York, on September 6, 1901. (McKinley actually seemed to be recovering for the first week, until gangrene set in. He died September 14.) Both presidents are interred in mausoleums suitable for Roman emperors, Garfield's in Cleveland and McKinley's in Canton, Ohio.

As many as 300,000 people lined Pennsylvania Avenue on November 24, 1963, to see the horse-drawn caisson that carried John F. Kennedy's body from the White House to the Capitol. Despite near-freezing temperatures, a quarter of a million people waited hours for a chance to file by Kennedy's casket in the Rotunda. That Monday, another million lined the route from the Capitol back to the White House, then to St. Matthew's Cathedral for the funeral service. Thanks to television, untold millions worldwide were watching when the president's son, young John, saluted his father's coffin as it left the cathedral, maybe the most poignant single visual in broadcast history.

But for sheer drama prolonged to the breaking point, nothing has ever matched the funeral train that carried Abraham Lincoln home to Illinois. The train started out on April 21, heading north from Washington to Baltimore and Harrisburg, Pennsylvania; due east through Lancaster (where James Buchanan and Thaddeus Stevens both saw it pass by—Buchanan from a buggy at the depot, Stevens standing by a tunnel entrance) to Philadelphia; northeast to New York; and straight north to Albany. At Albany, the Illinois-bound train at last turned west, to Buffalo; southwest around the bottom of Lake Erie to Cleveland and Columbus, Ohio; on to Indianapolis; north to Chicago; and southwest again, to Springfield, arriving May 3, the day before the president's interment.

The funeral train was in fact a collection of different trains, different engines, different engineers and crews, each provided anew whenever the tracks passed from the jurisdiction of one railroad company to another. A pilot engine ran in front, making sure the tracks were clear and whole. Behind it came the funeral train itself: engine, tender, then a string of cars, always ending with the specially built forty-two-foot United States, the railcar bearing Lincoln's coffin and that of his son, Willie, who had been buried in Washington in 1862 and now would be reinterred with his father.

The train stopped for five hours in Baltimore and almost three in Harrisburg before overnighting in Philadelphia, besieged by crowds the whole time. In New York City, where the train sat for a day and a half, the president's coffin was loaded onto a ferry to cross the Hudson River, then carried to City Hall, where it was placed on a dais in the rotunda beneath an arch of black, white, and silver. An estimated half-million people lined up for a look. Many waited all night long—at midnight a thousand German singers began chanting dirges. Although the mourners were ushered in at the rate of 6,000 an hour, there simply wasn't time enough for most to get near the coffin. Afterward, the coffin was placed in a fourteen-foot-long hearse drawn by sixteen horses to the Hudson River ferry depot, for passage across to the train. Guns fired in honor and church bells tolled the entire time. "It is the most imposing and impressive spectacle ever witnessed," a *Washington Evening Star* reporter wrote. Back on its journey, the train passed slowly through small towns at five and ten miles an hour while church bells tolled and the people gathered by the tracks or on hillsides to watch it roll by. In Lebanon, Indiana, bonfires still lit up the town when the train finally arrived at one thirty in the morning on May 1.

Planned by Stanton and administered by his aide, General Edward D. Townsend, who traveled on the train, the procession reversed the route of the whistle-stop tour Lincoln had taken east in 1861, on his way to assuming the presidency. Stanton had more than nostalgia in mind, however. By repeating that earlier, winding route, the war secretary sought to maximize public exposure to the murdered Lincoln: a reminder, now that peace was at hand, of the horrible crime that had promoted Andy Johnson to the highest office in the land. To that end, as an exercise in political propaganda, the funeral procession was choreographed to perfection. Booth was at large when the cortege started out. As Lincoln's assassin lay dying by a smoldering barn near Port Royal, Virginia, the president's corpse was spending the night in Albany, New York, the 190th of 444 communities in seven states the cortege would ultimately pass through. The train was nearly at the end of its two-week-long journey on May 2, when Johnson announced his $100,000 reward on the head of Jefferson Davis and the lesser rewards for Booth and Powell's alleged co-conspirators. For two weeks, the assassination and its aftermath—the lonely train bearing the dead president and his disinterred son to their final resting place—dominated the front pages of the nation's newspapers as no event ever had. To the Copperheads who had pilloried Lincoln in life and lent aid and comfort to the enemy, and who even now agitated on the South's behalf, the warning was clear. Let them beware now that he was murdered.

In fact, Stanton and the others probably needn't have worked so hard at their plan. For a period in the early May of 1865, the disincentives to letting the South up easy and the goads to revenge had trouble topping each other.

———

On Tuesday, May 2, as the Lincoln funeral train sat in state at the Chicago station, the *Philadelphia Inquirer* reported on a Rebel plot to burn the City of Brotherly Love to the ground the previous Sunday evening. No fire was set, but the threat echoed a November 1864 scheme, launched by Confederate agents in Canada, to put New York City's business district to the torch. Philadelphia authorities had been on the highest alert, the *Inquirer* wrote. "All the hotels of the city were warned to use extra caution, and the different floors of the principal ones were patrolled so closely during the entire night that not a guest could leave his room without his movement being made the subject of strict scrutiny." A week later the *Washington Evening Star* announced that William R. Donaldson, "well known in this and other cities as a circus clown and negro delineator [a blackface clown]," had been arrested by military detectives who had traced him from Philadelphia to the national capital. "Donaldson's trunks were taken possession of by the military authorities, and a large number of letters were found therein from parties in the South, but whether they implicate him with the plot we have not been informed."

Between the Philadelphia scare and the "negro delineator's" arrest came word via newspapers in Bermuda of a "devilish rebel plot" to introduce yellow fever into major Northern cities. Luke Pryor Blackburn, a surgeon under Confederate general Sterling Price and later a Confederate agent in Canada, had traveled to Bermuda in April 1864 following an outbreak of yellow fever there, volunteered his medical services, and stayed until October, when the outbreak eased off. That much was true. That Blackburn had gathered clothing from victims of the disease and stored it in trunks for eventual transport to Boston, Philadelphia, Washington, and the Union-controlled ports at Norfolk, Virginia, and New Bern, North Carolina, seems less likely, yet in the postassassination hysteria of late April and early May 1865, it was taken far and wide across the victorious North as near gospel.

A witness named Godfrey Joseph Hyams told the military tribunal hearing the case of Booth's alleged co-conspirators that he had met

Blackburn in Toronto, where the doctor had offered him $100,000—and as much as ten times that had the plot succeeded—to accompany the trunks to the target cities and "dispose of [the contents] at auction...on a hot day, or of a night," presumably when the disease would spread the fastest. (One of the benefits of a military tribunal over a civil one was that it could cast a wider net. In addition to trying Powell, Herold, Atzerodt, and the others, this one served as a kind of Warren Commission for the Lincoln assassination conspiracy.)

Blackburn even suggested, according to Hyams's testimony, that he send a special batch of clothes infected by both yellow fever and smallpox "by express, with an accompanying letter, as a donation to President Lincoln." As for protecting himself against the fever and the pox, Hyams testified, Blackburn prescribed that he chew camphor, smoke strong cigars, "the strongest you can get," and wear gloves at all times. For further verisimilitude, a yellow fever outbreak in New Bern the previous summer had killed an estimated 2,000 Union soldiers and local residents, exactly what Blackburn hoped to accomplish, according to Hyams.

The science doesn't hold up under modern scrutiny. While smallpox can be spread by contact with infected articles of clothing, we now know that yellow fever is spread by the *Aedes aegypti* mosquito. Despite all the alluring detail he provided to the military tribunal, Hyams was one of those people of low character who always seem to emerge at the margins of sensational stories such as this. As for Blackburn, he was indeed arrested in Canada, tried there, and acquitted in October 1865 for lack of evidence. In 1872, still besmirched by his celebrity, he finally returned to the United States. Six years later, as an indication of how much the debate had changed and how far the issue of Reconstruction and Lincoln's martyrdom had retreated, Blackburn was elected governor of Kentucky.

Blackburn, though, was almost the least of it. The *Washington Evening Star* looked at that false report in the *Chattanooga Rebel* (then being published in Selma, Alabama) that Andrew Johnson and Edwin Stanton had been murdered by a Washington mob and saw in it proof positive that the editors had foreknowledge of Booth's plan and had printed the expected result, including the public uprising that would follow the assassination. In Richmond, the officer of a New York regiment sifting through files left behind by the fleeing government found a bill introduced in the Confederate House of Representatives that seemed—so the newspapers reported—to lay the framework for both the assassinations and the abuse of Union prisoners. "Resolved...that we do adhere to our opinion that the so-called Emancipation Proclamation of the President of the United States, and the enlistment of negro slaves in the several Federal armies, now opposed to us, are not among the acts of legitimate warfare, but are properly classed among such acts as the right to put to death prisoners of war without special cause, the right to use poisoned weapons, and the right to assassinate, and, if persisted in, will justify this Government in the adoption of measures of retaliation."

It was a stretch to get from one vague measure introduced by an Alabama congressman to a full-blown plot to murder the president and abuse the helpless prisoners of war, but everything was being stretched at that moment. The nation had fallen into a kind of extended exaggeration. Hyperbole had become commonplace.

With Jefferson Davis finally shackled at Fort Monroe, the *New York Times* summarized the arc of the Confederate president's career as follows:

> At one time ruling with vigorous hand over an empire of vast extent, and over a people of singular bravery and independent character—having at his absolute command the resources of one of the richest of lands—having at his service some of the ablest generals that ever led armies, and some of the ablest statesmen and diplomatists that ever sat in council—soon after friendless among the people of his own States, deserted by his officers, forsaken by his councilors, deserted even by the petty escort whose services he secured for a day by stolen gold, and

finally betrayed into the hands of his pursuers by one of his own conscripts....It seems but yesterday that this great nation was appalled by his power—to-day he and his power are the school-boy's scorn.

The prose is beautiful, the generosity to the South as a whole remarkable, but Davis never climbed that high nor sank quite so low. Nor, despite all the rumors, the jokes, and the little ditties that broke out all over the North, was he captured dressed head to toe in his wife's finery. That, however, did not prevent a representative of P. T. Barnum from offering government officials $500 for the frock in which Davis was said to have been captured; or keep two Chicago representatives of the great North-Western Fair from seeking the same article of feminine apparel; or prevent the *Lancaster Daily Express* from noting in a little column filler, "The rebel Jeff is not satisfied with having caused the women of the country more tears and sorrow than all other men, but must insult them by taking refuge beneath their skirts."

As the *Boston Advertiser* noted, Lincoln's assassination, the prisoner abuse, the plot to burn Philadelphia, and the yellow-fever plot were part of the same barbarism that included slavery, oppression of "laboring men," loss of religion, dueling, "starvation of the poor," "debasement of women," and so on. "There was no need, therefore, for Booth to scream out the motto of Virginia, as he fled from the scene of the murder. With her credentials or without them, no one would have doubted that he represented her interest and was true to her system."

In one of the most poetic passages in his lengthy diary, Gideon Welles says much the same thing, though in gentler tones. The war, the deaths, the destruction, the destitution were all the inevitable working out of the South's primal sins and vanities. The young men of the Southern aristocracy, he wrote on May 29 from Charleston, "had read [Sir Walter] Scott's novels, and considered themselves to be knights and barons bold, sons of chivalry and romance, born to fight and to rule." Knowing cotton was king and "slavery created cotton," they enlisted "weak minds" in a war to preserve their way of life and found "weak and willing tools to pander to them in certain partisans of the North." The results, Welles observed, were to be seen all around "in this ruined city and this distressed people. . . . Having sown error, [the South] has reaped sorrow. She has been, and is, punished. I rejoice that it is so."

The clergyman and orator Henry Ward Beecher went a step further in comments reported in the *Boston Transcript* of April 25, 1865. Even the South's natural resources had been tainted by slavery. "Its products are rotten. No timber grown in its cursed soil is fit for the ribs of our ships of state or for our household homes." To the *Chicago Tribune* of May 30, all the degradations of war that had been visited on Dixie—the great estates abandoned, stocks and crops destroyed, levees broken, rivers out of their banks, young men killed and old men impoverished—represented "the accumulated vengeance of Heaven, due to outraged law and humanity, to licentious living and long years of cruelty and gilded barbarism."

Of all the testaments to the cruelty of the war only then ending, and of all the goads to a punitive peace and lasting bitterness on both sides, none were more pointed than the prisoner of war camps, Northern and Southern. The Union POW camp at Elmira, New York, to cite one example, was an absolute sump. Almost 9,000 Rebel prisoners were being held there when an Army surgeon inspecting the camp discovered a stream that he described in his report as "a festering mass of corruption, impregnating the entire atmosphere of the camp with the pestilential odors." At current death rates, he estimated, the entire prison population would likely have to be admitted to hospitals within the year, and more than one in three would die. Already, he wrote, "the hospitals are crowded with victims [bound] for the grave."

Both sides had to deal with hideous overcrowding, especially after the North canceled the prisoner exchanges that had been commonplace in the opening years of the war. (Union armies could replace their lost warriors; Rebel ones couldn't—a fact not lost on Ulysses Grant.) Sanitation was primitive. The Confederate prison at Cahaba was housed in a partially finished cotton warehouse that had been built on a flood plain, between two rivers that overflowed their banks so regularly that the first Alabama capital had fled the place after only a few years. Especially in the South, food was scarce, in many cases almost nonexistent. Among Union prisoners, starvation grew commonplace as the war wore on. As early as June 18, 1864, *Frank Leslie's Illustrated Newspaper*, wildly popular in the North, was featuring drawings of eight recently released Federal prisoners, all desperately emaciated.

"The releas'd prisoners of war are now coming up from the Southern prisons," Walt Whitman wrote in his diary near the end of April 1865, while he was still serving as a nurse in Washington.

> I have seen a number of them. The sight is worse than any sight of battlefields, or any collection of wounded, even the bloodiest. There was . . . one large boat load of several hundreds, brought about the 25th, to Annapolis; and out of the whole number only three individuals were able to walk from the boat. The rest were carried ashore and laid down in one place or another. Can those be *men*—those little livid brown, ash-streak'd, monkey-looking dwarfs?—are they really not mummied, dwindled corpses? They lay there, most of them, quite still, but with a horrible look in their eyes and skinny lips (often with not enough flesh on their lips to cover their teeth.) Probably no more appalling sight was ever seen on this earth.

The Confederate camp at Andersonville in Georgia was a hell on earth for the ages. Of the 45,000 Union soldiers confined there during the scant fourteen months of the camp's existence, 13,000 died while in prison, a mortality rate of Great Plague proportions. Many were released at war's end barely alive. On May 21, under the headline THE FEETLESS MEN, the *New York Times* reported that Union captain John J. Geer was selling photographs of Andersonville's most pitiable survivors to raise money for their care:

"Nothing could give a more harrowing or realizing sense of the awful sufferings endured by our gallant volunteers in those diabolical prison pens of the Confederacy than these photos," the front-page article read. "Constant contact with the cold sand caused the blood to stagnate, and the feet of 287 of these prisoners actually rotted off, and of this wretchedly stricken band only 45 survive."

The Andersonville commander, Henry Wirz, would be executed in Washington on November 10, 1865, the only Confederate soldier put to death for war crimes in a war that set new standards for barbarity on both sides.

The North won the war. It held the trials. But the North was only part of the equation of what would become a newly stitched-together America. The soon-to-be–ex-Confederacy had its own version of recent events, as real to many Southerners as the newspaper accounts of Andersonville's feetless men. Some of the bitterest pages of Jefferson Davis's memoirs are devoted to allegations of Northern barbarism, the "constantly recurring atrocities of the invader," as Davis calls them: "Aged men, helpless women and children appealed in vain to the humanity which should be inspired by their condition, for immunity from arrest, incarceration, or banishment from their homes. Plunder and devastation of the property of the non-combatants, destruction of private dwellings, and even of edifices devoted to the worship of God, expeditions organized for the whole purpose of sacking cities, consigning them to flames, killing the unarmed inhabitants, and inflicting horrible outrages on women and children."

Davis goes on to cite page after page of testimony drawn from letters and journals of the time: families stripped clean of their food, prized servants hanged by their necks on makeshift gallows until the ladies of the plantation brought forth their hidden jewels and silver, meticulously assembled natural-history libraries put to the torch for no good reason other than the cruelty of it, "scenes of licentiousness, brutality, and ravishment that have scarcely had an equal in the ages of heathen barbarity." All this was written more than twenty years after the fact, fueled by a rage that never ceased burning. Davis's dark recitation of Yankee inhumanity would linger for generations. It was commonly assumed in the South that the Northern industrialists who supported the war were at least as interested in stealing a cheap labor pool as they were in liberating blacks from the yoke of slavery, and that in the end they would treat their workers worse than they had ever been dealt with in the plantation society.

Of all the memoirs and diaries to emerge from this remarkably literate war, none seems on the surface more clearheaded than that produced by the Confederate nurse Kate Cumming. First published in 1866, her journal provides a detailed account of the Confederate hospital system, wartime medical practices, and her own daily rounds. Like nurses everywhere, Cumming was a pragmatist, ready to cobble a dressing out of whatever was handy or trade whiskey for flour so that she could make biscuits for her next posting. Yet in the margins, and especially toward the end, Cumming's journal reads almost like a companion piece to Davis's memoirs. In her entry for May 4, 1865, for example, Cumming recounts without blinking a story told her by a Mr. Yerby, of the enemy's atrocities in Mississippi: "It was a common thing for them to kill negro children, so as to carry off the parents with greater facility...many a negro child had been left to starve in the woods." Eleven days later, she passes on accounts of Confederate prisoners of war frozen to death in their beds, starving men forced to wait within sight of a table heaped with food until they took the oath of allegiance to the United States, one prisoner shot to death for "pick[ing] up a handful of snow to put to parched lips."

In that same entry for May 15, Cumming tells of having read a few days earlier a newspaper account of Andrew Johnson's April 20 address to the Indiana delegation, the one where he promised—at least at the top of the speech—that "traitors must be made odious.... Their social power must be destroyed." "It seems to have struck dismay to many a heart," she writes. "... If President Johnson wants the Southern people to be more inimical to the North than even this war has made them, he will carry out the policy indicated in that speech; but, if he wishes the North and South to be united in spirit, as well as in the form, he will adopt another.... What wound was ever healed by continual irritation?"

That really was the choice before Andy Johnson, the question staring him in the face: Reunion or retribution? Reintegration or subjugation? The Confederacy had stretched from south of the nation's capital to the Rio Grande. Including slaves, it counted for about a third of the nation's population at the start of the war and some of its best agricultural land. Of the nation's then seventeen presidents, ten, including the current one, had been born within the borders of what became the Confederacy. Washington, Jefferson, Madison, Monroe—they were the pillars the nation had been built on, and they were Virginians every one. What to do with such a place, after such a war?

Before that could be resolved, though, the war had to finally and officially come to a close.

On May 10, 1865, Johnson issued a proclamation declaring hostilities between the two Americas—the United States and the Confederate States—to be at an end. Three days later, on May 13, the last skirmish was fought, at Palmito Ranch in Texas, near the mouth of the Rio Grande River—ironically, a Confederate victory. For added irony, or perhaps just poignancy, the routed Federal force included the Sixty-second U.S. Colored Troops. Private John Jefferson Williams of the Thirty-fourth Indiana was the sole fatality of the fighting that day.

That wasn't the end of it. Some 2.7 million soldiers had spent four years in often fierce combat against one another, one in every eleven people in the land. (Imagine a war today that had 27 million Americans in uniform.) Better than one in three of the combatants had been killed or wounded, with the former outstripping the latter by a three-to-two margin. Prison camps were emptying out. The slaves had been freed, to a future still to be determined. A month earlier, Johnson's predecessor had been assassinated; the secretary of state, disfigured and nearly murdered. The economic toll of the war, especially on the defeated and ruined South, was immense. Shelby Foote noted that in the twelve months after the end of hostilities, the state of Mississippi spent a fifth of all its scant revenues on artificial limbs for returning veterans. For combatants and noncombatants alike, the bills—emotional and social, psychological and political—would continue to come due for decades, arguably for generations. The American Civil War wouldn't end with a single edict, a last bit of conflict, a final death.

Johnson issued another proclamation on May 22, this one removing blockade restrictions and opening trade to nearly all Southern ports except those in Texas. On June 2, General Edmund Kirby Smith, who had been severely wounded fighting for the South at the First Battle of Bull Run, boarded the Federal steamer *Fort Jackson* offshore at Galveston, Texas, and surrendered the Confederacy's last army and its last political entity, the Trans-Mississippi Department, which Jefferson Davis had been trying to reach when he was captured. Even that didn't close the books. More than a year would pass before Johnson could proclaim, on August 20, 1866, that the insurrection in Texas was officially at an end and "peace, order, and tranquility, and civil authority now exist in and throughout the whole United States of America."

But for a practical date to declare the war at an end, May 10 will do. Jefferson Davis was captured; the Confederate Congress, scattered. Richmond was a charred hulk of itself. The South had neither a government nor a seat to govern from. All that remained was the grand review, one last hurrah for the victorious Union army. Then Andrew Johnson would reveal the terms of peace.

CHAPTER 7

War & Peace

$\mathcal{P}$ IERRE CHARLES L'ENFANT, the Parisian who laid out the basic plan for the nation's capital, including its radial avenues, is one of history's malcontents. A wheedler, a whiner, a sycophant, haughty and vain, as brilliant as he was unbearable, L'Enfant was appointed by none other than George Washington to design the city that would bear Washington's name. The appointment was dated January 29, 1791. Thirteen months later, L'Enfant was fired in a letter drafted by Alexander Hamilton and signed by Thomas Jefferson. In between, the irascible planner managed to enrage just about everyone who came in contact with him. He would remain in the Washington area the rest of his life, and die there virtually penniless and almost entirely forgotten, in 1825.

L'Enfant liked to think *en grand,* according to Jules Jusserand, who helped rescue his countryman's reputation while serving as French ambassador to the United States from 1902 to 1924. L'Enfant's plan for the federal city is full of the evidence. The Capitol, as he saw it, was to be approached from the east, along sidewalks that would pass beneath "an Arched way under whose cover Shops will be most conveniently and agreeably situated." On the west front of the Capitol, Tiber Creek (now channeled underground) would form a "Grand Cascade" as it tumbled down to a canal running to the Potomac along the present line of Constitution Avenue. The "Grand Avenue"—what we know today as the National Mall, home to the Smithsonian museums and the monuments to Washington and Lincoln—was to be "bordered with gardens, rising in a slope from the houses on each side." All L'Enfant's radial avenues were oversized by the standards of the day, but Pennsylvania Avenue—designed to create a visual as well as transportation link between the "Presidential Palace" and the Capitol—was nearly epic in scale: an eighty-foot-wide carriageway, flanked on either side by thirty-foot-wide gravel walkways planted with trees, and beyond that, by ten-foot-wide pavements.

Grand it was, every inch of the way. L'Enfant had visions of Versailles dancing in his head. Washington was no Paris, however. The great plan was realized only in fits and starts. Funds never materialized. L'Enfant's elegant "reciprocities of sight"—his phrase—suffered one blow after another, including the new Treasury Department, begun in 1838, which destroyed the visual connection between the White House and the Capitol. Large parts of the federal city simply sat undeveloped and untended. A third of the way through the nineteenth century, the Portuguese ambassador took to calling Washington the City of Magnificent Distances. In his 1842 tour of America, Charles Dickens amended that to the City of Magnificent Intentions: "Spacious avenues, that begin in nothing, and lead nowhere ... ornaments of great thoroughfares, which only lack great thoroughfares to ornament."

The Civil War did nothing to improve the capital's appearance or elevate its populace. So many prostitutes crowded into the blocks south of Constitution Avenue that the area became known as Hooker's Division, in tribute to the supposed frequent visits of General Joe Hooker and his men, popularizing what had been a seldom-used nickname for the oldest profession. Hookers, pickpockets, drunks, grifters, railroad touts, camp followers, politicians—the whole place was a mess. But on May 23 and 24, 1865, the war gave Washington what it had never had before: a spectacle finally worthy of Pierre Charles L'Enfant's design.

On May 18, ten days after Andrew Johnson had declared hostilities at an end, the War Department issued Special Order No. 239, announcing a grand review of all the Union armies in any proximity to Washington, to begin a mere five days later. Troops began gathering almost immediately. Across the Potomac in Alexandria, where Sherman's men bivouacked, Anne Frobel could barely believe her eyes. "To day we see tents and camps spring up in every quarter," she wrote. "The roads filled with soldiers as far back as we can see through the woods, coming-coming-coming, thousands and tens of thousands. I hardly thought the world contained so many men and the wagons."

In Washington proper, the crowd was even thicker. "The city is full of soldiers, running around loose," recorded Walt Whitman. "Officers everywhere, of all grades. All have the weather-beaten look of practical service.... You see them swarming like bees everywhere." And not only soldiers. The *Washington Evening Star* reported on the twenty-third that train-passenger traffic into the capital had more than tripled in the days before the review. Steamers tying up at Alexandria groaned under the weight of their extra loads. (Shades of the *Sultana,* but without the terrible aftermath.) As for foot and horse-and-coach and mule traffic, "The roads leading to the city [are] thronged by country people from far and near. Such a concourse never assembled in Washington."

Unable to find lodging, thousands spent the night before the festivities camped out in the open air. At sunrise, as the fire department was watering Pennsylvania Avenue in a vain effort to hold down the dust of a dry spell, just about everyone who didn't have an assigned or reserved place to watch the review scrambled for the best vantage points. Accompanied by trustees and teachers, and preceded by a band, the District's public school children—girls in all-white, boys in white pants and black jackets—marched to the Capitol, where they sang "Battle Cry of Freedom" ("We will welcome to our numbers the loyal, true and brave... And although they may be poor, not a man shall be a slave"), "When Johnny Comes Marching Home" ("The men will cheer and the boys will shout, and the ladies they will all turn out"), and other favorites to entertain the crowd until the parade got underway. The day, by all accounts, was brilliantly sunny.

Four reviewing stands had been thrown up in front of the White House, including one for wounded veterans brought in from the city's hospitals. The main one, on the south side of Pennsylvania Avenue across from Lafayette Square, was for the president. Johnson waited there in the company of Grant and Stanton, other members of the cabinet, heads of the major military and civilian departments, and the foreign diplomatic corps. Like the other stands, the president's was draped with American flags and battle banners.

The troops had been converging half the night long. At nine that morning, they finally began to move out. Day one was set aside for Washington's defenders, the Army of the Potomac, under the command of Lee's nemesis at Gettysburg, Major General George Gordon Meade: 80,000 infantrymen, trained in close-order drill, marching twelve abreast, rifles on shoulder. "Slanted bayonets, whole forests of them, appearing in the distance, approach and pass on, returning homeward," wrote Whitman, who seems to have set himself up near the reviewing stands along Lafayette Square. "Moving with steady motion, swaying to and fro, to the right and left, / Evenly, lightly rising and falling, as the steps keep time."

After the infantrymen came the artillery pieces, hundreds of them; an engineering brigade; other brigades; most impressively, a seven-mile-long column of mounted cavalrymen that took an hour to pass the reviewing stand. In all, it was precisely the sort of spectacle L'Enfant had designed the federal city to stage, and when George Armstrong Custer's mount bolted almost directly in front of Johnson's reviewing stand, the day had a crowning stroke of drama worthy of events. "Suddenly a thrill ran through the vast assemblage as a magnificent stallion dashed madly down past the President and his associates, General Custer, with a large wreath hanging upon his arm, his scabbard empty, and his long hair waving in the wind, vainly striving to check him," the *Star* reported late that afternoon. "On swept the horse, the throng rising from their seats in breathless suspense that changed to a murmur of applause at the horsemanship of the rider, and finally giving place to a long loud cheer as the General checked his frightened steed, and gracefully rode back to the head of his column, the third cavalry division." Custer would carry to his grave the question of whether his mount had bolted on its own or been spurred by its rider. Either way, one has little trouble imagining him keeping his best profile to the crowd.

The next day, the twenty-fourth, belonged to William Tecumseh Sherman, a different matter altogether. His 65,000-man army, drawn primarily from what was then considered the West, had slogged some 2,000 miles from beyond the Appalachians to the Atlantic. Now it had seventeen more miles to go. Sherman's men did what they could to improve their uniforms for the review, but compared to the crisp appearance of the Army of the Potomac, they were still in rags. They'd had little time either for the drill work that so sharpened Meade's contingent. On May 19, in a note to Johnson, Sherman described his men as "in good order and condition for parade, Review or fighting." By the twenty-third, he was calling them a "tatterdemalion" bunch, an antiquated word that sounds exactly like what it means. Ragtag or not, Sherman intended for them to make an impression, and by his own rigid standards, they did. "When I reached the Treasury-building, and looked back, the sight was simply magnificent," he wrote. "The column was compact, and the glittering muskets looked like a solid mass of steel, moving with the regularity of a pendulum." Watching it, he would add later, "there was no wonder that it had swept through the South like a tornado."

General Reub Williams, who returned to the Warsaw, Indiana, area after the war and spent a half century editing the *Northern Indianian* newspaper there, led his regiment out onto the avenue right at the start of the procession, with the crack of the third signal gun—another brilliantly sunny day. "I had not moved a hundred feet into Pennsylvania Avenue...until my horse was fairly covered from the saddle forward with great wreaths of flowers, fully as large as the collar horses wear in harness, while bouquets were showered upon the moving men in endless profusion." In fact, flowers seem to have been everywhere. As much as $15,000 had been appropriated for them—over $175,000 in current dollars, a king's ransom at a time when the mid-Atlantic states were full of blooms.

People were everywhere, too. An estimated 60,000 lined Pennsylvania Avenue. With the marchers and the remnants from Meade's army of the day before, there might have been 200,000, perhaps 250,000 people on, alongside, or not far off the parade route: about one in every 150 people in America, equivalent, given today's population, to a crowd on the order of 2 million. Nearly a century and a half later, Washington has seen few spectacles to equal it.

Reub Williams wrote that he led his regiment past the stand where Andy Johnson and the others waited in review, then turned command over to a lieutenant colonel and backtracked a third of the way down Pennsylvania Avenue to the Willard Hotel to have a look at the spectacle himself.

After stabling my horse, I sought a position on a third-story balcony, where the whole line of march was in full view. On stepping through the window I was surprised to discover that it contained thirteen Confederate officers, who had sought the same place to inspect the soldiers as they passed. They were so interested in viewing the parade and their attention was so wholly engrossed with the sight that they had not noticed my presence, and as the Western troops came down the avenue with that swinging step so noticeably different from the well-drilled veterans of the East, one of these Confederates—a brigadier general's mark on his coat collar—looking away up the two-mile line of troops, made the remark, as though it had been forced from him involuntarily—"Great God," said he, "we never could have whipped them in the world."

So indeed it must have seemed, exactly as Sherman had predicted, but the realization came four years too late. One quarter of all white

Southern males of military age had been killed. Meanwhile, the victors marched, one witness remarked, "like the lords of the world." Grant put their average age at about twenty-three years old. The *New York Times* lauded their "healthfulness, strength and size [about an inch taller on average for the Westerners than for Meade's Army of the Potomac], their litheness and vigor, their freedom from superfluous fat and muscle, the firmness of their tread and force of their movement," as if the war had been an extended physical education class. "In silence [we] marched as only tired veterans of many battles can march," Allen L. Fahnestock, a colonel with the Eighty-sixth Illinois Volunteer Infantry, wrote in his diary that evening.

For entertainment, day two offered up two curiosities not seen in the opening parade and largely unknown to a Washington audience: Sherman's Pioneer Corps composed of ex-slaves clad for the event in fresh uniforms and marching abreast in double ranks and perfect step, armed with picks and shovels, and four or five companies of bummers, or camp followers, mostly the families of freed slaves—women and children, some on foot, some on mules hung with hams, leading a motley assortment of pigs, sheep, calves, gamecocks, and chickens. Like the camp followers, the Pioneers were cheered lustily and with good cause, Reub Williams wrote, "for they were a very essential feature in Sherman's march from Atlanta to the sea.... They had rebuilt hundreds of destroyed bridges, and laid miles upon miles of corduroy on the line of march, and thus enabled Sherman's troops to move forward at a speed that surprised the Confederates."

The drama on day two featured Sherman himself, not grandstanding for the crowd à la Custer but settling his score with Stanton over the war secretary's public rebuke of his peace terms with Joe Johnston. Nearing the reviewing stand on horseback, Sherman noticed William Seward, the secretary of state, sitting heavily bandaged in an upper window of his house on Lafayette Square, and removed his hat in salute. Sword raised, Sherman then led his army past the presidential reviewing stand. As was the custom, he turned afterward on to the White

House grounds, dismounted, and climbed on to the reviewing stand, where his own family was sitting. "I shook hands with the President, General Grant, and each member of the cabinet," Sherman recalled in his memoir. "As I approached Mr. Stanton, he offered me his hand, but I declined it publicly, and the fact was universally noticed." Well noticed, too, was that Sherman's face went beet red, while Stanton's remained its usual emotionless mask. The slight delivered, Sherman and Johnson—the Scourge of Atlanta and Melville's Avenger—stood shoulder to shoulder for six and a half hours while the Army of the West marched by.

In the wake of Lincoln's assassination, Washington had fallen into a turmoil of grief and revenge, even of fear that the conspiracy had yet to fully play itself out. The aftermath of the great parade added extravagant public drunkenness to the mix. The soldiers were at the tail end of a grueling campaign, waiting to be mustered out, and the capital was never a hard place to find a drink. On May 28, the provost-marshall-general of Washington ordered all establishments selling intoxicating beverages to close between the hours of seven P.M. and seven A.M., not much more than a finger in the dike but about all the authorities dared to do. The military tribunal remained in session, too, and would for another month. On the day the grand review got underway, newspapers trumpeted a document recovered from the archives of the Confederate War Department in which a man named Alston offered "to rid my country of some of her deadliest enemies, by striking at the very heart's blood of those who seek to enchain her in slavery." Jefferson Davis had presumably endorsed the proposal, which supposedly included assassinating the Union civilian leadership.

Still, a corner had clearly been turned. The war was past tense; peace, the present tense; Reconstruction, not military victory, the business at hand. The White House was finally vacant, too, ready for the new president to move in. While the armies of the Union were marching in review, Mary Todd Lincoln together with her surviving sons,

Robert and Tad, and a threadbare traveling party boarded the afternoon train for Chicago.

On May 29, 1865, five days after the review had ended and forty-five days after he had been sworn in as president, Andrew Johnson unveiled for the nation his vision of the America that was to emerge from the slaughter.

RESTORATION trumpeted the *Times* in its May thirtieth headline, in not quite end-of-the-world type. PRESIDENT JOHNSON'S AMNESTY PROCLA-MATION. RESTORATION OF RIGHTS OF PROPERTY EXCEPT IN SLAVES. AN OATH OF LOYALTY AS A CONDITION PRECEDENT. And on and on, the headlines and subheads and sub-subheads stacked one on top of an-other down the left-hand side of page one for more than nine inches, practically to the fold.

Johnson, in fact, issued two proclamations on the twenty-ninth. In the lesser of them, appointing a provisional governor for North Caro-lina, Johnson opened with his usual bombast, decrying "the rebellion, which has been waged by a portion of the people of the United States, against the properly constituted authorities of the Government thereof, in the most violent and revolting form." Then he got down to business. The provisional governor of the Tar Heel State was to be William Woods Holden. Like Johnson, Holden had risen from humble origins. The editor of the Raleigh-based *North Carolina Standard*, he had been a leading light of the antebellum Democratic Party in the state. Party af-filiation aside, Holden had stood by the Union until Fort Sumter was fired on. Even after he endorsed secession, Holden continued to use his pages to lambaste the government of Jefferson Davis, and in 1864 he ran unsuccessfully for governor of the Confederate state of North Carolina as a peace candidate.

Holden's duties, as laid out in the proclamation, were straight-forward. He was to assemble at the "earliest practical period" a conven-tion composed of delegates chosen by "that portion of the people of said

State who are loyal to the United States, and no others." The convention would then alter North Carolina's constitution in such manner and particulars as to restore the state to its proper relation to the federal government, specifically by repealing the ordinances of secession adopted in 1861, by repudiating all debts run up by North Carolina during the war, and by ratifying the Thirteenth Amendment to the Constitution of the United States, outlawing slavery. As to who could vote for the delegates to be chosen for the convention, in addition to requiring loyalty, Johnson set the bar at those who had been eligible to vote in 1861, before the onset of hostilities.

In the second and greater of the proclamations—this one taking up the twin issues of amnesty and loyalty—Johnson opened with a broad stroke, though one thick with caveats. The proclamation granted "to all persons who have, directly or indirectly, participated in the existing rebellion, except as hereinafter excepted, amnesty and pardon, with restoration of all rights of property, except as to slaves, and except in cases where legal proceedings, under the laws of the United States providing for the confiscation of property of persons engaged in rebellion, have been instituted." The price of readmission was a simple oath, which Johnson directed should be of the "tenor and effect following":

> I, _____, do solemnly swear, (or affirm,) in the presence of Almighty God, that I will henceforth faithfully support, protect, and defend the Constitution of the United States, and the union of the States thereunder; and that I will, in like manner, abide by, and faithfully support all laws and proclamations which have been made during the existing rebellion with reference to the emancipation of slaves. So help me God.

Excepted from the general amnesty and pardon were fourteen separate classes of rebels, ranging from civilian officials of the Confederate government to all military officers above the rank of colonel in the army and lieutenant in the navy, any rebel soldier or sailor educated at the public expense at West Point or Annapolis, any federal judge who had deserted his post to aid the rebellion, all so-called governors of the so-called states of the "pretended" Confederacy (since to Johnson, the Confederacy had never lawfully existed), all those who left their homes within the jurisdiction of the United States and passed through Federal lines to aid the aforementioned pretended Confederate States, pirates and raiders who had preyed on Union vessels, and "all persons who have voluntarily participated in said rebellion, and the estimated value of whose taxable property is over twenty thousand dollars"—about $236,000 in today's terms, a figure that almost certainly would have included Johnson himself had he sided with the Rebels.

Even to the excepted classes, Johnson extended an olive branch, providing "that special application may be made to the President for pardon...and such clemency will be liberally extended as may be consistent with the facts of the case and the peace and dignity of the United States."

The North Carolina proclamation made no mention of extending suffrage to blacks; indeed, by omission if not commission, it seemed to specifically exclude the possibility. Stanton and the Radicals had lost, at least in this first round of Reconstruction, since North Carolina was to be the model for reintegrating all the entities of the defeated South. It was as if the breakaway states had gone into a kind of anticonstitutional coma for four years while war whirled around them and their sons died by the tens of thousands, and now they were awakening again. Time to plump the pillows, throw open the windows, give the poor sick states some nourishment, and get back to the way things were—minus slavery, the one concession to a changed world.

Nor would the "conscious traitors" be stretching hemp or atoning for their odious crimes by forfeiting their property (other than slaves) or even their citizenship. Johnson had spent his first six weeks in the presidency thundering like Amos, but the worst he had done when he was through was to require his former enemies to prostrate before him and ask the nation's forgiveness, a softer fate by far.

Jefferson Davis, for one, would never bring himself to do it, yet even Davis, the head devil of them all, never paid the price that Johnson had seemed to vow was his due. New York senator Edwin Morgan, the state's former governor, wrote Johnson on May 29 that "there can be no question...[Davis] deserves death." The treatment of Union prisoners at Andersonville, the slaughter of black troops at Fort Pillow in Tennessee, the yellow-fever plot, the earlier attempt to torch New York City—they all could be laid at Davis's feet, Morgan argued, and they all demanded the ultimate punishment. Johnson himself wrote Chief Justice Chase on August 10 to ask his advice on "the time place and manner of trial of Jefferson Davis." Two weeks later, Johnson raised the issue with his cabinet, but the trial was never held. In May 1867, Jefferson Davis was released on bail bond; by then, his wife was living with him at Fort Monroe, in improved quarters. A year and a half later, on Christmas Day 1868, Johnson issued a general pardon "unconditionally and without reservation, to all and to every person, who directly or indirectly, participated in the late insurrection or rebellion...against the United States"; and the treason case was dropped altogether. Davis left for Canada, then England, then settled for a while in Memphis, where he was president of an insurance company until it went under in the Panic of 1873 and carried his savings down with it. Davis died in New Orleans in 1889 and was given, by some accounts, the grandest funeral ever in that city of grandly overdone events.

The Democratic press was naturally ecstatic about the president's proclamations. Johnson had been magnanimous, the *New York Sun* declared. His words were chock-full of "wise, just, and humane sentiments," according to the Washington-based *National Intelligencer*. The president had showed the nation that he was not likely "to stand idle, while black stars were substituted for white in the banner of the Union," wrote the *Daily News* of Petersburg, Virginia, a compliment heavy with ugly undertones.

For once, the bitter divide between the nation's newspaper didn't seem so wide. In Johnson's two proclamations, prowar papers and Copperhead ones alike could find something to applaud. *The New York Times*—along with the *New York Herald,* Johnson's most consistent supporter from one end of the war to the other—took the president to task ever so slightly for failing to include among the excepted classes "the editors and proprietors of the principal rebel sheets" for their role in stirring the population to the "madness of the rebellion. . . . Never, since the art of printing was discovered, has the art ever been put to the work of hell with such vigor or such unscrupulousness." On the whole, though, the *Times* and its editors couldn't have been more satisfied. "President Johnson has well done a very difficult piece of work," the paper said on May 31. "An amnesty of some sort was a necessity. Statutory punishment of all who have committed treason would bring to death nearly every man and woman in the South, for nearly all have either 'levied war' against the United States, or given those who did so, 'aid and comfort.' A universal amnesty, on the other hand, would have been a full absolution of the greatest crime of the age, and the greatest of all injuries to the authority and majesty of law." In finding a golden mean between these two extremes, the president had acted "in the best manner possible."

The North Carolina proclamation's neutral stance on suffrage seemed sound to the *Times,* as well. The President "imposes no conditions but those of simple obedience to the laws and support of the proclamations of the national government. He leaves the question of suffrage—without regard to negroes or whites—to be determined by the convention, or the Legislature constituted and organized by that body"—as if the question of suffrage with "regard to negroes" had not already been predetermined by the very simplicity, the crisp cleanliness of the solution.

The leading figures of the day were less certain than the press that Reconstruction had gotten off to a proper start. Political centrists like Ulysses Grant, who worried that Johnson had gone too far in his denunciations of the rebel leaders and would visit too cruel a peace on a broken land, were mostly nonplussed by what Grant would later refer to as the president's "complete revolution of sentiment." Was this the same man who had put a $100,000 price tag on Jefferson Davis's head and stood complicitly by while the Confederate president was thrown into chains? Stevens, Wade, Sumner, Julian, and the other congressional Radicals, meanwhile, were utterly beside themselves. On the most critical issue of the immediate postwar period—one of the most critical moments in American history—Johnson had acted unilaterally. Not only had the president failed to heed their individual counsel, he had refused to call Congress back into special session so that he might benefit from its collective wisdom.

Thus, Johnson had assured that Reconstruction would be a fight not only between Republicans and Democrats, between North and South, between pro- and anti-Negro factions, but also between Congress and the executive branch. Of all the fights he could have picked, the last was the one he was most certain to lose. Congress was quicksand, and no president was more sure than Andy Johnson to thrash his way to the bottom.

On June 3, less than a week after Johnson had delivered his edicts, Stevens wrote Sumner, wondering whether it was possible "to devise any plan to arrest the government in its ruinous career?" Two days later, Sumner heard from Carl Schurz, the German American leader. The president, Schurz wrote, had shown him a draft of the North Carolina proclamation, and Schurz had attempted to strike out the passage limiting suffrage to only those qualified under the prewar constitution. "He listened so attentively that I was almost sure he would heed my advice," Schurz went on. Even now that it was clear Johnson had not listened, Schurz urged Sumner to return to Washington and pressure the president personally. "[His] opinions are quite unsettled on the most vital points. I fear he has not that clearness of purpose and firmness of character he was supposed to have." Like so many others, and particularly among the Radicals, Schurz calculated Johnson by what he wanted the president to be.

Thaddeus Stevens wrote Sumner again on the fourteenth of June: "Is there no way to arrest the insane course of the President in Washington?" On the twenty-second, in a written reply to Schurz, Sumner referred to Johnson's emergent Reconstruction as "a defiance to God and Truth . . . an imbecile and shameful policy." Only two months had passed since Black Easter, with Lincoln barely dead, when Ben Wade crowed: "Johnson, we have faith in you. By the gods, there will be no trouble *now* in running the government!"

No group was more directly affected by the combined weight of Johnson's proclamations than the ex-slaves themselves, and no group saw with greater clarity the future that awaited as a result. On June 29, a month to the day after the proclamations had been issued, a contingent of South Carolina blacks sent Johnson a petition, imploring him to change his mind on suffrage. "The power to tax, and legislate generally by one class only of a commonwealth, distroys the safeguard of the disenfranchised," the petitioners wrote, "and undermines the piller of Civil liberty upon which rests their prosperity happiness and improvement, and impairs the quietude and Strength of the Goverment." In the particular case of South Carolina, denying the ex-slaves the vote puts them in "a anomelous position as citizens," a majority within the state ruled by a minority. (The petition included a lengthy calculation showing that blacks outnumbered whites in the state by 119,911, out of a total population, black and white, of 417,641.) The document concludes:

"For the foregoing and other cogent reasons, your humble petitioners anxiously desire to be put, by your excellency politically, in a position that would inable them to protect their Rights and interest against the probably Encroachments of a power that would have no nutralizing influences should they be denied the right of suffrage."

The petition bore 1,456 names. The next day, Charles Sumner forwarded to the president a second petition on the matter, this one signed by 300 Georgia blacks.

As for Johnson—the unlikely new hope of Southern Democrats (although he had been one all his adult life), and the unlikely fresh despair of Northern Radical Republicans, who had embraced him like a brother four years earlier when he rose up in the Senate to denounce secession—he was in the most profound sense just being himself.

Johnson did seek counsel before he issued his proclamations: with Carl Schurz; with William Holden, his choice to be North Carolina's provisional governor, whom he had asked to come to Washington for the purpose; and with three other prominent North Carolinians, including the president of the university at Chapel Hill. On April 21, only a week after Lincoln was shot, Johnson had sent a letter to Attorney General James Speed, asking for his legal opinion on such matters as the president's power to grant pardons and the proper construction of whatever proclamations he might ultimately issue. Johnson had had Speed's lengthy reply in hand since May 1. In the seven weeks since Lincoln's death, he sat through cabinet sessions on all these issues, endured endless meetings, large and small and one-on-one, in which Republicans and Democrats alike sought to bend his ear and swing him to one side or another. None of it was hasty. Nor was Johnson or his plan imbecilic, despite what Charles Sumner had to say. Rather, his Reconstruction strategy was inseparable from the man who was making it. Surrounded on all sides by advice, Johnson took Reconstruction deep into himself, and in the end he emerged with a policy so steeped in his best and worst traits, so much the essence of the man, and so tone deaf to the political world around him that the policy couldn't help but doom him. Reconstruction was his short road to the ash heap of history.

Why did he do it? How did he emerge from all that deliberation with a policy so certain to fail and drag him down with it? Perhaps the simplest answer is that Johnson was a caretaker president and saw it as his duty to carry on Abraham Lincoln's policies. Not that he simply deferred to his martyred predecessor or adopted Lincoln's policies wholesale—that wasn't Johnson's style. But both proclamations were rooted firmly in Lincolnian doctrine and more generally in the spirit of the sixteenth president.

Johnson's North Carolina plan was Lincoln's ten-percent solution stripped of its wartime trappings and modified to reflect a nation now at peace: rally the loyalists, shrove the state of its sins and relieve it of its baggage (the ordinances of secession, the Confederate debt), recognize that the postbellum world would not be the same as the antebellum one (by ratifying the Thirteenth Amendment), and get on with the business of electing senators and representatives. Congress could or could not choose to seat whoever was elected. That was Capitol Hill's trump card; the power of Congress in these matters is absolute. The process itself could take months or years. The North Carolina template came with no timetable, a ray of sunshine for those who hoped for a long and painful penance. But Johnson had set in place the mechanics to restore the wayward Rebel states to the Union, and to do so without undue humiliation.

His pardon and amnesty provisions were no less faithful to his predecessor. In Lincoln's amnesty proclamation of December 8, 1863, he spelled out a lumbering, 125-word loyalty oath drenched in legalese. (Lincoln's would-be loyalists, for example, had to swear to uphold the Emancipation Proclamation "so long and so far as not modified or declared void by decision of the Supreme Court.") Johnson kept the first third of Lincoln's oath verbatim, then pared the final two-thirds down to a trim twenty-two words. The lawyer-talk disappeared—that was Lincoln's profession, not his—but the gist of both oaths is identical: I will protect and defend the Constitution. I will abide by and support emancipation. "With malice toward none, with charity for all, with firmness in the right as God gives us to see the right" the then-vice president had been too inebriated to take in those words when Lincoln spoke them at his second inaugural. But surely this was as close as Andy Johnson could get to an absence of malice, to charity for all. Firmness in the right was his home turf, the fruit of his stony and inflexible intellect. But the point is that Johnson would let the South up easy, just as Lincoln had advised.

If he hadn't seen it coming, Attorney General James Speed had at least tried in his legal opinion to focus the new president's attention on this issue of excessive leniency, of too slavish an attention to Lincoln's wishes. "A profound respect for the opinions of that great and good man, Abraham Lincoln, late President of the United States, induces me to ponder long and well before I can venture to express an opinion differing even in a shade from his," Speed writes, foreshadowing his intentions every inch of the way. "But all who had the good fortune to know him well must feel and know that from his very nature he was not only tempted but forced to strain his power of mercy. His love for mankind was boundless, his charity all embracing, and his benevolence so sensitive that he was sometimes as ready to pardon the unrepentant as the sincerely penitent offender." The words drip with honey, but one can also taste the venom behind them (and almost see Edwin Stanton bent over Speed's shoulder as he writes). How much greater, then, the shock when the lion and the lamb laid down together?

Differences existed. Lincoln had excluded six classes of Confederates from his December 1863 amnesty proclamation. Johnson more than doubled the exceptions and ended with wealthy landowners, a group whose inclusion must have been based, at least in part, on sheer class rage. Lincoln never would have done it, never would have thought of it. Johnson's heart was not his predecessor's equal in magnanimity. A meanness seemed always to be gnawing at the edges of his calculation. Lincoln never would have come up with a full fourteen classes of excluded Rebels, either. His mind was too supple to get caught up in some endless cataloging of guilt. Not Johnson. He saw the world in black and white: a place for everything, everything in its place.

Then there was the difference with regard to enfranchisement, or the supposed difference. Pressed hard by Sumner, Wade, Julian, and Stevens, as well as by Stanton, Chase, Schurz, and dozens of others to make some sort of nod toward black sufffrage, Johnson went almost entirely in the opposite direction. Slavery was abolished, but as for the franchise, the prewar status quo held firm. Surely Lincoln would have done it differently. He was too decent to have acted otherwise, too savvy to let the ex-slaveholders sneak back into power through a lily-white ballot box, too compassionate. In the eyes of the ages to which he was handed over, a halo effect spreads broadly over the actions that Booth's derringer never allowed Lincoln to take.

Lincoln, however, had spoken quite pointedly on the subject in a speech in Columbus, Ohio, on September 1859. Reacting to a report in the *Ohio Statesman* that he had endorsed black suffrage during his debates with Stephen Douglas the previous fall, Lincoln told the crowd that "I am not, nor ever have been, in favor of bringing about in any way the social and political equality of the white and black races; that I am not, nor ever have been, in favor of making voters or jurors of negroes, nor of qualifying them to hold office, or intermarry with the white people."

Is it fair to hold Lincoln to words spoken before he was president— before the Civil War, that great divide in American history? Not really. Unlike Johnson, Lincoln was always a work in progress, always growing, always uncovering new dimensions in that vast mansion of his character. Evidence suggests that as the war drew to a close, Lincoln was moving toward black enfranchisement. Eric McKitrick cites a message the president sent to Michael Hahn in March of 1864, shortly after Hahn had been appointed governor of Louisiana under Lincoln's ten-percent plan: "Now you are about to have a convention which among other things will probably define the elective franchise. I barely suggest for your private consideration whether some of the colored people may not be let in, as for instance the very intelligent and especially those who have fought gallantly in our ranks." "Probably...barely...private consideration...may not be let in"—the qualifiers are abundant, especially given that Lincoln was writing to the governor of a state that already had 10,000 free blacks living in New Orleans before the war, many of them well integrated into the fabric of the city. But Lincoln had at least walked up to the subject. For him, taking the next step seems wholly imaginable.

Johnson made his own pass at black suffrage in much the same way Lincoln had—in a message to the provisional governor of Mississippi, William L. Sharkey, sent in mid-August 1865. "If you could extend the elective franchise to all persons of color who can read the Constitution of the United States in English and write their names, and all persons of color who own real estate valued at not less that two hundred and fifty dollars, and pay taxes thereon, you would completely disarm the adversary and set an example the other States will follow." Note, however, the profound difference in the two president's approaches. Though Johnson is suggesting black suffrage, he lades on so many requirements that not more than one Mississippi black in a thousand would have been eligible to vote in the summer of 1865, maybe one in 5,000. Both presidents clearly were moved in part by practical consideration, but with Johnson the politics are so naked, so obvious for everyone to see, that any hint of underlying compassion disappears. Whatever higher subjects he might have sought to address—and he never raised the issue again after Sharkey informed him on August 20 that suffrage was best left to the state legislature—Johnson is at heart being a pol. The Lincoln enshrined on the National Mall, beneath whose carved visage Martin Luther King Jr., delivered his "I Have a Dream" speech; the Lincoln impressed on every penny; the author of the Gettysburg Address—that man was a pol to be sure, yet his politics were ultimately transcendent.

Johnson had nothing like Lincoln's footwork, his humor, his facility with words, his soul; and he has paid dearly in the near century and a half since for the inevitable comparison. Nonetheless the reality is that in the only chance Lincoln got to make an official public determination concerning suffrage in the Rebel states, in his December 1863 proclamation, the Great Emancipator limited voters to those qualified "by the election law of the State existing immediately before the so-called act of secession, and excluding all others." Eighteen months later, on May 29, 1865, Johnson said almost the exact same thing. On every key point in the proclamation that launched him on the short road to oblivion, Johnson aped his predecessor. It wasn't policy, in short, that would bring him down so much as it was lack of political skills. Lincoln, one suspects, could have pulled it all off. Johnson couldn't.

Johnson was also a strict constructionist. Indeed, of all the clues to Johnson's essence, the ways in which he was likely to shape the peace, and the particulars of what he was ultimately to propose, it seems oddest that the Radicals so bitterly disappointed by the May 29 proclamations missed this most salient fact: The Constitution of the United States of America was Johnson's divine word.

It was for the Constitution that Johnson rose up in the Senate late in 1860 and through the spring and summer of 1861 to denounce his fellow Southerners and thereby brand himself a pariah. To protect and defend the Constitution, he risked life and limb for the three long years in Nashville, saw his property confiscated and his wife and youngest son abused by the enemy, lost a son-in-law and indirectly a son. The Constitution, not the Bible, was Johnson's text when he railed against traitors, when he thundered about stretching hemp. Treason was bad enough. Treason against a Union so perfectly conceived was odious. And the Constitution—as Johnson read and understood it—underlay every inch of the Reconstruction plan he offered up to the nation at the end of May 1865.

His treasury secretary, Hugh McCulloch, was absolutely right: Johnson's off-the-cuff remarks were intemperate, alarmingly so; yet give him time to fashion a response, to reason it out, to grind the issues in that gristmill of a mind, and he could be clarifying in the extreme. So it was with the State of the Union message he sent to the Thirty-ninth Congress on December 4, 1865, at the opening of its first session. "To fulfill my trust I need the support and confidence of all who are associated with me in the various departments of Government and the support and confidence of the people," Johnson wrote. "There is but one way in which I can hope to gain their necessary aid. It is to state with frankness the principles which guide my conduct, and their application to the present state of affairs." And in a little over 9,000 words of frank, sometimes even elevating prose, he went on to do that—to "unfold the principles on which I have sought to solve the momentous questions and overcome the appalling difficulties that met me at the very commencement of my Administration." (The quality of the writing, in this instance, probably owes much to the help of the historian George

Bancroft, but the principles he speaks of are clearly his own. Johnson never let anyone else think for him.)

The foundation of his Reconstruction policy, Johnson wrote, was "the supreme authority...the fundamental and unchanging principles of the Constitution," and they began with statehood, with what it meant and what obligations it entailed. Because the Constitution did not allow states to secede—a poison pill that Washington, Jefferson, and the others never would have agreed to—secession and the Confederate States of America had never happened. "The perpetuity of the Constitution brings with it the perpetuity of the States. Their mutual relation makes us what we are, and in our political system their connection is indissoluble. The whole can not exist without the parts, nor the parts without the whole. So long as the Constitution of the United States endures, the States will endure. The destruction of the one is the destruction of the other; the preservation of the one is the preservation of the other."

From that hard rock of reasoning, Johnson went on to lay out his entire argument. The states could not be treated as conquered territories, as Thaddeus Stevens and so many other Radical Republicans had wanted, because they had never ceased to be states. "The pretended acts of secession were from the beginning null and void.... The States attempting to secede placed themselves in a condition where their vitality was impaired, but not extinguished; their functions suspended, but not destroyed." What's more, since they were still states, still a part of the whole however worn and battered, the first duty of a responsible government was to return them to full health and function, and at the earliest possible moment. The perpetuation of martial law in the South would have had the opposite effect. "Military governments, established for an indefinite period, would have offered no security for the early suppression of discontent, would have divided the people into the vanquishers and the vanquished, and would have envenomed hatred rather than have restored affection."

Nor was it proper or even possible to impose on states that had never ceased to be states voting requirements that didn't apply to all states equally, any more than it would be proper or possible for the federal government today to impose a law on, say, Minnesota that didn't apply equally to California or New Jersey. In the case of suffrage this was especially true, since the Constitution so explicitly vested to each state the right to determine its own electors. "A concession of the elective franchise to the freedmen by act of the President of the United States must have been extended to all colored men, wherever found, and so must have established a change of suffrage in the Northern, Middle, and Western States, not less than in the Southern and Southwestern. Such an act would have created a new class of voters, and would have been an assumption of power by the President which nothing in the Constitution or laws of the United States would have warranted."

In this address, as he never did in his extemporaneous comments, Johnson recognized the risk of his approach. The states themselves must acquiesce to his terms; they must renew their allegiance to the United States. He had acted quickly to return the states and their people to full membership and citizenship because he felt he must, but the states and people must come along quickly with him. To allay the risk, to bring them along, he offered the full beneficence of his office: the power of pardon and amnesty. And to unite the people, North and South, Union and Confederate, in common purpose, he offered them all the chance to participate in the highest calling of the citizenry under the Constitution—the chance to amend that great document. "The evidence of sincerity in the future maintenance of the Union shall be put beyond any doubt by the ratification of the proposed amendment to the Constitution, which provides for the abolition of slavery forever within the limits of our country," Johnson wrote. "This is the measure which will efface the sad memory of the past; this is the measure which will most certainly call population and capital and security to those parts of the Union that need them most.... The adoption of the amendment reunites us beyond all power of disruption; it heals the wound that is still imperfectly closed: it removes slavery, the element which has so long perplexed and divided the country; it makes of us once more a united people, renewed and strengthened, bound more than ever to mutual affection and support."

The logic of all this can be painful to swallow. If raising militias and binding together to wage war against the Union didn't carry the states of the pretended Confederacy beyond the Union's bounds, then what could? (Johnson's answer, presumably: nothing.) And if the states had never left the Union, then how was it that the executive, or any other branch of government, now had the power to dictate terms whereby, in effect, the rebellious states could be returned to full membership?

The bulldog reasoning, the refusal to recognize, as Carl Schurz noted, that the Civil War was a circumstance "unforeseen in the Constitution," the determined steamrolling of one logical inconsistency after another is vintage Johnson. Yet the depth of his conviction was unquestionable. These were not just words. The Constitution was Johnson's one true thing, and in defense of it and the principles he drew from it, he came in his December 1865 State of the Union address as close to poetry as he was capable—a measure, one suspects, of his sincerity and the depth of his feeling, but not of his entire character.

The ugly side of Johnson's Reconstruction policy is the ugly side of the man himself. He was a racist, and not just by a modern understanding of the term. Johnson owned slaves. He apparently swapped one of them—something you do with farm equipment, perhaps, or furniture, not with people. Like all of us, he was a deeply flawed human being. Unlike all but a handful of us, his flaws found their way into the national debate at a tipping point in American history.

The same State of the Union address that speaks so eloquently about healing the wound of slavery "still imperfectly closed," the one that urges Americans North and South to abolish slavery so that we can again be a "united people...bound more than ever to mutual affection and support" can barely be bothered when it comes to the practical matters of how an uneducated and penniless people ripped from their homelands and compelled into labor are now to secure the blessings of life, liberty, and the pursuit of happiness. "It is one of the greatest acts on record to have brought 4,000,000 people into freedom," wrote Johnson. "The career of free industry must be fairly opened to them.... Good faith requires the security of the freedmen in their liberty and their property, their right to labor, and their right to claim the just return of their labor." With that, though, Johnson basically stops promising and starts preaching.

The freedmen's "future prosperity and condition must, after all, rest mainly on themselves," he went on. "If they fail, and so perish away, let us be careful that the failure shall not be attributable to any denial of justice." Is there a more darkly haunting phrase in all the literature of presidential addresses than "and so perish away"? In his Gettysburg Address, Lincoln had turned "perish" into a cry of hope—"that government of the people, by the people, for the people, shall not perish from the earth." Here, Johnson makes the word feel almost like a premonition. To avoid failing, Johnson went on, so they don't "perish away," the freedmen must show "patience and manly virtues," and they should look for their solace not to the federal government that freed them but to the states that once held them in slavery. "When the tumult of emotions that have been raised by the suddenness of the social change shall have subsided, it may prove that they will receive the kindest usage from some of those on whom they have heretofore most closely depended."

Johnson had offered this theory before, in his response to the National Equal Rights League. By the time he dragged it out again, in his State of the Union address, it was already discredited. Two days earlier, the Mississippi legislature had passed the first of the notorious Southern Black Codes—a collection of state laws that imposed plantation discipline on supposedly free workers and thus extended the virtual bondage of the descendants of so many former slaves for another century. Alabama and South Carolina would follow suit before the year was out. Meanwhile, the federal government at Johnson's urging seemed to be taking back with one hand what it had offered with the other. In late July 1865 the Freedmen's Bureau, newly launched under General

Oliver O. Howard, ordered that land then under cultivation by ex-slaves in the South need not be returned to its owners—one small leg up in the long struggle to economic self-sufficiency. That September, Johnson commanded Howard to rescind the order and restore all lands to their owners. In October, he did the same with the coastal lands Sherman had set aside for the freedmen after his march to the sea.

In part, Johnson's own story must have figured in here. Other than the tailor's customer who introduced him to that book of speeches, no one had ever raised a finger to help him. Still half a boy, he'd walked from Raleigh across the Great Smokies into Tennessee, carrying his family, almost literally, on his shoulders. He'd pulled himself up from nothing to the governor's mansion, the Senate, by chance the White House, all by dint of his own fierce determination. This was America, land of the self-reliant—Johnson was its emblem, its poster boy, its proof. Let the ex-slaves do the same if they could.

There was also, again, the Constitution to be considered, the right of the executive, the right of anyone to seize land and redistribute it. The rebel states had not ceased to be states. Their citizens need only take a loyalty oath to be forgiven for their crimes and restored to the full rights of citizenship. With the exception of slaves, Johnson's North Carolina proclamation had returned their property. The president's hands were tied by no less than the Founding Fathers and their great document.

So goes the argument on Johnson's behalf, yet something darker and uglier was at work. In his address and in his actions, Johnson willfully ignored the history that had landed Africans on American soil and held them here against their will. In his December 1866 State of the Union address, Johnson barely mentioned slavery, black suffrage, or the freedmen. He was obsessed with Congress' continuing refusal to seat the senators and representatives elected by his loyalist governments. A year later, though, in his 1867 address, Johnson came back to the subject with a vengeance, goaded by Congress' determination to enfranchise Southern blacks despite the president's wishes, and with his own reputation plunging into ruin. "If anything can be proved by known facts, if all reasoning upon evidence is not abandoned, it must be acknowledged that in the progress of nations Negroes have shown less capacity for government than any other race of people. No independent government of any form has ever been successful in their hands. On the contrary, wherever they have been left to their own devices, they have shown a constant tendency to relapse into barbarism."

Eric Foner suggests that the passage might be the most racist statement ever to appear in the official state papers of any American president. There's no defending it. The most that can be said is that Johnson's racism, while generic and rooted in the time, was also quite specific and singular to his own experience.

That brings us to the fourth reason Johnson's Reconstruction strategy failed so spectacularly and why he has been judged so harshly by history. To Johnson, the war was not about slavery or African Americans; it was an economic and class struggle among whites. There's a passage midway through Johnson's December 1865 State of the Union address that is both so revealing of the man and so central to the way he looked at the war and at the landscape of American history that it's worth quoting at some length.

> Now that slavery is at an end, or near its end, the greatness of its evil in the point of view of public economy becomes more and more apparent. Slavery was essentially a monopoly of labor, and as such locked the States where it prevailed against the incoming of free industry. Where labor was the property of the capitalist, the white man was excluded from employment, or had but the second best chance of finding it; and the foreign emigrant turned away from the region where his condition would be so precarious. With the destruction of the monopoly, free labor will hasten from all parts of the civilized world to assist in developing various and immeasurable resources which have hitherto lain dormant.

The eight or nine States nearest the Gulf of Mexico have a soil of exuberant fertility, a climate friendly to long life, and can sustain a denser population than is found as yet in any part of our country. And the future influx of population to them will be mainly from the North or from the most cultivated nations in Europe. From the sufferings that have attended them during our late struggle let us look away to the future, which is sure to be laden for them with greater prosperity than has ever before been known. The removal of the monopoly of slave labor is a pledge that those regions will be peopled by a numerous and enterprising population, which will vie with any in the Union in compactness, inventive genius, wealth, and industry.

Note who wins in this pollyannish vision of a postbellum South: the mechanic, the artisan, the working man who had been shut out of the old plantation economy, and the cultivated European eager to use hands and sinew to carve out a place in the New World—in short, Johnson's people. And look who loses: the monopolizer and the monopolized, masters and slaves, oligarchs and the new freedmen.

This is Andrew Johnson's Civil War. To protect their monopoly on labor, the planters urged secession. When Lincoln refused to let the states go peacefully, the slave owners duped the Southern yeomanry into believing the war was about other causes—states' rights, honor, chivalry, the sanctity of womanhood, satanic Lincoln—and there followed the bloodiest four years ever seen on the North American continent. Now, as one letter writer put it, the South lay "desolate, a horrible sacrifice to the insatiate ambition of a Class of unprincipled men." In the North, the sentiment was widespread. With Johnson, it was an article of faith. "Thank God that the tyrants [sic] rod has been broken," Johnson exulted in a January 13, 1865, letter to Lincoln, informing him that a Tennessee convention had approved an amendment forever abolishing slavery in the state. Tellingly, all the emphasis is on the tyrant's rod, not the slave beaten with it. That, too, is a stuck record with Johnson.

"Damn the Negroes!" he had shouted in that famous (or infamous) speech. "I am fighting those traitorous aristocrats, their masters!"

Johnson was thinking of the Southern workers cut off by the labor monopoly from the right to compete for wages when he declared in Nashville in October 1864 that the war "has freed more whites than blacks." And it was his vision of a wondrous new Tennessee purged of the planters, the common man at last ascendant, that he painted in October 1864 for that same Nashville crowd. "I say if [the] immense plantations were divided up and parceled out amongst a number of free, industrious, and honest farmers, it would give more good citizens to the Commonwealth, increase the wages of our mechanics, enrich the markets of our city, enliven all the arteries of trade, improve society, and conduce to the greatness and glory of the State." Fourteen months later, in his annual message to Congress, Johnson said essentially the same thing, and the freedmen still weren't part of the plan. A hidebound conservative in so many ways, Johnson was also a kind of racist Marxist: From the oligarchs according to their means, to the white workers according to their needs. What a union leader he might have made in a later era.

It is today almost heresy to talk about the Civil War as a class struggle. High-school textbooks, documentaries, and indeed the whole machinery by which history gets transmitted to future generations all tend to agree: The war was fought to right the awful wrongs of slavery. In the early 1860s, though, the idea that war had been a class struggle was anything but far-fetched. "Why do you not offer resolutions in Congress boldly affirming that this war will free the poor white man?" a New York lawyer and reformer named Lorenzo Sherwood wrote Johnson early in the conflict, not long after he had first claimed public attention. "...It is the poor white man, in shirt sleeves, who must be protected from the Southern oligarchy."

The *New York Times* chimed in its agreement, too, at the front and the back ends of the war. "Our readers will bear in mind that we have from the beginning of the war urged that this struggle was essentially a struggle between classes—the slave aristocracy and the people," ran an editorial on April 29, 1865. "We have always maintained that only as this feature is considered both in legislation and executive action, can we hope for a permanently successful issue." And in Johnson, the *Times* argued, the nation had a president uniquely suited to understand this critical element. "He has felt 'the cold shade' and heavy hand of a barbaric but able and desperate aristocracy; he has suffered untold wrong from them; he has been the object of their boundless scorn and contempt."

The *Times* would sour on Johnson soon enough—just about everyone would—but in those first forty-five days of his presidency, the *Times* saw a consistent logic emerging from all that ponderous thinking. Use the pardon—granted unconditionally by the Constitution to the president—to isolate the aristocracy and break its "social power" (another of Johnson's favorite phrases); appoint provisional governors in the Southern states who will be receptive to government of, by, and for the white working class (best of all, governors who, like William Holden in North Carolina, had risen up from the mudsill); keep the old planters busy in Washington petitioning the president for the full restoration of their citizenship; and let a New South blossom, an Eden of honest labor and perhaps not coincidentally a broad political base that Andy Johnson could ride to a full elected term in 1868 and reflected glory for centuries to come.

The plan failed miserably. Johnson had hoped that, in seeking pardons, the Southern aristocracy might dwell on the enormity of its crimes. Instead, it used the pardons to pursue the political power that had been stripped from it. Repentance wasn't in the aristocracy, or, so it seemed, in the South generally. "There is the same arrogance, the same materialistic mode of thought, which reckons the strength and value of a country by the amount of its crops rather than by the depth of political principle which inspires its people, the same boyish conceit on which even defeat wastes its lessons." So lamented the noted poet, social and literary critic, and diplomat James Russell Lowell in an 1865 essay titled "Scotch the Snake, or Kill It?" (Ambassador to both Spain and England in his later years, Lowell is part of the same distinguished New England family as the twentieth-century poets Amy Lowell and Robert Lowell.) Johnson, at least, seemed to get the gist of Lowell's message. By the end of August 1865, he was pointedly relaying to his provisional governors complaints that instead of appointing loyal Union men, they were "giving a decided preference to those who have participated in the Rebellion."

Nor was there any economic base for Johnson's glorious revolution to spring from. The ex-Confederacy was tapped out, its human capital depleted along with its bank balances, its institutions in shambles. "The war has left [the Southern states] nothing they can fairly call their own politically but helplessness and confusion," Lowell wrote in the same essay. The noble common man the president so idealized proved in practice more apt to join the Ku Klux Klan than to extend a welcome, upward-lifted hand of friendship to the former slaves. And the freedmen were barely that, an unfinished business that would weigh on the region for generations.

One question remains about Johnson's pardons: To what extent, consciously or otherwise, were they meant to extract a measure of grim personal satisfaction? From his childhood on, Johnson had indeed felt the cold shade and heavy hand of the aristocracy. Now the holders of those vast estates that were economically viable only with forced and unpaid labor, the genteel and the blue-blooded, all had to come to him and tell America they were sorry and ready to mend their ways.

They did arrive, by the thousands, as Johnson knew they would. Among the first to apply for a pardon was a soldier who had half expected to be indicted instead on treason charges by a grand jury meeting in Norfolk, Virginia: Robert E. Lee. In a June 13 letter to the president, Lee catalogued in almost telegraphic fashion his many exclusions from the general amnesty: "I graduated at the Mil: Academy at W. Point in June 1829. Resigned from the U.S. Army April '61. Was a General in the Confederate Army, & included in the surrender of the Army of N. Va: 9 April '65." To Southern die-hards, Lee's request amounted to a capitulation to an illegal authority. For most excluded ex-Confederates, though, the general's request served as a seal of approval. If Lee, why not us? There were practical considerations, too. Only loyal citizens could gain work in the new civilian governments, and in the broken economy of the postwar South, paying work was in desperately short supply.

Between June and August 1865, Johnson awarded nearly 5,300 pardons for residents of Alabama, North Carolina, and Virginia alone. Figure in the rest of the states, the rest of the pardon seekers, and there could have been little time for anything else. The White House was so crammed with pardon seekers during the summer and fall that pardon brokers sprang up to grease the process and their own palms. Scandal spread, as was only to be expected under the circumstances; the whole business begged for corruption. By October, even the Confederate vice president, Alexander Stephens, fresh out of prison at Fort Warren in Boston Harbor, had received his absolution from the president. Four months later, Stephens was elected to the U.S. Senate from his native Georgia, although the Senate declined to seat him.

By all accounts, Johnson received his petitioners with the same good manners that were forever surprising those who expected the drunken boor portrayed in the Southern and Copperhead press. Sometimes, he even bantered with his callers, as if it were a social visit, as if he hadn't commanded their presence. Having launched the pardoning marathon, the president became almost a slave to it. He rose with the sun, was in his office by nine and worked until four, almost all that time spent on pardons for the legions clamoring in his anterooms. Johnson returned to his office around nine in the evening, after dinner and a spot of fresh air, and worked away until eleven. As always, he was a grind.

Johnson's biographer Hans Trefousse writes that it is at least "debatable" whether the president took great pleasure in responding to these "pleas of haughty Southerners." The power to pardon was the one Constitutional tool he had in his kit. Why not use it? Eric McKitrick, by contrast, paints the president as almost giddy with revenge: "How sweet would any words of contrition have sounded in his ears!"

At this remove, and without better evidence, it's hard to say either way, but there must surely have been some satisfaction in it. Bottom rail was on top in this way, too, but like that other bottom rail the ex-slaves talked about, this one wouldn't stay on top for long.

In fashioning his version of Reconstruction, Johnson might also have listened to some of the better angels of his own nature. This is sheer speculation, but it's hard to resist the idea that in the final tweaking of his May 29 proclamations, Johnson was influenced by the grand review that had ended five days earlier. Possibly, as he stood there on the reviewing stand shoulder to shoulder with Meade, Sherman, and the others, Johnson was struck by something like the same sentiment that Ulysses Grant expressed so powerfully to his wife, Julia, in an April 25 letter sent from Raleigh:

"The suffering that must exist in the South the next year, even with the war ending now, will be beyond conception. People who talk now of further retalliation [sic] and punishment, except of the political leaders, either do not conceive of the suffering endured already or they are heartless and unfeeling and wish to stay at home, out of danger, whilst the punishment is being inflicted."

Johnson was almost certainly one of those Grant was writing about in his letter home, but unlike Stevens, Wade, Julian, and the other Radicals whose chorus the president seemed to be leading, Johnson had also been in the thick of the battle and in great physical danger for almost three years. Far more so than any Washington-bound politician, he had seen close up the devastation that already existed in the South. And it was, after all, his native land. In the end, perhaps all that came together. Maybe Johnson let 'em up easy not just because he was listening to the better angels of Abraham Lincoln's nature, but because he, too, had been touched. Certainly, that's the kindest interpretation that can be put to his actions and policies.

———

A final reason to throw into the mix: Johnson couldn't help himself. It's easy enough to say that Andy Johnson was a Jacksonian and thus, like Jackson, was bound to butt heads with Congress, but the issue goes deeper than that. Johnson sought out conflict the way a desert traveler seeks out an oasis. Conflict nourished him. It animated him and stoked the furnace of his intellect. Johnson's rhetorical tools had been sharpened on the stump. His personal courage had been tested and found whole on the killing fields of Tennessee. Conflict, not serenity, made life meaningful for him. And conflict is exactly what he got.

The ink was barely dry on Johnson's elegant December 1865 State of the Union address before he and the Congress he had so intentionally ignored fell into a series of running skirmishes that led inevitably to what one historian has termed "the savage years of the tragic era." The newly elected senators and representatives from the ex-Confederate states arrived in Washington only to find Congress unwilling to recognize their legitimacy. The president vetoed bills, including one to extend the Freedman's Bureau; Congress passed them over his opposition. Used to taking matters to the people, Johnson reminded one and all of his humble origins, then denounced Senate and House leaders in terms more fit for a barroom shouting match than a political debate. (In an 1866 essay on the president, James Russell Lowell drolly noted that the electorate was more interested in where Johnson "had arrived at than where he started from.") The people responded by packing Congress even more fully with Johnson's growing list of enemies. The civil authority the president sought to establish in the ex-Confederate states yielded to the martial law the Radicals had wanted from the first.

"A few of our people are in their element now—perfectly happy," Massachusetts congressman Henry L. Dawes wrote to his wife on March 31, 1866. "They can cry and howl and...alarm the country at the terrible crisis the President has involved us in, and he is fool enough, or wicked enough...to furnish them with material fuel for the flame, depriving every friend he has of the least ground upon which to stand and defend him." In fact, things would only get worse.

On March 2, 1867, on its second-to-last day in session, the Thirty-ninth Congress passed, over Johnson's veto, a truly awful piece of legislation: the Tenure of Office Act, which forbade the president from removing any official, including cabinet members, who had been appointed with the consent of the Senate. As sure as the tides, Johnson responded by vowing, according to his private secretary, Colonel William G. Moore, that if he could not be president in fact, he would not be president in name alone. On August 5, Johnson asked for the resignation of Edwin Stanton, and with that, the last battle was on. "The whole Senate seemed to catch hysterics of nervous bucking without apparent reason," Henry Adams wrote in his famous autobiography. "Great leaders, like Sumner, and Conkling, could not be burlesqued; they were more grotesque than ridicule could make them." Johnson was impeached by the House on eleven articles. Eight of them had to do with Stanton, who had finally barricaded himself in his office—more burlesque for a theater already full of it. A ninth article was a trumped-up charge involving the Army Appropriations Act. Number ten held that Johnson had delivered "intemperate, inflammatory and scandalous harangues . . . as well against Congress as the laws of the United States"—every word of it true, and true to Johnson's character, but none of it a firing offense. For the eleventh and concluding article, Thaddeus Stevens cobbled together a grab bag of items meant to give political cover to senators who didn't want to tackle the president directly on the main issue of Stanton.

Tried in the Senate over ten weeks, from March 5 to May 16, 1868, during which he studiously avoided the proceedings, Johnson escaped conviction by a lone vote—an act of conscience that would earn the senator who cast it, Edmund Ross of Kansas, his own chapter in John F. Kennedy's *Profiles in Courage*, and kept in office a president who had been otherwise thoroughly stripped of his powers, the lamest of lame ducks. The Tenure of Office Act, which kicked off the entire spectacle, would remain in effect for nearly two more decades, and bedevil other presidents, until it was repealed in 1887.

What would it have taken for Johnson to strike at least a tentative truce with the Radical Republicans before the miserable spectacle got underway? Some sort of delay mechanism attached to his plan for provisional governments—a probationary period so that states recently at war with the Union weren't rushed back into it? Maybe a simple nod to black suffrage would have done the job—something like the plan he outlined to Mississippi's William Sharkey two months after he had delivered his proclamations—or some kind of recognition of black entitlement to plantation lands formerly worked by slaves. All the freedmen were asking was a chance to feed their families by the sweat of their own brows. Perhaps Johnson could have called a brief special session of Congress to glean its sense before he acted. At the least, he might have made an effort to explain his reasoning face to face to the Radicals in May, rather than through his annual message in December. Any bone of conciliation would have been better than none.

Although Johnson had come to office as Lincoln's vice president, he had almost no leverage within the Republican Party itself. To win Congress over to his vision of a reconstructed nation, he needed the Republican leadership on his side. Working together, they might even have come up with something novel—a proto-Marshall Plan, say, for the devastated South, a public expenditure to build up the economy and win the loyalty of freed slaves and white workers alike. Almost anything would have been better than what Reconstruction actually became.

Andy Johnson didn't have it in him: neither conciliation nor creativity. His synapses didn't leap that way; his neurons wouldn't fire in that direction. It was his way or the highway, and his way seemed always to be right through a brick wall. "Who, four years ago, looking down the stream of time, could have delineated that which has transpired since then?" Johnson told a delegation on April 21, 1865, six days after he was sworn in as president. "Had any one done so, and presented it, he would have been looked upon as insane, or it would have been thought a fable—fabulous as the stories of the Arabian Nights, as the wonders of the lamp of Aladdin, and would have been about as readily believed."

Johnson was talking about the war, but he could have equally been talking about himself. Looking down that stream of time, who would have thought it possible that an iconoclastic Tennessee senator would do so much to steel Northern resolve in those dark days of 1861, or that when the fighting was finally over, the same Southern ex-slaveholder and Democrat would be sitting in the White House.

Andy Johnson was the greatest man of his age, the *Times* had decreed at the start of the war. He was the Avenger, heaven-sent, to right the worst wrongs of American history. Pulpit after pulpit rang with that message on that Black Easter after Lincoln's death. Johnson was also his own worst enemy, almost pathologically obstinate, inflexible as pig iron. In the end, this is what ruined him. Fate handed Andrew Johnson the position he had so long wanted at a time in American history when he was certain to fail, and do so spectacularly. He inherited Lincoln's challenges without Lincoln's capacities to see them through. Johnson couldn't take his place. No one could. The result was a tragedy for the nation and for African Americans. It remains a cautionary tale.

Epilogue

The failure of Reconstruction was less a matter of poor policy than of immoderate men living in incendiary times facing intractable problems. It wasn't only Abraham Lincoln who wanted to let the South up easy, and it wasn't only Robert E. Lee and the *New York Times* editors who thought Andrew Johnson had struck the right balance.

Senator Henry Wilson of Massachusetts would later take his place among the Radical Republicans who sought Johnson's scalp, but in an 1865 letter to his fellow senator, James Warren Nye of Nevada, Wilson wrote, "I do not consider it either generous, manly, or Christian, to nourish or cherish or express feelings of wrath and hatred toward [the South]." Henry Ward Beecher—the most famous clergyman of his day, a leader of the antislavery movement, and brother of Harriet Beecher Stowe—echoed Wilson in an October 22, 1865, sermon preached before what the newspapers described as an "immense audience." "Nothing better than a generous and trustful spirit to those who have been in error can crown our victories," Beecher told parishioners at his Plymouth Congregational Church in Brooklyn. "... When the crime of slavery blotted our fair page, charity was a mistake and a witness against us in favor of slavery. Now things are changed. The cause of trouble is removed, and it has become our privilege and duty, as it is my pleasure, to plead for a large measure of good will and love towards all men."

What's more, Beecher went on, "it is best for us that restoration should at once commence" and that "all men should partake actively in the administration of civil affairs." No dawdling. No prolonged occupation. This was essentially what Andy Johnson had ordered up, and Beecher was quick to acknowledge the debt. "We have never had a man in the Presidential chair who has proven himself more wise in the solution of questions brought to him than President Johnson....Let me express my gratitude to God that He had appointed without our forethought, and almost without our knowledge, a man singularly fitted to take up the work where his martyred predecessor left it."

Even those who couldn't contain their wrath toward the former enemy—those who, in Winston Churchill's words, wanted to subject the late Confederacy "to Army rule of the kind that Cromwell had once imposed on England"— weren't quite ready to overturn Southern institutions completely, at least not in the early going. Thaddeus Stevens wanted to do more than redistribute the land of former slaveholders and impose Union rule at the point of a sword; he wanted to "revolutionize [the] feelings and principles" of the South. "Do not they deserve humiliation?" Stevens once asked. "If they do not, who does? What criminal, what felon deserves it more?" Yet on the matter of black suffrage, Stevens was willing to wait "four or five years...when the freedmen shall have been made free indeed, when they shall have become intelligent enough, and there are sufficient loyal men there to control the representation from those states." Principle was one thing; having the slaves vote Democratic like their former masters was another matter entirely.

Less than a year away from some of the most shameful diatribes ever delivered by an American president, Andy Johnson was sounding positively statesmanlike as the summer of 1865 turned into fall. "We must not be in too much of a hurry," he told George Stearns in a lengthy White House interview. "It is better to let them reconstruct themselves than to force them to it; for if they go wrong, the power is in our hands and we can check them...and oblige them to correct their errors. We must be patient with them. I did not expect to keep out all who were

excluded from the amnesty, or even a large number of them, but I intended they should sue for pardon and so realize the enormity of the
crime they had committed."

On enfranchising blacks, Johnson told Stearns that his position as
president was different than it would be were he still governor of Tennessee. "There, I should try to introduce negro suffrage gradually—first
those who had served in the army; those who could read and write, and
perhaps a property qualification for others, say $200 or $250." To introduce universal suffrage now, Johnson said, was both unconstitutional
and ill considered. "The negro will vote with the late master whom he
does not hate, rather than with the non-slaveholding white, whom he
does hate. Universal suffrage would create another war, not against us,
but a war of races."

This was not entirely Henry Ward Beecher's position, nor that of
Thaddeus Stevens—Johnson as always was looking out for his own
base: the workers and small farmers of his eastern Tennessee redoubt.
But they were not that far apart, either. Politics, after all, is the art of
seizing common ground.

Yet whatever tendency there was toward moderation, toward something approaching a middle way, was swept up in the magnitude of the
problem: almost half the land mass east of the Mississippi in shambles;
Texas still uncertain; four million refugees set loose on a barren land—
nearly one-hundred times those displaced by Hurricane Katrina by way
of comparison—and in an area far greater than the Gulf region. And
this was in a nation with almost no permanent federal infrastructure.
The magnitude of the problem was, in turn, magnified by the inelastic-
ity of those charged by law and duty with solving it.

If Andrew Johnson could have looked forward to that "stream of
time" he talked about in April and seen what his version of Reconstruction would so quickly become—Black Codes, empty loyalty oaths,
power seized not by Johnson's long-suffering commoners but by the
planter class—would he have done anything more to correct course
than send additional hectoring letters to his provisional governors? And

if Thaddeus Stevens could have done the same with the Reconstruction he so longed for—could have seen that it would end for African Americans in bad faith and broken dreams—would he have acted differently? One doubts it in both cases. This train was headed off a cliff from the moment it left the station.

Presidential Reconstruction was dead and gone by the end of 1866. Johnson's effort to kill the Freedmen's Bureau, the one government agency specifically charged with ameliorating the lot of the former slaves; his veto of the Civil Rights Bill, the first veto of a major piece of legislation ever overturned by Congress; what became known as his "swing around the circle," a collection of intemperate stump speeches he never should have delivered; and the overwhelming evidence that the new order of the South was pretty much the same old gang—all this dried up public support and finally drove voters into the Radicals' fold. Johnson stood by his principles until he had barely a patch of ground to call his own, until he was in effect providing aid and comfort to the very traitors he had sworn vengeance on. That, too, was in his fundamental nature.

The elections that November handed Reconstruction to Congress, which couldn't wait to get started. Instead of provisional state governments and a quick march toward a renewed Union, the ex-Confederacy was divided into five military territories. The first public schools were established in the South. Manhood suffrage replaced race suffrage: Below the Potomac, at least, it was only women, black or white, who couldn't vote now. The state governments that reemerged were Republican ones, protected by the full authority of the United States military. Blacks served on juries; they took their place in state legislatures. In 1869, in perhaps the high point of Congressional Reconstruction, Mississippi's Hiram Revels, the first black man elected to the U.S. Senate, won the seat formerly occupied by none other than Jefferson Davis.

Capital reappeared in the South, too: in the form of Yankee speculators and financiers, eager to secure for themselves the blessings of land and resources that the cash-starved ex-planters had once worked with slave labor. Public improvement projects followed, many of them having to do with railroads; and greed and scandal came trailing behind, as they always do, following the loose money. It was the usual mix of doing good and doing well, fortified in this case by the stakes—a race of people, a whole section of the country—and darkened by the Klan and other expressions of the deep resentment that white Southerners felt at having a future imposed on them. (Already the South was practicing the massive resistance that would emerge with such vehemence a century hence, in the civil rights struggles of the 1960s.)

Then the Panic of 1873 merged with the scandals, the KKK terror campaign, and the philanthropic fatigue that had already started to settle in—a perfect storm—and the problems of the South and of the former slaves and their still-precarious existence began to seem both very expensive and, for most non-Southerners, very remote. Having nearly destroyed the delicate balance of power between Congress and the executive branch in its rush to impeach and remove Andrew Johnson, the House and Senate disgraced themselves further by bartering away the results of the presidential election of 1876.

Although the Democratic candidate, Samuel Tilden, had won the popular contest by 250,000 votes (of about 4.3 million cast) and appeared to have won the electoral count as well, two Southern states, Florida and Louisiana, submitted multiple, competing results. To resolve the impasse, a congressional committee composed of eight Republicans and seven Democrats met and awarded all the disputed votes to the Republican candidate, Rutherford B. Hayes, just enough to give him a one-vote victory in the Electoral College. In return for conceding that fiction, Democrats secured from Hayes an agreement to withdraw federal troops from the South and allow the last Republican state governments to fall. (Only three remained: Florida, Louisiana, and South Carolina.) And that really was it for Reconstruction. The Republicans kept the White House, and Southern blacks were left to the tender mercies of all-white legislatures and courts and juries, on which once more they could no longer serve.

Andrew Johnson didn't attend Ulysses Grant's inauguration as America's eighteenth president on March 4, 1869. Grant refused to ride in the same carriage as his predecessor. Now, although a second carriage waited to take Johnson from the White House down Pennsylvania Avenue to the Capitol, he refused at the last minute to take it. Two weeks later, on March 18, Johnson, Eliza, his daughter Martha Patterson and son Robert, and a handful of others left Washington by train for Greeneville. In Charlottesville, Virginia, he was cheered so lustily that he felt compelled to give a brief speech. More cheering crowds waited in Lynchburg, where eight years earlier Johnson had been burned in effigy and nearly assaulted in his train car by an angry mob. From Bristol to Greeneville, where Rebel raiders had once dogged his steps, Johnson was carried home like some Roman emperor. Now that Congress was in charge of Reconstruction, the Scourge of the South had become its champion, maybe the greatest oddity of all of that odd and trying time.

Johnson was gone from Washington when Grant named Edwin Stanton to fill a vacant seat on the Supreme Court, a recognition of a brilliant legal mind but also a reward for Stanton's role in helping bring Johnson to the brink of removal from office. (Ben Wade of Ohio, the president pro tempore of the Senate, would have taken over the presidency had Johnson been convicted, but by then the Radicals were already running government with a rarely encumbered hand.) Johnson was gone from Washington, too, on December 24, 1869, when Stanton died there four days after having his appointment confirmed by the Senate. But Washington was never far from Andy Johnson's mind. Politics was what he knew, political battle was his raison d'être, and he had long ago outgrown the quiet ways of Greeneville.

That October, Johnson barely missed being returned to the Senate by the Tennessee legislature. Three years later, in 1872, he finished a dismal third in the race for a House seat. The following summer, still in Greeneville, he was so sickened with cholera that he penned what he thought were his last words: "Here I will rest in quiet and peace beyond the reach of calumny's poisoned shaft—the influence of envy and jealous enemies—where treason and traitors in state, backsliders and hypocrites in church can have no place."

Johnson did recover, though, and in January 1875, he was returned to the U.S. Senate on the fifty-fifth ballot cast by the Tennessee legislature. "I feel it is the greatest victory of your life," Martha wrote him, and so it must have felt to Andy Johnson when he first took his Senate seat on March 5, at a desk covered with flowers, to the thundering applause of his colleagues and from the gallery. Sweet vindication, though brief.

In late July 1875, with Congress adjourned, Johnson traveled by train, then by horseback seven hours in the hot sun to join Eliza at the farm of their daughter Mary, near Carter's Station, Tennessee. At four P.M. on the afternoon of his arrival, Johnson suffered a stroke that left him paralyzed on his left side. Two days later, seemingly on the road to recovery, came a second stroke. He died at two thirty the following morning, July 31, four months shy of his sixty-seventh birthday.

"It is not often that kindly mention is made of him upon the platform or in the press," Hugh McCulloch wrote in his 1888 memoir. "Among those who have filled high places with ability, or rendered distinguished services to their country, his name is rarely classed; and yet when the history of the great events with which he was connected has been faithfully written, there will appear few names entitled to greater honor and respect than that of Andrew Johnson."

That, of course, has not happened. Nor is it ever likely to. There was too much missing in the man. His weaknesses and the parallel ones of the Congress he battled for so long left us with unresolved issues of race that haunt the nation to this day. "If we only emancipate [the negro], he will not let us go free," James Russell Lowell warned in his 1865 essay on Reconstruction. That's what happened, and Johnson must always bear part, perhaps even the brunt, of that blame. Little wonder that history, so far from Hugh McCulloch's prediction, should remember our seventeenth president so poorly and ignore him so thoroughly—a strange fate for a man so impossible to ignore in his own day.

The Civil War was the watershed moment in American history, the great testing point of the founding document, a Constitution that had existed for less than seventy-five years when the war began. The nation survived the challenge—survived all the killing, the bitterness, the disunity. The United States, plural, became the United States, singular, a remarkable achievement. Reconstruction was the chance to do more—to heal the wounds of history, to correct America's worst sins, to let not just a restored nation but a better one flourish. That test, the nation failed. The war, it seemed, brought out the better angels in many leaders, Lincoln most profoundly. It magnified his virtues and projected them onto a stage with the world as his audience. Reconstruction did the opposite. It evoked the demons in Lincoln's successor and in his enemies in Congress. It let loose their worst qualities and provoked a second constitutional crisis that would serve to diminish the executive branch for decades to come and leave us with a string of presidents so forgettable that even A history students are challenged to name them all. (Ulysses Grant was the exception, but only because of his war reputation.) Worse by far, Reconstruction failed the Americans who had suffered most under the Old South's yoke, an unforgivable breach of duty. The goal of this book has never been to exonerate Andrew Johnson for his role in that. Far from it. The goal has been to show how central Johnson was to the drama and to the times that surrounded it. His failures are with us still.

Acknowledgments

This book has benefited immeasurably from the work of a vast array of historians and biographers, including—to cite only the most obvious—Hans L. Trefousse, Eric L. McKitrick, and Eric Foner. I'm grateful to every one of them, and I hope I've done their work justice. The multivolume *Papers of Andrew Johnson*, published by the University of Tennessee Press and edited first by LeRoy P. Graf and Ralph W. Haskins and later by Paul H. Bergeron, are a model of scholarship. When I began this book, I had no idea that my wife's great-grandfather, Robert W. Winston, had written a full biography of Andrew Johnson. Thanks to his grandson Robert Winston "Judge" Carr for mentioning the work, and thanks to my father-in-law, George Watts Carr Jr., for providing me with his copy, including the author's handwritten notes. It will be returned to its owner the worse for wear. The Library of Congress, where I conducted much of my research, is a paragon of quiet excellence and a national treasure. I'm grateful to so many staff members for their help and patience. The public-library systems in Montgomery County, Maryland, and Frederick and Clarke counties, Virginia, and the Kiplinger Research Library at the City Museum of Washington, D.C., were also valuable resources. Thanks, too, to the Lancaster County (Pennsylvania) Historical Society for its collection of Civil War–era newspapers. In his later years, my father volunteered at the Historical Society, so I already knew how dedicated the staff is. The online Valley Project, created by Edward L. Ayers, provides ready access to a treasure chest of original Civil War sources in Augusta County, Virginia, and Franklin County, Pennsylvania.

Without the help of my agent, Rafe Sagalyn, *The Avenger Takes His Place* would never have been written; and without the help of my editor at Harcourt, Timothy Bent, it would never have been written anywhere near so well. The flaws are mine; the deft touches, Tim's. Working with him has been an object lesson in what good editing is all about.

Thanks to so many friends for listening to me ramble on about Andrew Johnson and for asking the pointed questions and suggesting books and articles that helped shaped my thinking and led me in directions I would not have found on my own. Any attempt to list everyone here would be woefully incomplete. I'll have to trust that you know how thoroughly I value your support. Special thanks, though, to Ben Lamberton, Dan Rapoport, and to Brewster Willcox; and to John Larson, for calculating the number of days that elapsed between the assassinations of Abraham Lincoln and John F. Kennedy. The answer, 36,016, didn't reveal much, but getting there without John's help would have taken me days. My brother and sister, Tom Means and Mary Ellen Willcox, were, as always, encouraging. So were my daughter and son, Ihrie and Nathan, and Nathan's partner, Xan Hamilton. Halfway through the writing of this book, Caper Hamilton Means came into this world and provided added inspiration and sheer joy. May he never live in times as terrible as those that brought Andrew Johnson to the presidency and ruined his reputation. My first reader and critic, chief photocopier, inexhaustible sounding board, and total stalwart in every way has been my wife, Candy. All credit to her.

Endnotes

Preface

Nearly a century and a half after John Wilkes Booth's derringer: *The New York Times*; Aug. 1, 1875; p. 1.

With Andy Johnson, what you saw was what you got: All quotes from Oliver Temple can be found in *Notable Men of Tennessee: From 1833 to 1875* (Cosmopolitan Press, 1912).

Remarkable, indeed, especially those vast "causality" protuberances: Shelby Foote quotes are from pp. 181–183, *The Correspondence of Shelby Foote and Walker Percy*, ed. Jay Tolson (W. W. Norton, 1997).

Four months later, alarmed by two extended illnesses: Until the ratification of the Twenty-fifth Amendment to the Constitution in February 1967, any vice president who succeeded to the presidency served out his term without a number two. Gerald Ford, chosen to succeed the disgraced Spiro Agnew, was the first nonelected VP. Nelson Rockefeller, who took over the office when Ford rose to the presidency with Richard Nixon's resignation, was the second.

Johnson was the only president to be entirely self-taught: *The Papers of Andrew Johnson*, volume 1 (University of Tennessee Press, 1967), p. 14.

Johnson was the third vice president: The parallels and congruences between the Lincoln and Kennedy assassinations have been bantered around ever since 1963. Both were succeeded by vice presidents named Johnson. Both Johnsons were Southern Democrats and former senators, with an unlucky thirteen letters in their combined first and last names. Now, thanks to the Internet, the speculation, like viruses, replicates endlessly. One Web site maintains that both assassinations were "bipartisan Masonic coups." (Andrew Johnson had been made a Mason in 1851.) By way of support, it offers up the astounding "fact" that in 1865 at least two newspapers published "highly detailed stories of the Lincoln assassination several hours before it ever took place." (See www.freemasonrywatch.org for an example.) It could also be noted that Lincoln and Kennedy died exactly 36,016 days apart and that Lyndon Johnson, the end point of this unholy alliance of numbers, was the thirty-sixth president and Abraham Lincoln, its beginning, the sixteenth, or that the digits of 36,016 add up to sixteen, as in Lincoln the sixteenth president.

The final battle of the war: Such was the state of medicine during the Civil War that soldiers who were wounded or fell seriously ill had a better chance of dying than surviving. Figures for Iowans who fought in the war are representative of the armies on both sides: Of the roughly 13,000 Iowans killed in the Civil War, 3,540 died in battle, another 515 perished in prisoner of war camps, and nearly 8,500 died of disease. By the First World War, American combatants who suffered nonmortal wounds exceeded fatalities by nearly two to one. It should be noted, too, that casualty figures for the Confederacy are of necessity approximations and tend to vary fairly widely. Record keeping in the South was never the equal of record keeping in the North. The numbers used in this book represent a middle ground from multiple sources.

Into this volatile mix now stepped Andy Johnson: In all, Johnson owned eight or perhaps nine slaves. He paid $500 for the first one, a young girl named Dolly, purchased in 1842. Dolly, so the story goes, asked Johnson to buy her after having a good look at other prospective owners at the auction where she was being sold. Johnson later bought her half brother, Sam, as well. Legend has it that Johnson never sold a slave, but he does appear to have traded a thirteen-year-old male named Henry in 1851. For more, see Hans L. Trefousse, *Andrew Johnson: A Biography* (W. W. Norton, 1989), p. 45 and elsewhere; and David Warren Bowen, *Andrew Johnson and the Negro* (University of Tennessee Press, 1989). As Bowen points out, at various times Johnson maintained he owned anywhere from seven to ten slaves.

Johnson's politics were always hard to pin down: Banished by Lincoln to the South, Vallandigham eventually traveled to Bermuda and Canada, from where he conducted an unsuccessful campaign for Ohio governor. He returned to the U.S. in June 1864 and helped write a radical peace plank at that summer's Democratic presidential convention.

Chapter 1: Kirkwood House

Almost alone among the crowd at Fords Theatre: The Dictionary of Wisconsin History, an online resource, cites the 1960 *Dictionary of Wisconsin Biography*.

Leonard Farwell, Johnson's would-be savior: Information on Leonard Farwell's role as a civic promoter comes from an article by Stuart Levitan in the January 2005 issue of *Madison Magazine*, the first installment of a multipart series celebrating the 150th anniversary of the city. Farwell's role in naming Madison's lakes is courtesy of the Dade County (Wisconsin) Lakes and Watershed Commission.

The U.S. Capitol had two new wings: The Capitol dome was completed in 1863, thanks to Lincoln's insistence that the work go on despite the war.

Seven weeks later, on June 3, 1865: All quotes from testimony before the military commission are from the three-volume set entitled *The Conspiracy Trial for the Murder of the President*, edited by Benjamin Perley Poore (J. E. Tilton, 1865). Farwell's testimony begins on p. 174 of volume 3.

The challenge of sorting out the actual conspirators: See Michael W. Kauffman, *American Brutus* (Random House, 2004), pp. 154–55.

The task of murdering Seward: Powell would ultimately be indicted, tried, and executed under the name Lewis Paine, the alias he used in January 1865 when he took an oath of allegiance to the Union. See Kauffman, p. 165.

"The assassin then rushed into the chamber . . .": This item, the otherwise reliable *New York Herald* reporter seems to have muffed. According to Kauffman (pp. 231–32), Major Clarence Seward was not in Washington the night of April 14, 1865.

A modern account of the same events: Kauffman, pp. 22–24.

Mad, he might well have been: The $7.2 million paid for Alaska translates to about $90 million in today's dollars, a shade more than 10 percent of what a group led by Daniel Snyder spent in 1999 to purchase the Washington Redskins football franchise. As to why Booth included William Seward among those to be assassinated: Under the terms of the Presidential Succession Act of 1792, which still applied when Booth and his colleagues struck, assassinating both Lincoln and Johnson would have decapitated the executive branch until a new president could be chosen by special session of the Electoral College. As secretary of state, Seward would have been responsible for calling the electors together, a further incentive to add Seward to the list of those to be murdered. The Presidential Succession Act of 1886 made the secretary of state—as head of the oldest of the cabinet departments—the next in line for the nation's highest office should the president and vice president die or be killed in office or be incapacitated.

Atzerodt did check into the Kirkwood House: *The Conspiracy Trial*, Lee's testimony begins on p. 62, volume 1.

Just as clearly, Atzerodt had set about: *The Conspiracy Trial*, Nevins's testimony begins on p. 277, volume 2.

"I told him I would have a glass of beer . . .": *The Conspiracy Trial*, Fletcher's testimony begins on p. 326, volume 1.

An hour or so later: *The Conspiracy Trial*, Briscoe's testimony begins on p. 402, volume 1, and resumes on p. 507, volume 2.

By no later than one that evening: *The Conspiracy Trial*, Walker's testimony begins on p. 390, volume I.

Atzerodt would later testify that the weapons: The Frederick Road of 1865 is modern-day Wisconsin Avenue, Rockville Pike, and Maryland State Route 355.

Forensically, the note was—and remains—meaningless: John Matthews, the friend and fellow actor to whom Booth entrusted the letter, opened it backstage at Ford's Theatre, where he was among the performers on the night of Lincoln's assassination, and promptly burned the evidence.

If the latter was his aim, it worked: Orne was the wife of a prosperous Philadelphia carpet-maker. It's worth noting, too, that the definition of a "miserable inebriate" had changed dramatically in Andrew Johnson's lifetime. In 1830, when Johnson was in his early twenties, white American males age fifteen and older consumed on average about five ounces of 100-proof alcohol a day. By the 1850s, a succession of temperance movements had cut the average consumption by almost two-thirds. In *Mary Todd Lincoln: A Biography* (W. W. Norton, 1987), Jean H. Baker suggests that Willie's fatal typhoid fever might have been caused by the lack of sanitation in a city that had drastically outgrown its infrastructure as the war progressed.

Mrs. Lincoln was not the only one in the president's box: Clara Harris Rathbone was the daughter of a U.S. senator from New York. At age seventeen, Henry Rathbone had inherited $200,000 upon his father's death, after which his mother married Clara's father. Thus, Henry and Clara were step-siblings as well as husband and wife. The Rathbones' sad story is told in Thomas Mallon's novel *Henry and Clara*.

It's possible, even, to argue that the assassination: An article in the May 28, 1865, *New York Times* took note of the European roots of the assassination. In the fifteen years before Lincoln was gunned down, at least ten kings, queens, and emperors were either shot at or otherwise assaulted by would-be assassins: Queen Victoria of England, clubbed by a retired lieutenant of the Tenth Hussars in June 1850, the fourth attempt on her life; two Prussian kings; the Duke of Parma, stabbed and murdered as he was returning from an excursion; Francis Joseph I, the Austrian emperor; Queen Isabella of Spain, a second try; the king of Naples, bayoneted by one of his own soldiers while reviewing troops; Napoleon III of France, so often that it became commonplace; the queen of Greece; and Victor Emmanuel II of Rome. For more on Seward and Speed, see Doris Kearns Goodwin, *Team of Rivals* (Simon & Schuster, 2005), p. 718.

In the heat of the moment, though: See Kauffman, pp. 29 and 259.

"I had retired to bed about half past ten . . .": *Diary of Gideon Welles*, volume 2 (W. W. Norton, 1960), p. 283 ff.

Senator Sumner was seated on the right: Charles Sumner had experienced firsthand the violence of politics. In May 1856, three days after he had delivered a fiery speech on Kansas, Sumner was attacked in the Senate by Representative Preston Brooks of South Carolina, who wielded a metal-topped cane. Although Sumner retained his seat, he was absent from the Senate for the next three and a half years while he recovered from his injuries. Brooks resigned his seat after a failed attempt by the House to censure him, and was soon reelected.

Sometime after one in the morning: Hans L. Trefousse adds Leonard Farwell to the party that accompanied the vice president to the dying Lincoln's bedside. See Winston, p. 267, and Trefousse, p. 194.

The infuriated crowd, through some chance: Walt Whitman, *Memoranda During the War* (Electronic Text Center, University of Virginia Library) pp. 48–49. Whitman's memoranda are also available in a 1990 edition from Applewood Books.

Then there are those who contend: William M. Stewart, *Reminiscences* (Neale Publishing, 1908), pp. 193–95, 198.

Back at Kirkwood House, again behind closed doors: Shelby Foote, among others, has questioned whether Stanton really spoke those famous six words at the moment of Lincoln's death or "later saw to it that he was quoted as having said..." Shelby Foote, *The Civil War, a Narrative: Red River to Appomattox* (Vintage, 1974), p. 986.

Johnson suggested that the swearing in: It's a measure of Johnson's diminished role in history that while everyone agrees on the exact moment Lincoln died (7:22 A.M.), no one seems quite certain when Johnson officially succeeded him. Foote (p. 986) has the swearing in taking place at ten A.M. Hans Trefousse (p. 194) sets it "between ten and eleven." Robert W. Winston, *Andrew Johnson: Plebeian and Patriot* (Henry Holt, 1928), p. 268, has the ceremony at "about eleven o'clock." According to the *Washington Evening Star* of April 15, 1865—the closest authority to the actual event—the swearing in took place at eleven. John Tyler had taken over for William Henry Harrison after only a month in office; Millard Fillmore assumed the presidency when Zachary Taylor died sixteen months into his term. Tyler, the first vice president to achieve the highest office through death, was popularly known as His Accidency, in honor of his serendipitous rise to the top. A Virginian, Tyler also became the only ex-U.S. president to serve in the Confederate Congress.

On its Web site, the Joint Congressional Committee: See inaugural.senate.gov/history/chronology/ajohnson1865.htm.

Chapter 2: *Apprentice Boy*

Hans L. Trefousse's *Andrew Johnson: A Biography* is considered the standard work on the seventeenth president. This account of Johnson's early years draws from multiple sources, but especially Trefousse's scholarship, books and newspaper accounts published during Johnson's lifetime, and *Andrew Johnson: Plebeian and Patriot*, Robert W. Winston's 1928 account of the seventeenth president. Jauntily written, Winston's biography is much less reliable than Trefousse's, but Winston, who was a teenager when Johnson died, was a prominent North Carolinian of generally liberal sentiments, and his book reflects attitudes toward Johnson largely lost in our own day. I should add that Robert W. Winston is my wife's great-grandfather. His book was unknown to me when I began this project.

Left nearly penniless with two boys: Earlier accounts hold that Johnson was indentured in February 1822, at age thirteen, but Hans Trefousse argues convincingly that Johnson was apprenticed in November 1818, even though the papers weren't recorded until 1822.

Tailoring gave Andy Johnson a way: The story must have been commonplace in Raleigh and Chapel Hill because Winston was only seven years old when Johnson spoke. As part of the ceremony, Johnson presented a watch and chain to Winston's brother, valedictorian of the UNC class of 1867.

Like the fire-iron story just above: Through a mistaken usage of "former" and "latter," the notice as posted by Selby seems to ascribe the "black hair, eyes, and habits" to Johnson's brother. Even as a boy, Johnson was not fair, blond, freckled, and fleshy.

The trek ended in September 1826: Willie Johnson would hang around Greeneville for a few years before eventually heading off to Texas, where he became a surveyor and lived just long enough to see his brother become president of the United States. (Willie died in a hunting accident in the fall of 1865.) As tied together as they had been during their flight from Raleigh, the two boys seemed to have nothing like the same ambition or talent or determination. Selby the Tailor, recall, had offered ten dollars for both boys *or* for Andy alone. That puts an effective recovery value of zero on the older brother.

First Lady lore is filled with fairy tales: Betty Boyd Caroli's *First Ladies* (Oxford University Press, 1987) and *The Smithsonian Book of the First Ladies*, edited by Edith P. Mayo and with a foreword by Hillary Rodham Clinton (Henry Holt, 1996), both cover the territory. Of the two, the Smithsonian survey is more user friendly.

Where they differed most dramatically: Odd to consider the First Ladies who surrounded and filled the Civil War: Buchanan, our only bachelor president, whose niece Harriet Lane Johnston, served as White House hostess; the haunted Mary Todd Lincoln, who would lose a second son while the war raged and a husband at its end; Eliza Johnson, whose refusal to appear in public achieved almost mythic proportions. Maybe heightened epochs of history produce odd domesticities at 1600 Pennsylvania Avenue.

The record is uncertain: Johnson never got a chance to defend his skein of ten straight electoral victories in the 1868 presidential election. Instead, after an excruciating twenty-two ballots, the Democratic Party handed the nomination to New York governor Horatio Seymour, a man so reluctant to accept it that he became known as the Great Decliner. Ulysses Grant, the Republican nominee, slaughtered him in the election.

Financially, Johnson went from strength to strength: *The Papers of Andrew Johnson*, volume 2, p. xxix. Collectively, the introductions to the sixteen volumes in the series provide a quick and reliable overview of Johnson's life.

"My dear, dear Father": *The Papers of Andrew Johnson*, volume 7, p. 560.

"[Johnson] was announced to speak . . .": *Life, Speeches and Services of Andrew Johnson* (T. B. Peterson, 1865), pp. 112–113.

Not only would Johnson have known the book: Helper's numbers need a little help. Nonslaveholding whites in the secession states totaled about 5.14 million, not six million. Of the roughly 350,000 Confederate Southerners who did hold slaves, half owned fewer than four. An estimated 1,800 Southerners, about .03 percent of the total Confederate population and .5 percent of the slaveholding segment, owned more than one hundred slaves. When Johnson and Helper rail against the oligarchs, these are the planters they're referring to. For an easy-to-use online reference on these matters, see http://pbsvideodb. pbs.org/resources/civilwar/mapsandgraphs/.

Time and again, in the House and in the Senate: Winston, pp. 260–61 and pp. 228–29.

Abolition was about the slaveholders: Winston, p. 204.

On the far harder question of what to do with the slaves: *Life, Speeches and Services of Andrew Johnson*, p. 32.

Johnson eventually embraced the language of abolition: "I am for my government . . ." is cited in Trefousse, pp. 168–69. Lincoln was responding by letter to an editorial in the *New York Tribune* in which Greeley implied that the president and his administration lacked resolve.

Having declared himself for emancipation: "I will indeed be your Moses" can be found in Winston, p. 260. Francis Blair's letter appears in volume 7 of *The Papers of Andrew Johnson*, p. 293

By the fall of 1864: Winston, p. 118.

Political back-and-forth is at least as old as Greece: Maury's account—a journal of her travels in Virginia, New York, and elsewhere in 1715–16—can be found in *Memoirs of a Huguenot Family*, translated and edited by Reverend James Fontaine.

These were not the tepid, scripted affairs debates have become: By comparison, the transcript of the second of the three George W. Bush–John Kerry debates staged during the 2004 presidential campaign runs to a little over 16,500 words, including commentary from moderator Charles Gibson and questions from the audience, assembled on the campus of Washington University in St. Louis. (The debate had a vaguely town-meeting format.) Assuming the other debates to be of roughly equal length, the combined transcript might fill about 120 printed pages, about a third of the Lincoln-Douglas record but with very little of the spontaneity of that earlier, famous exchange.

Chapter 3: Triumph & Disgrace

To say that America was an unsettled place in mid-December 1860: In all, four candidates, including Henry Clay and William Crawford, competed for the presidency in 1824 under the loose banner of the Democratic-Republican Party. The election was thrown into the House because none of the four won an electoral majority.

A compromise capital that compromised strongly: Constance McLaughlin Greene, *Washington: Village and Capital, 1800–1878* (Princeton University Press, 1962), p. 272. W. W. Corcoran's $1.25 million in 1862 dollars converts to about $25.7 million in our own day.

"There seems to be no one, neither at the North nor at the South...": For more on Maryland at the brink of the Civil War, see Carl Bode's *Maryland: A History* (W. W. Norton, 1978), pp. 118 ff.

The *New York Herald* reported that Johnson: Thomas Clingman was expelled from the Senate in 1861 for supporting the rebellion. Almost sixty years old at the time, he went on to serve as a brigadier general in the Confederate Army.

On the pro-Union side: See Trefousse, p. 131 ff., for more on the response to Johnson's December 18 speech.

Back home, Johnson's February speech: Denied the vice presidency four months earlier—on the Southern Democratic ticket led by John C. Breckenridge—Joseph Lane was in his final days as a U.S. senator. Johnson had stumped for Breckenridge in 1860, but lukewarmly at best, perhaps because he himself had hoped to be the nominee.

Within a span of only a few months: Temple, p. 467.

Throughout the spring of 1861: Winston, p. 194.

Johnson arrived in Nashville in the second week of March 1862: Winston, p. 227.

So frail was Eliza's health that two months later: Winston, pp. 232–33.

Thus, Johnson went on for the better part of three years: Stanton's March 3 letter was in response to Johnson's letter of the same day, resigning his positions as brigadier general and military governor so he could assume the vice presidency. Given that John Hunt

Morgan had bedeviled Johnson so thoroughly for much of the war, it seems fitting that the famed raider died on the streets of Greeneville, a block and a half from the A. Johnson Tailor Shop and a few blocks from the home Eliza and Frank had been expelled from two and a half years earlier.

For the rest of the party, Lincoln was the nominee: "No Peace Without Victory, 1861–65"—the presidential address delivered by James M. McPherson at the 2003 annual meeting of the American Historical Association—provides an excellent overview of the political backdrop to the Civil War.

More complex answers tend to make Johnson's selection: David Herbert Donald, *"We Are Lincoln Men": Abraham Lincoln and His Friends* (Simon & Schuster, 2003), p. 218.

Inevitably, Johnson came to the ticket with baggage: For a document of such historic significance from a president of unsurpassed prose grace and power, the Emancipation Proclamation itself is oddly flat and technical, excluding, for example, eight Louisiana parishes and the city of New Orleans, as well as forty-eight Virginia counties—modern West Virginia—and eight current Virginia counties, plus the cities of Norfolk and Portsmouth, already in Union hands.

Earlier that spring, Lincoln had sent General Dan Sickles: Sickles is one of those intriguing rapscallions of American history. After he lost his leg at Gettysburg, he had it shipped to what is now the National Museum of Health and Medicine in Washington, D.C., where he would occasionally pay the lost limb a visit. Sickles was acquitted for the murder of Philip Barton Key on the grounds of temporary insanity, the first person in America to successfully employ such a defense. His attorney: Edwin M. Stanton, later Lincoln's war secretary. For an enlightened fictional treatment of the Baltimore convention and Johnson's selection, see Gore Vidal's *Lincoln: A Novel* (Random House, 1984), pp. 530–33.

On the Democratic side, the pressure to pursue peace: *New York World*, July 25, 1864. Sarah Butler's June 19, 1864, letter to her husband, General Benjamin Butler, is cited by McPherson in his 2003 presidential address to the American Historical Association.

Two days after his memo, Lincoln met: *The 13 Keys to the Presidency* by Allan J. Lichtman and Ken DeCell (Madison Books, 1990) is a very useful resource for understanding presidential elections and the factors that influence them.

As surely as they had seemed bound for victory at the polls: *The Papers of Andrew Johnson*, volume 7, pp. 237–38.

Best of all, the vice-presidential candidate had events on his side: Perhaps the Electoral College result wasn't as one-sided as the numbers suggest. Historian Mark Grimsley of Ohio State University has calculated that a shift of just 60,300 votes across ten states—about 1.5 percent of all votes cast—would have given McClellan a victory of almost equal dimensions. But considering where the matter had stood only nine weeks earlier, this was an astounding turnaround.

Like the war itself, the election had been won in the trenches: See McPherson's AHA address for more.

Johnson, who remained on duty in Nashville: "Old" is a relative term, of course. The average life expectancy for all white Americans in 1860 was about forty-one years.

A modern account by the Senate's own Historical Office: See Mark O. Hatfield, with the Senate Historical Office, *Vice Presidents of the United States, 1789–1993* (U.S. Government Printing Office, 1997), pp. 213–219.

Outside, the day was wet and raw: Of the many accounts of Johnson's drunken inauguration, the one provided by George Fort Milton in *The Age of Hate: Andrew Johnson and the Radicals* (Coward-McCann, 1930), p. 145 ff., is perhaps the most colorful and extensive. See also Trefousse, p. 189 ff.

Like many unattributed quotes, then and now: See Milton, p. 150, for the full text of the doggerel verse.

On the fourteenth of April, about three in the afternoon: See Trefousse, p. 192, and Foote, p. 977.

Chapter 4: Center Stage

On the eighth of July, Adams received separate letters: For more, see L. H. Butterfield's excellent article, "The Jubilee of Independence: July 4, 1826," in the April 1953 issue of *The Virginia Magazine of History and Biography*, available from the Virginia Historical Society of Richmond.

The lamb was gone. The lion was waiting: See the opening chapter of Edward J. Blum's *Reforging the White Republic: Race, Religion, and American Nationalism, 1865–1898* (Louisiana Sate University Press, 2005).

At that same Trinity Church in New York: After God ordered Saul to destroy the Amalekites and all their possessions for ambushing the Israelites as they fled Egypt, Saul led an army more than 200,000 strong to do God's bidding, but Saul spared the Amalekite king, Agag, and the best of the sheep and cattle. When Samuel learned of Saul's leniency, he personally murdered Agag, then departed from Saul, never to return again. Reverand Francis Vinton and Abraham Lincoln had some history together. Vinton visited the White House in March 1862, several weeks after the president's eleven-year-old son Willie had died of typhoid fever. According to legend, Vinton not only lifted the president from a deep depression by reminding him that Willie lived in heaven but actually converted Lincoln to a belief in the doctrine of resurrection and the immortality of the soul. The visit was real enough; its effect on Lincoln, including the alleged conversion, is open to question.

In Crane's telling, Johnson's part: It's hard not to be reminded here of Shakespeare's *Henry IV,* part 1, ii, 217. Like Prince Hal in the Henry cycle, Johnson had allowed "the base contagious clouds / To smother up his beauty from the world / That . . . being wanted, he may be more wondered at."

Lincoln's tenderness, his "wonderful caution": Recall that while Moses led the Jews out of Egypt, he died (at age 120) before they could conquer Canaan and enter the Promised Land. That duty fell to the military leader, Joshua, whom Moses had chosen as his successor.

For many in the North, the question in those first days: The quote can be found in *The Humble Conqueror: A Discourse Commemorative of the Life and Services of Abraham Lincoln,* preached April 23, 1865, at Cambridgeport (Massachusetts) Parish by Reverend Henry C. Badger.

A visitor to the capital, the Marquis de Chambrun: The French diplomat Charles Adolphe de Pineton, the Marquis de Chambrun, wrote of Lincoln, after meeting him at a reception: "He dominates everyone present and maintains his exalted position without the slightest effort." See *Impressions of Lincoln and the Civil War: A Foreigner's Account* (Random House, 1952), pp. 21–23.

As many as 40,000 blacks had poured into the District: From *The National Freedman,* March 1, 1865, p. 60; quoted by Constance McLaughlin Green. Chapter 11 of Green's history, "Contrabands, 'Secesh.', and Impending Social Revolution, 1861–65," is a superb introduction to the subject at hand. If the ninety gallons of soup the writer mentions were distributed among, say, 5,000 needy, each person would receive about 2.3 ounces.

Between the freedmen and the Southern sympathizers: For the most part, this second, intra-North front was a war of words, of dueling editorials and razor-edged sermons, but not always. On July 13, 1863, just nine days after Lee's army was thwarted at Gettysburg, New York City was scene to some of the most intense and bloody rioting in American history. The proximate cause was the National Conscription Act, creating a draft to stock the depleted Union army, but the greatest victims, by far, were African Americans. With shouts of "burn the niggers nest," hundreds of New Yorkers, many of them Irish, attacked the Colored Orphan Asylum and set the building afire. In some cases, black men were hung from lampposts and their bodies mutilated afterwards.

In fact, the two men couldn't have been much different: Full disclosure: I was born and raised in Lancaster, Pennsylvania, in a home not much more than a hard line drive from

James Buchanan's Wheatland. For most of the 1940s and '50s, my Alabama-born father planted and tended a victory garden virtually in the shadow of Wheatland. My maternal great-grandfather served in the Civil War with the 122nd Pennsylvania Volunteers, organized in Lancaster.

On April 15, the day of Lincoln's death, the _Daily Express_: Civil War–era copies of the _Lancaster Daily Express, the Lancaster Intelligencer,_ and the weekly _Lancaster Examiner & Herald_ are available on microfilm at the Lancaster County (Pennsylvania) Historical Society, just about on the site of my father's former victory garden. I'm indebted to the excellent staff there for their help with this book.

At noon that first day, Johnson met with the cabinet: The Welles family was busy on April 15, 1865. Not only was Gideon attending Johnson's swearing in and first cabinet meeting, his wife, though recovering from illness, was twice summoned to the White House by the devastated Mrs. Lincoln to be at her side. The second time, Welles records in his diary, she "had yielded and imprudently had gone although the weather was inclement. She remained at the executive mansion throughout the day." Welles had just visited with his wife at the White House and was leaving with Attorney General Speed when they were spotted by Lincoln's young son. "Tad . . . seeing us, cried aloud in his tears, 'Oh, Mr. Welles, who killed my father?' Neither Speed nor myself could restrain our tears, nor give the poor boy any satisfactory answer."

The final meeting of the Thirty-eighth Congress: Gideon Welles, "Lincoln and Johnson: Their Plan of Reconstruction and the Resumption of National Authority," first paper, p. 8,298. Available through the Manuscript Division of the Library of Congress.

For Johnson, there was no choice: By contrast, Evelyn Lincoln, John F. Kennedy's secretary, had cleared his personal effects out of the Oval Office by noon on Saturday, November 23, 1963, a day after JFK's assassination. Lyndon Johnson didn't move into the office until after the funeral on November 25. On the twenty-sixth, Jackie Kennedy and Lady Bird Johnson met to discuss details of transferring the living quarters. On its official Web site, the Department of the Treasury notes that "as a courtesy to Mary Todd Lincoln, Johnson delayed moving into the White House, allowing Mrs. Lincoln time to recover and plan her departure." If euphemisms didn't already exist, Washington would have invented them.

For an office, Johnson might have used: Hugh McCulloch, _Men and Measures of Half a Century_ (Da Capo Press, 1970), p. 374.

The same day, Johnson met with a delegation of black citizens: Educated at Oberlin College and trained as a lawyer, Langston established the Howard University Law School after the war and served as its dean. Langston was appointed U.S. minister to Haiti by Rutherford B. Hayes and, in the closing days of Reconstruction, served briefly as the first black member of the House of Representatives from Virginia.

Chapter 5: "Bloody-Minded Tailor"

The North simply had more of almost everything: See Bruce Catton's *Glory Road* (Doubleday, 1956), p. 254 ff., and Foote, p. 1,041. There's also an excellent Internet resource—http://www.civilwarhome.com/transcom.htm—that draws on E. B. Long's *The Civil War Day by Day*. For more on the role of salt in the war, see Mark Kurlansky's *Salt: A World History* (Penguin, 2003), p. 257 ff. Kurlansky's book is filled with fascinating information, including the fact that a 200-pound sack of imported salt that sold for fifty cents on the pier in New Orleans at the start of the war was commanding $25 on the docks of Savannah by January 1863.

Of all the advantages the Federals enjoyed, the telegraph: One more irony of an irony-filled war: Samuel F. B. Morse, who invented the magnetic telegraph that gave the North such a profound advantage in the Civil War, violently opposed the president who prosecuted it. As Kenneth Silverman notes in his fine biography *Lightning Man: The Accursed Life of Samuel F. B. Morse* (Alfred A. Knopf, 2003), Morse considered Lincoln "inhuman," "wicked," and "irreligious." "What can be expected of a President without brains?"

Before the war, Joseph Addison Waddell: Waddell's voluminous diaries (or the surviving portion) begin in 1855, with the innocent observation that he had taken his wife and a friend by carriage that morning to the beautifully named Tinkling Spring Church, and end in October 1865, when he finally ran out of paper. The diaries are available online through the remarkable Valley Project. Created by Edward L. Ayers and administered through the Institute for Advanced Technology in the Humanities at the University of Virginia, the Valley Project examines in minute detail, through original sources such as Waddell's diary, the Civil War as it played out in two opposing valley communities: Augusta County, Virginia, and Franklin County, Pennsylvania. For more, see http://valley.vcdh.virginia.edu.

So it would continue for days and days: This was the second time Waddell had recorded Johnson's possible death in his diary. The entry for June 14, 1862, reads in part: "For several days past it has been reported that Andrew Johnson, the Lincoln Governor of Tennessee, was assassinated at Nashville." The persistence of these rumors would seem to be a good index of just how loathed Johnson was in his native South once the war got underway.

The lyceums, in turn, encouraged libraries: See Carl Bode, *The American Lyceum: Town Meeting of the Mind*. Houghton Mifflin's online "The Readers Companion to American History" (http://college.hmco.com/history/readerscomp/rcah/html/rc_027601_ieducationto.htm) provides a useful introduction to the subject.

Perhaps the second most persistent rumor: Noah Andre Trudeau, *Out of the Storm: The End of the Civil War, April–June 1865* (Little, Brown, 1994), p. 261.

It all sounds insane: See Douglas Southall Freeman, *R. E. Lee*, volume 4 (Scribner's, 1935), chapter 5: "The Threat of Starvation."

The Confederacy was bled dry: Foote, p. 1,042.

In the days just after Lincoln's murder: Whether Sherman's army or the retreating Confederate forces bear primary responsibility for the February 17, 1865, conflagration that nearly destroyed Columbia is one of the Civil War's still-unanswered questions. Marion B. Lucas's *Sherman and the Burning of Columbia* (Texas A&M University Press, 1976) gets high marks for treating the issue impartially and thoroughly.

Later that day in Raleigh, Sherman: See volume 2, chapter 24, of the *Memoirs* of *Gen. W. T. Sherman, Written by Himself* (Charles L. Webster, 1891) for more.

"I think we have permitted ourselves amid great excitements...": Welles, pp. 296–97. The Usher quote is from John P. Usher, *President Lincoln's Cabinet* (privately printed: Omaha, Nebraska, circa 1925), pp. 22–24. Perhaps the worst thing Usher has to say about Edwin Stanton is that he stiffed his own son—a man "of a most lovable character" and a "lawyer of note"—in his will. "One would suppose that Stanton would have at least, in the making of his will, bestowed upon him his library, but when his will came to be published it was found that he had not given him a cent or a scrap of any kind, book or anything else. Yet Mr. Stanton was possessed of a considerable fortune, his estate amounting to nearly one hundred thousand dollars. How will you account for this?"

Newspapers favorable to the administration jumped on the cause: If ever there was a dwindling asset, it was the fleeing Confederate treasury. On May third, near the Savannah River, a part of the money was distributed to Davis's restless cavalry contingent. On the fourth, more was disbursed to high civilian officials to aid in their escapes and to the loyal cavalrymen who hadn't extorted their share a day earlier. Another $86,000 was hidden in the false bottom of a carriage so that it might eventually be shipped out of country. That left about $26,000 cash on hand. (See Trudeau, pp. 289–290.) When Davis was finally captured, he had in his possession about $10,000 in gold and silver coin. "That thirteen millions of treasure, with which Jeff. Davis was to corrupt our armies and buy his escape, dwindled down to the contents of a hand-valise!" Sherman crowed in his *Memoirs*. (volume 1, p. 373.)

Sherman, not surprisingly, would never forgive Stanton: See Bruce Catton's *This Hallowed Ground* (Doubleday, 1956), pp. 391 ff.; Foote, pp. 988 ff.; and Craig L. Symonds's biography *Joseph E. Johnston* (W. W. Norton, 1992), pp. 355 ff. for more. "In the course of time it would all wash off," Catton writes of the Stanton smear campaign. "The South would forget that Sherman had nearly ruined himself by his effort to befriend it, and the North would forget it also, and after a few years he would be complete villain to one section and unsustained hero to the other." In his later years, Joe Johnston made an avocation of attending the funerals of his former enemies. He was a pallbearer at Grant's funeral in 1885 and for George McClellan later that year. In 1891, Johnston served as an honorary pallbearer at Sherman's funeral, insisting on standing hatless by the graveside despite the bitter February weather. He died the next month of a cold brought on by the exposure.

On May 13, two and a half weeks after he had struck: Sherman, pp. 375–76.

Maryland congressman Henry Winter Davis wrote Johnson: By rushing the case to a military court, the War Department also might have compromised its own vast store of evidence in the case. Michael Kauffman argues that had Stanton's people thoroughly sifted through their files, another five or more of Booth's cohorts might have been placed on trial.

Against this advice and these concerns: In fact, Speed's opinion wasn't delivered in writing until July 1865, by which time all the conspirators had been judged guilty and four hanged, but one assumes the arguments contained in the opinion were delivered orally by Speed to Johnson before the president's decision to use a military tribunal, especially since he specifically cites Speed at the outset of his own order.

Message three was the most personal: Messages one, two, and three, I should add, don't imply any concerted strategy on Johnson's part or on the part of any of his advisers. The messages and the numbers are my own mathematics and interpretation, my own effort to summarize and categorize events of those forty-five days.

On the advice of Robert E. Lee, Davis and his cabinet: So rough was the roadbed and so dilapidated the rolling stock that the train carrying Davis south needed half a day to cover the 140 miles to Danville, Virginia. About two hours short of the destination, the floor collapsed in a troop carrier running in front of Davis's train, throwing a half-dozen soldiers under the wheels. In retrospect, the disaster seems an apt metaphor for the whole enterprise, but Richmond at least was behind them. Noah Andre Trudeau provides an excellent and meticulously detailed account of the closing months of battle in *Out of the Storm.* See in particular chapter 7, "Heads of State."

On the fifteenth, the day Lincoln died, the day Andy Johnson was sworn in: The *Richmond Whig* of April 25, 1865. A Confederate mouthpiece during the war, the *Whig* was taken over by Union supporters immediately after the fall of the capital.

Time never softened Davis's position: Jefferson Davis, *The Rise and Fall of the Confederate Government,* volume 2 (Thomas Yoseloff, 1958), p. 683. Davis and Johnson had been born less than six months apart—Davis in July 1808 and Johnson in December. The only Confederate president would outlive the seventeenth Union one by fourteen years.

For Davis, whom the proclamation: The math here is probably more fun than meaningful, but in the final years of the Civil War, U.S. federal budget outlays spiked to about

$1.4 billion annually. Thus, Johnson's $100,000 reward for Jefferson Davis amounted to about .0007 percent of total outlays. Given that current federal budget outlays run to more than $2.2 trillion, a proportional reward would then equal .000007 x $2.2 trillion, or just shy of $150 million.

The Confederate newspapers talked longingly: Cited in Ken Burns's PBS series *The Civil War*, episode nine, "The Better Angels of Our Nature."

From the vantage point of the twenty-first century: About the only person North or South who seems not to have taken the possibility of sustained Confederate opposition seriously was one of the Southern generals most worth fearing. At a May third meeting of Rebel military leaders called to plan a retreat across the Mississippi and the establishment of an ongoing military presence somewhere beyond its far shore, Nathan Bedford Forrest dismissed the idea out of hand: "Any man who is in favor of a further prosecution of this war is a fit subject for a lunatic asylum, and ought to be sent there immediately." See Trudeau, p. 261.

The shackles would last for less than a week: See Jefferson Davis, pp. 703–705, and McCulloch, pp. 409–412.

In Camden, South Carolina, the acid-tongued diarist: *Mary Chestnut's Civil War* (Yale University Press, 1981), p. 824.

Chapter 6: Waiting Game

As wartime policy and propaganda, Lincoln's ten-percent plan: For more, see Eric Foner, *Reconstruction: America's Unfinished Revolution*, chapter 2, "Rehearsals for Reconstruction," (Perennial Classics, 2002), pp. 35 ff. Foner has the twin gifts of being both an excellent scholar and a lucid writer.

Lincoln did direct cabinet members: Gideon Welles felt much the same. In his diary entry for April 7, Welles writes that while "it is desirable Lee should be captured...his true course would be to desert the country he had betrayed, and never return."

And yet what one heard from Andy Johnson: McCulloch, p. 374.

The new president was back at it again on April 21: See the *Washington Evening Star* of April 22, 1865. I've contracted the *Star*'s account of Johnson's remarks here into a kind of greatest-hits compilation. The Grant quote is from Ulysses S. Grant, *Memoirs and Selected Letters* (Library of America, 1990), pp. 751–52.

When he visited Sherman at Morehead City: John Sherman would serve almost three full terms in the Senate before becoming treasury secretary in the administration of Rutherford B. Hayes. Afterward, he served another three terms in the Senate. William Sherman's quote is from Sherman, pp. 373–74. Chase had come south on the revenue

cutter *Wayanda* with his daughter. Still fuming over the war bulletins faulting his han-
dling of the Johnston peace terms, Sherman went aboard the *Wayanda* to complain to
Chase about Stanton.

Inevitably, too, each faction, each cabal worried: See Eric L. McKitrick, *Andrew Johnson
and Reconstruction* (Oxford University Press, 1988), p. 53 ff., for an excellent and enlighten-
ing discussion of the fluid meaning of radicalism in the context of Reconstruction politics. As McKitrick notes, by the summer of 1865, the closest one could come to defining
a radical was to say that he (or she) was for Negro suffrage, against a quick return of
the Rebel states to the bosom of the Union, and by now generally opposed to Andrew
Johnson.

Johnson was, first of all, incorruptible: McCulloch, pp. 377–78. In his May 22, 1865, letter declining the gift, Johnson wrote the merchants, "While I fully appreciate the purity
of your motives in thus generously tendering me such substantial evidence of your regard, I am compelled solely from the convictions of duty I have ever held in reference to
the acceptance of presents by those occupying high official positions, to decline the offer-
ings of kind and loyal friends."

As military governor of Tennessee, he had an autocrat's powers: McKitrick provides a
brief but excellent summary of Johnson's attempts at wartime reconstruction in Tennessee. See pp. 126–28.

Temple, who spent the war years in Nashville: Brownlow and Johnson's alliance in
Nashville is one more instance of war making for strange bedfellows. Over the years,
Brownlow had denounced Johnson in the pages of his newspaper as a "toady," a "villain-
ous blackguard and low-bred scoundrel," and an "unmitigated liar and calumniator."
Brownlow also informed his readers that Johnson's father was suspected in Raleigh of
being a chicken thief, and that a Johnson cousin had been hanged there for stealing and
murder. The chicken thief part of that was pure slander, but Jacob Johnson's nephew,
Aaron, was indeed hanged for killing a man in a barroom brawl. Their truce, it should be
noted, lasted only so long as the war. Once Johnson was president, Brownlow resumed
his relentless attacks. The Oliver Temple quote is from Temple, p. 409.

It all reads like a scene out of a comic opera: McCulloch, p. 405; Temple, p. 456.

Johnson lost his father at age three: James David Barber does not include Johnson in *The
Presidential Character: Predicting Performance in the White House* (Prentice-Hall, 1972), but his
discussion of what he calls "rigidification"—centered around Woodrow Wilson and the
League of Nations, Herbert Hoover and the Depression, and Lyndon Johnson and Vietnam—sounds a good deal like Andy Johnson and Reconstruction, too. See p. 42 ff.

Oliver Temple saw that, too: Temple, p. 453. Richard G. White was earnest on this occasion, but he spent much of the war years turning out a series of anonymous satires that

collectively amounted to a political allegory of the Civil War. Among his titles, *The New Prophet of Peace According to St. Benjamin* in multiple volumes and the *Book of the Prophet Stephen, Son of Douglas, Wherein Marvelous Things are Foretold of the Reign of Abraham.*

Welles, who seemed to get ants in his pants: Welles, pp. 302–303.

The generals who had liberated the South's slaves: The Sherman quote is from volume 2 of his memoirs, chapter 14. Both volumes of the memoirs are available, in searchable form, online at www.sonshi.com/sherman24.html. Grant's quote can be found at Grant, p. 752. In his later years, after leaving the presidency, Grant was first impoverished by the failure of a financial firm in which he served as partner, then diagnosed with incurable throat cancer. His memoirs, written to pay off his debts and provide for his family, were in the final pages a race against death, but they did earn him posthumously nearly half a million dollars, almost $10 million in current dollars.

All that was basis for speculation: Foner, p. 182.

Charles Sumner, who had worked so hard: See Trefousse, p. 214 ff.

But for sheer drama prolonged to the breaking point: The Web site of the Lincoln Highway National Museum and Archives—http://www.lincoln-highway-museum.org—is a cheerfully cluttered treasure trove of details about the funeral procession. See also Scott Trostel's *The Lincoln Funeral Train* (Cam-Tech Publishers, 2002) and Kauffman, pp. 302–303. I've also made free use here of a column on the funeral train by Bob Kriebel for the January 26, 2003, edition of the Lafayette (Indiana) *Journal and Courier.* Thanks to him as well.

In one of the most poetic passages in his lengthy diary: Welles, pp. 312–13.

I have seen a number of them. The sight is worse: Whitman is cited in *A Perfect Picture of Hell: Eyewitness Accounts by Civil War Prisoners from the 12th Iowa,* edited by Ted Genoways and Hugh H. Genoways (University of Iowa Press, 2001), p. 259. The Genoways' book makes for harrowing reading.

The North won the war. It held the trials: Davis, pp. 709 ff.

Of all the memoirs and diaries to emerge: Kate Cumming, *Kate: The Journal of a Confederate Nurse* (Louisiana State University Press, 1959), pp. 278 ff.

That wasn't the end of it: Foote, p. 1041.

Chapter 7: War & Peace

Pierre Charles L'Enfant, the Parisian: "Daily thro' the city stalks the picture of famine L'enfant [*sic*] and his dog," the great engineer Banjamin Latrobe wrote in his journal.

"The plan of the city is probably his, though others claim it.... This singular Man, of whom it is not known whether he was ever educated to the profession, and who indubitably has neither good taste nor the slightest practical knowledge, had the courage to undertake any public work whatever that was offered to him. He has not succeeded in many, but was always honest, and now miserably poor. He is too proud to receive any assistance, and it is very doubtful in what manner he subsists." That was in August 1806. The miserable L'Enfant still had nearly two decades ahead of him.

L'Enfant liked to think *en grand*: For more on Pierre Charles L'Enfant, see the author's "L'Enfant Terrible," *Washingtonian* magazine, January 1990, pp. 85 ff.

On May 18, ten days after Andrew Johnson had declared: No sooner had his army settled into Alexandria than Sherman petitioned Grant for permission to move to the north side of the Potomac. The spaces assigned to him, Sherman would write, "had been used so long for camps that they were foul and unfit."

In Washington proper, the crowd was even thicker: Cited in *The Better Angel: Walt Whitman in the Civil War*, by Roy Morris Jr. (Oxford University Press, 2000), pp. 223–24. Morris's book is both a history of the times told through a unique lens and a celebration of the deep humanity and vast empathy of this "poet of the people."

The troops had been converging half the night long: From "Spirit Whose Work Is Done," Number 138 of Whitman's epic *Leaves of Grass*.

General Reub Williams, who returned to the Warsaw, Indiana, area: All quotes from Reub Williams are from his recollections of the grand review, published in the *Northern Indianian* July 7, 1904, available online at http://yesteryear.clunette.com/warmemories070704.html.

People were everywhere, too: By comparison, an estimated 500,000 people took to the streets of Washington to celebrate VJ Day at the end of World War II.

So indeed it must have seemed, exactly as Sherman had predicted: For more, see chapter 17 ("They march like the lords of the world") of Trudeau's *Out of the Storm*, pp. 321 ff. The "they march..." comment belongs to Thomas Corwin, a Sherman family friend and a former U.S. senator and representative. Corwin served as U.S. ambassador to Mexico from 1861–64.

Johnson, in fact, issued two proclamations on the twenty-ninth: After his brief term as North Carolina's provisional governor, William Woods Holden helped organize the Republican Party in the state, backed expanded rights for blacks in North Carolina and throughout the South, and was elected full-time governor in 1868. As governor, he ran afoul of the rising power of the Ku Klux Klan and was eventually impeached by conservative legislators on charges of public corruption and removed from office.

Thaddeus Stevens wrote Sumner again on the fourteenth of June: *Speeches, Correspondence and Political Papers of Carl Schurz*, ed. Frederick Bancroft (G.P. Putnam, 1913), pp. 258 ff.

Johnson did seek counsel: See Hans Trefousse, pp. 216–218, for more on the influences on Johnson and for the public reaction to his proclamations. I've made free use of Trefousse's scholarship here.

His pardon and amnesty provisions were no less faithful: Perhaps Johnson had learned that leaner is better from his experience in Nashville, where he had come up with an unwieldy loyalty oath that required prospective voters to swear, among other clauses, that "I ardently desire the suppression of the present insurrection and rebellion against the Government of the United States, the success of its armies, and the defeat of all those who oppose them."

Is it fair to hold Lincoln to words spoken: McKitrick, note, p. 56. The Johnson quote that follows is from the same source.

Johnson made his own pass at black suffrage: Like William Holden, William L. Sharkey is practically a condensed history of the early stages of Reconstruction. A lawyer and distinguished Mississippi jurist, Sharkey stood firm for the Union at the time of secession, rare among the leaders of the state. Johnson rewarded Sharkey by appointing him provisional governor on June 13, 1865. Four months later, having called a state constitutional convention and met the criteria laid down in the North Carolina proclamation, Sharkey was defeated in the race for governor. The new legislature named Sharkey to serve as one of the state's U.S. senators, but outraged by Mississippi's new Black Codes and the failure of the legislature there to ratify the Thirteenth Amendment, Congress refused to seat any of the state's delegation.

Nor was it proper or even possible to impose on states: By December 1865, when Johnson delivered his first State of the Union address, five Northern states—Maine, Massachusetts, New Hampshire, Rhode Island, and Vermont—had removed any legal barriers to voting on the basis of race. In New York, blacks with a freehold worth at least $250 could also vote. In October and November 1865, voters in Connecticut and Wisconsin rejected by roughly three-to-two margins amendments to their state constitutions that would have granted the franchise to blacks. Minnesota voters also rejected a similar amendment at the same time, but by a narrower margin—2,670 votes out of 27,010 votes cast. See McKitrick, notes pp. 58–59, for more.

The bulldog reasoning, the refusal to recognize: See Eric Foner, p. 179. Foner cites a wonderful 1867 quip from the railroad magnate and future university beneficiary Leland Stanford. "To say because [the states] had no right to go out therefore they could not does not seem to me more reasonable than to say that because a man has no right to commit murder therefore he cannot."

This is Andrew Johnson's Civil War: Letter to Johnson from George L. Stearns, sent from Boston on May 17, 1865. Stearns had been the Union recruiting commissioner for black troops. *The Papers of Andrew Johnson*, volume 8, pp. 83–85.

It is today almost heresy to talk about the Civil War: Winston, p. 220.

The plan failed miserably: James Russell Lowell, "Scotch the snake, or kill it?" *Political Essays* (Houghton Mifflin, 1888), p. 224.

Between June and August 1865, Johnson awarded: *The Papers of Andrew Johnson*, volume 8; p. xxix.

Johnson's biographer Hans Trefousse writes: Trefousse, p. 227; McKitrick, p. 140.

"The suffering that must exist in the South...": Grant, p. 1,089. Grant was in Raleigh to personally inform Sherman that his peace terms with Johnston were unacceptable. He signed the letter to his wife, "Love and Kisses for you and the children, Ulys."

The ink was barely dry on Johnson's: Harry Williams, *Lincoln and the Radicals*, p. 384. Cited in McKitrick, p. 53.

"A few of our people are in their element now...": Cited in *Andrew Johnson and the Negro*, p. 138.

On March 2, 1867, on its second-to-last day in session: Henry Adams, *The Education of Henry Adams* (Houghton Mifflin, 1918), p. 261. "Conkling" is Roscoe Conkling, of New York, then serving as a U.S. senator.

Andy Johnson didn't have it in him: Speech to an Indiana delegation headed by Governor Oliver P. Morton. See *The Papers of Andrew Johnson*, volume 7, p. 611 ff., for the complete text.

Epilogue

Senator Henry Wilson of Massachusetts: Henry Wilson's letter and Henry Ward Beecher's sermon are both cited in Paul H. Buck's *Road to Reunion: 1865–1900* (Little, Brown, 1937). See p. 4 ff. for more. Henry Wilson was elected vice president during Ulysses Grant's second term and served in that capacity until his death, in November 1875. A foreshortened version of Henry Ward Beecher's sermon can be found on p. 1, column 2 of the *New York Times* of October 23, 1865, under the headline GREAT POLITICAL SERMON.

Even those who couldn't contain their wrath: The Winston Churchill quote is from *A History of the English Speaking People: The Great Democracies* (Dodd, Mead & Company, 1958) p. 309. For more on radical reformers and black suffrage, see chapter 5 ("The Political Legacy of the First Reconstruction") of C. Vann Woodward's great work *The Burden of Southern History* (Louisiana State University Press, 1993), where the Stevens quotes can be found at pp. 92–93.

Johnson did recover, though: The "last statement," so reminiscent of Jonathan Swift's self-composed epitaph—"ubi saeva indignatio ulterius cor lacerare nequit" (where fierce indignation can no longer rend his heart)—is quoted in chapter 19 ("Ex-President") of Trefousse's biography, an excellent and detailed guide to Johnson's final years.

"It is not often that kindly mention is made of him...": McCulloch, p. 405.

That, of course, has not happened: Lowell, *Political Essays*, p. 190.

Selected Bibliography

Adams, Henry. *The Education of Henry Adams: An Autobiography*. New York: Oxford University Press, 1999.

Baker, Jean H. *Mary Todd Lincoln: A Biography*. New York: W. W. Norton, 1987.

Barber, James David. *The Presidential Character: Predicting Performance in the White House*. Englewood Cliffs, New Jersey: Prentice Hall, 1972.

Blum, Edward J. *Reforging the White Republic: Race, Religion, and American Nationalism, 1865–1898*. Baton Rouge: Louisiana State University Press, 2005.

Bode, Carl. *Maryland: A History*. W. W. Norton, 1978.

Bowen, David Warren. *Andrew Johnson and the Negro*. Knoxville, Tennessee: The University of Tennessee Press, 1989.

Buck, Paul H. *The Road to Reunion: 1865–1900*. Boston: Little, Brown, 1937.

Butterfield, L. H. "The Jubilee of Independence: July 4, 1826." *The Virginia Magazine of History and Biography*, volume 61, no. 2. April 1953.

Caroli, Betty Boyd. *First Ladies*. New York: Oxford University Press, 1987.

Catton, Bruce. *Glory Road*. Garden City, New York: Doubleday, 1956.

———. *A Stillness at Appomattox*. Garden City, New York: Doubleday, 1956.

———. *This Hallowed Ground: The Story of the Union Side of the Civil War*. Garden City, New York: Doubleday, 1956.

Chestnut, Mary. *Mary Chestnut's Civil War*, C. Vann Woodward, ed. New Haven: Yale University Press, 1981.

Churchill, Winston. *A History of the English-Speaking Peoples: The Great Democracies*. New York: Dodd, Mead & Company, 1958.

Cumming, Kate (ed. Richard Barksdale Harwell). *Kate: The Journal of a Confederate Nurse*. Baton Rouge: Louisiana State University Press, 1959.

Davis, Jefferson. *The Rise and Fall of the Confederate Government*, volume 2. New York: Da Capo Press, 1990.

Davis, William C. *An Honorable Defeat: The Last Days of the Confederate Government*. New York: Harcourt, 2001.

Donald, David Herbert. *Lincoln*. New York: Simon & Schuster, 1995.

———. *"We Are Lincoln Men": Abraham Lincoln and His Friends*. New York: Simon & Schuster, 2003.

Foner, Eric. *Reconstruction: America's Unfinished Revolution, 1863–1877*. New York: Perennial Classics, 2002.

Foote, Shelby. *The Civil War, a Narrative: Red River to Appomattox*, volume 3. New York: Vintage Books, 1974.

Freeman, Douglas Southall. *R. E. Lee: A Biography*, volume 4. New York: Scribner's, 1935.

Genoways, Ted, and Hugh H. Genoways, eds. *A Perfect Picture of Hell: Eyewitness Accounts by Civil War Prisoners from the 12th Iowa*. Iowa City, Iowa: University of Iowa Press, 2001.

Golay, Michael. *A Ruined Land: The End of the Civil War*. New York: John Wiley, 1999.

Goodwin, Doris Kearns. *Team of Rivals: The Political Genius of Abraham Lincoln*. New York: Simon & Schuster, 2005.

Gould, Lewis L. *Grand Old Party: A History of the Republicans*. New York: Random House, 2003.

Grant, Ulysses S. *Memoirs and Selected Letters: Personal Memoirs of U. S. Grant and Selected Letters 1839–1865*. The Library of America, 1990.

Green, Constance McLaughlin. *Washington: Village and Capital, 1800–1878*. Princeton, New Jersey: Princeton University Press, 1962.

Helper, Hinton Rowan. *Compendium of the Impending Crisis of the South*. New York: A. B. Burdick, 1859.

Hoehling, A. A. *After the Guns Fell Silent: A Post-Appomattox Narrative April 1865–March 1866*. Lanham, Maryland: Madison Books, 1990.

Holzer, Harold, ed. *The Lincoln-Douglas Debates: The First Complete, Unexpurgated Text.* New York: HarperCollins, 1993.

Johnson, Andrew. *Life, Speeches and Services of Andrew Johnson, Seventeenth President of the United States.* Philadelphia: T.B. Peterson & Brothers, 1865.

————. *The Papers of Andrew Johnson,* especially volumes 1 (1822–1851), 7 (1864–1865), and 8 (May–August, 1865). Paul H. Bergeron, LeRoy P. Graf, and Ralph W. Haskins, eds. Knoxville: The University Press of Tennessee, 1967 (volume 1), 1986 (volume 7), and 1989 (volume 8).

Kauffman, Michael W. *American Brutus: John Wilkes Booth and the Lincoln Conspiracies.* New York: Random House, 2004.

Kennedy, John F. *Profiles in Courage.* New York: Harper & Row, 1955.

Kimmel, Stanley. *Mr. Lincoln's Washington.* New York: Bramhall House, 1957.

Kunhardt, Dorothy Meserve, and Philip B. Kunhardt, Jr. *Twenty Days: A Narrative in Text and Pictures of the Assassination of Abraham Lincoln and the Twenty Days and Nights That Followed.* New York: Harper & Row, 1965.

Lichtman, Alan J., and Ken Decell. *The Thirteen Keys to the Presidency: Prediction Without Polls.* Lanham, Maryland: Madison Books, 1990.

Lowell, James Russell. *Political Essays.* Boston: Houghton Mifflin, 1888.

Mayo, Edith P., ed. *The Smithsonian Book of the First Ladies: Their Lives, Times, and Issues.* New York: Henry Holt, 1996.

McCulloch, Hugh. *Men and Measures of Half a Century: Sketches and Comments.* New York: Da Capo Press, 1970.

McFeely, William S. *Frederick Douglass.* New York: W. W. Norton, 1991.

McKitrick, Eric L. *Andrew Johnson and Reconstruction.* New York: Oxford University Press, 1988.

McPherson, James M. "No Peace without Victory, 1861–65." Presidential address delivered at the 118th annual meeting of the American Historical Association. Washington, D.C.: January 3, 2003.

————. *Ordeal by Fire* (volume 2 of *The Civil War*). New York: Alfred A. Knopf, 1982.

Milton, George Fort. *The Age of Hate: Andrew Johnson and the Radicals.* New York: Coward-McCann, 1930.

Moore, William G. "Notes of Colonel W.G. Moore, Private Secretary to President Johnson, 1866–1868. *American Historical Review,* volume 19, no. 1. October 1913.

Morris, Roy, Jr. *The Better Angel: Walt Whitman in the Civil War.* New York: Oxford University Press, 2000.

Oates, Stephen B. *The Whirlwind of War: Voices of the Storm, 1861–65.* New York: Harper-Collins, 1998.

Poore, Benjamin Perley, ed. *The Conspiracy Trial for the Murder of the President and the Attempt to Overthrow the Government by the Assassination of Its Principal Officers,* volumes 1, 2, and 3. Boston: J. E. Tilton, 1865.

Schurz, Carl. *Speeches, Correspondence and Political Papers of Carl Schurz,* Frederick Bancroft ed. New York: G. P. Putnam, 1913.

Sherman, William T. *Memoirs of Gen. W. T. Sherman, Written by Himself,* volume 1 and 2. New York: Charles L. Webster, 1891.

Silverman, Kenneth. *Lightning Man: The Accursed Life of Samuel F. B. Morse.* New York: Alfred A. Knopf, 2003.

Simpson, Brooks D., LeRoy P. Graf, and John Muldowny, eds. *Advice After Appomattox: Letters to Andrew Johnson, 1865–1866.* Knoxville: The University of Tennessee Press, 1987.

Smith, William Ernest. *The Francis Preston Blair Family in Politics,* volume 1. New York: Macmillan, 1933.

Stamp, Kenneth M., ed. *The Causes of the Civil War.* New York: Touchstone, 1986.

Stern, Philip Van Doren, ed. *The Life and Writings of Abraham Lincoln.* New York: The Modern Library, 1940.

Stewart. William M. *Reminiscences of Senator William M. Stewart, of Nevada.* New York: The Neale Publishing Company, 1908.

Swanson, James L. *Manhunt: The 12-Day Chase for Lincoln's Killer.* New York: William Morrow, 2006.

Symonds, Craig L. *Joseph E. Johnston: A Civil War Biography.* New York: W. W. Norton, 1992.

Temple, Oliver P. *Notable Men of Tennessee from 1833 to 1875: Their Times and Their Contemporaries.* New York: The Cosmopolitan Press, 1912.

Tolson, Jay, ed. *The Correspondence of Shelby Foote & Walker Percy*. New York: W. W. Norton, 1997.

Trefousse, Hans L. *Andrew Johnson: A Biography*. New York: W. W. Norton, 1989.

Trudeau, Noah Andre. *Out of the Storm: The End of the Civil War, April–June 1865*. Boston: Little, Brown, 1994.

Usher, John P. *President Lincoln's Cabinet*. Omaha, Nebraska: privately printed monograph, circa 1925.

Vidal, Gore. *Lincoln: A Novel*. New York: Random House, 1984.

Welles, Gideon. *Diary of Gideon Welles*, volume 2, Howard K. Beale ed. New York: W. W. Norton, 1960.

Winik, Jay. *April 1865: The Month That Saved America*. New York: HarperCollins, 2001.

Winston, Robert W. *Andrew Johnson: Plebeian and Patriot*. New York: Henry Holt, 1928.

Wise, John S. *Recollections of Thirteen Presidents*. New York: Doubleday, 1906.

Witcover, Jules. *Party of the People*. New York: Random House, 2003.

Woodward, C. Vann. *The Burden of Southern History*, third edition. Baton Rouge, Louisiana: Lousiana State University Press, 1993.

The WPA Guide to Washington, D.C. New York: Pantheon Books, 1983.

Index